The Norton Scores

Seventh Edition

VOLUME II

The Norton Scores

A Study Anthology

Seventh Edition
in Two Volumes

EDITED BY

KRISTINE FORNEY

Professor of Music
California State University, Long Beach

VOLUME II:
Schubert to the Present

W. W. NORTON & COMPANY
New York • London

Acknowledgments

The text translation for item 12 is from *The Ring of Words: An Anthology of Song Texts*, edited by Philip Miller (New York: W. W. Norton, 1973).
The text translation for item 28 is reprinted through the courtesy of London Records, a Division of Polygram Classics, Inc.
The text translation for item 41 is from Federico García Lorca, *Selected Poems*, translated by W. S. Merwin (New York: New Directions, 1955).

The text of this book is composed in Garamond Book
with the display set in Zapf Chancery
Composition by University Graphics, Inc.
Manufacturing by R. R. Donnelley

ISBN 0-393-96687-9

W. W. Norton & Company, Inc., 500 Fifth Avenue, New York, N.Y. 10110
W. W. Norton & Company, Ltd., 10 Coptic Street, London WC1A 1PU

1 2 3 4 5 6 7 8 9 0

Contents

Preface

This score anthology is designed for use in courses that focus on the great masterworks of Western music literature. The selections, which range from Gregorian chant through contemporary computer music, span a wide variety of forms and genres. Many works are presented in their entirety; others are represented by one or more movements or an excerpt. (In the case of some twentieth-century works, issues of copyright and practicality prevented the inclusion of a complete score.) Operatic excerpts and some choral works are given in piano/vocal scores, while other pieces are in full scores. Translations are provided for all foreign-texted vocal works; in operatic excerpts, these appear in the score as nonliteral singing translations. The anthology is arranged chronologically by the birthdate of the composer and, within a composer's output, by order of composition.

This collection of scores can serve a variety of teaching needs:

1. as a core anthology or ancillary for a masterworks-oriented music appreciation class, to aid students in improving their listening and music-reading abilities;
2. as a study anthology for a music history course, in which students focus on repertory, genres, and musical styles;
3. as an anthology for an analysis course, providing students with a variety of forms and styles for in-depth study;
4. as a central text for a capstone course in musical styles, in which students learn or review standard repertory through listening and score study;
5. as an ancillary to a beginning conducting course, where the highlighting aids students in following full orchestral scores.

In addition, *The Norton Scores* can function as an independent study tool for students wishing to expand their knowledge of repertory and styles, or as a resource for the instructor teaching any of the courses listed above.

The Norton Scores can be used either independently or with an introductory text. The repertory coordinates with that of *The Enjoyment of Music*, Seventh Edition, by Joseph Machlis and Kristine Forney. A package of recordings (eight CDs or cassettes) accompanies this seventh edition of *The Norton Scores*. (A sixth edition of this score anthology was bypassed in order to synchronize the edition numbers of *The Enjoyment of Music, The*

Norton Scores, and the recording package.) Also available is a new CD-ROM disk (*The Norton CD-ROM Masterworks,* vol. 1), which includes interactive analyses of twelve works chosen from *The Norton Scores,* spanning Gregorian chant through the twentieth century.

A unique system of highlighting is employed in the full scores of this anthology. The highlighting directs those who are just beginning to develop music-reading skills to preselected elements in the score, thus enhancing their listening experience. Students with good music-reading skills will, of course, perceive many additional details. Each system (or group of staves) is covered with a light gray screen, within which the most prominent musical lines are highlighted by white bands. Where two or more simultaneous lines are equally prominent, they are each highlighted. Multiple musical systems on a single page are separated by thin white bands running the full width of the page. (For more information, see "How to Follow the Highlighted Scores" on p. xiii.) This highlighting technique has been employed largely for instrumental music; in vocal works, the text serves to guide the less-experienced score reader through the work.

The highlighting is not intended as an analysis of the melodic structure, contrapuntal texture, or any other aspect of the work. In order to follow the most prominent musical line, the highlighting may shift mid-phrase from one instrument or vocal line to another. Since performances differ in interpretation, the highlighting may not always correspond exactly to what is heard in a specific recording. In some twentieth-century works, it is impossible to isolate a single musical line that shows the continuity of the piece. In these works, the listener's attention is directed to the most audible musical events, and the highlighting is kept as simple as possible.

The repertory chosen for *The Norton Scores* includes numerous mainstream works that reflect important cross-cultural influences from traditional, popular, and non-Western styles. Such mergers of musical styles occur in the following compositions: traditional and popular song or dance styles in John Gay's *Beggar's Opera;* Haydn's String Quartet, Op. 76, No. 2 *(Quinten);* Chopin's Polonaise in A flat, Op. 53; Brahms's *Vergebliches Ständchen (Futile Serenade);* Bizet's *Carmen;* Ives's *Fourth of July;* Bartók's *Music for Strings, Percussion, and Celesta;* Stravinsky's *Petrushka;* Copland's *Billy the Kid;* and Bernstein's *West Side Story;* and non-Western styles, instruments, and settings in Haydn's Symphony No. 100 *(Military);* Dvořák's Symphony No. 9 *(From the New World);* Tchaikovsky's *Nutcracker;* Mahler's *Das Lied von der Erde (The Song of the Earth);* Debussy's *Prélude à "L'après-midi d'un faune" (Prelude to "The Afternoon of a Faun");* Ravel's *Chansons madécasses (Songs of Madagascar);* and Crumb's *Ancient Voices of Children.* Specific information about the multicultural elements of each of these compositions can be found in *The Enjoyment of Music,* Seventh Edition, particularly in the text's new Cultural Perspectives.

The role of women in music is prominently reflected in the repertory chosen for this edition of *The Norton Scores*. Five pieces by women composers, covering the full chronological gamut, are included: a scene from Hildegard von Bingen's *Ordo virtutum (The Play of the Virtues);* a work from Elisabeth-Claude Jacquet de la Guerre's *Pièces de clavecin;* Clara Schumann's Scherzo, Op. 10, for solo piano; Ruth Crawford's song *Rat Riddles;* and Joan Tower's chamber work *Petroushskates*. In addition, several works written expressly for female performers emphasize the important historic role women have played as interpreters of music. These include Marenzio's madrigal *Cantate Ninfe,* written for the famous *Concerto delle donne* (referring to the Singing Ladies of Ferrara); Mozart's Piano Concerto in G major, K. 453, written for his student Barbara Ployer; and Babbitt's *Phonemena*, written for virtuoso singer Bethany Beardslee.

I should like to thank a number of people for assistance in preparing this, my first edition of *The Norton Scores:* Paula Sabin, Roger Hickman, and my husband, William Prizer, who have all made invaluable musical contributions to these volumes; David Hamilton, who has expertly guided the coordination of the recordings with the scores; Suzanne La Plante and Gabrielle Karp of W. W. Norton, who have ably edited this anthology; Claire Brook, who has generously counseled me throughout this endeavor; and Susan Gaustad, who has served as project coordinator at W. W. Norton. To all of them I express my heartfelt gratitude.

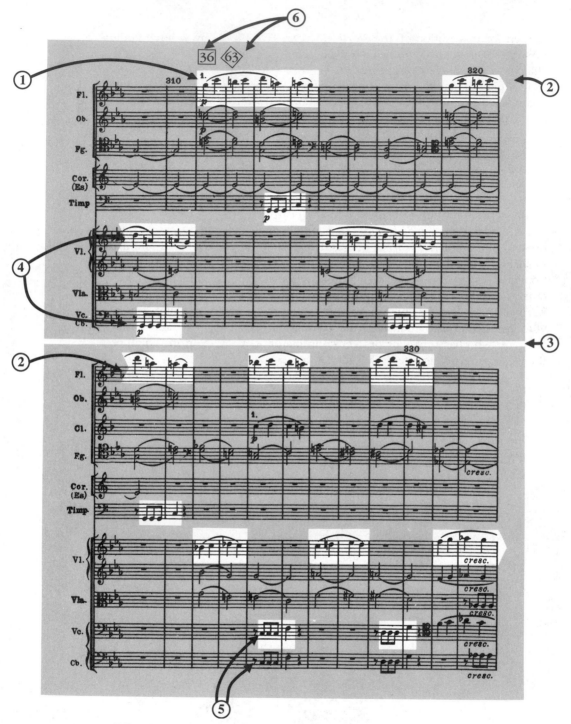

Editor's note: The track numbers in this illustration actually occur in measure 307 (see page 490 of *The Norton Scores,* volume one).

How to Follow the Highlighted Scores

By following the highlighted bands throughout a work, the listener will be able to read the score and recognize the most important or most audible musical lines.

1. The musical line that is most prominent at any time is highlighted by a white band shown against light gray screening.
2. When a highlighted line continues from one system (group of staves) or page to the next, the white band ends with an arrow head (>) that indicates the continuation of the highlighted line, which begins with an indented arrow shape.
3. Multiple score systems (more than one on a page) are separated by narrow white bands across the full width of the page. Watch carefully for these bands so that you do not overlook a portion of the score.
4. At times, two musical lines are highlighted simultaneously, indicating that they are equally audible. On first listening, it may be best to follow only one of these.
5. When more than one instrument plays the same musical line, in unison or octaves (called doubling), the instrument whose line is most audible is highlighted.
6. CD track numbers are given throughout the scores at the beginning of each movement and at important structural points within movements. They appear in a ☐ for the 8-CD set and in a ◇ for the 3-CD set, where appropriate.

A Note on the Recordings

Sets of recordings of the works in *The Norton Scores* are available from the publisher. There are five sets in all: an eight-cassette or eight-CD set that includes all the works in the two volumes of the anthology; a three-cassette or three-CD set that includes selected works from both volumes; and a CD-ROM disk that includes twelve of the works selected from the two volumes, with interactive analyses. The location of each work in the various recording packages is noted in the score to the right of the title.

Symbols employed:

Example (for Schubert's *Erlkönig*)

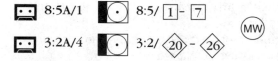

Following the cassette symbol: a numeral indicates whether the reference is to the eight- or three-cassette package; after the colon, a number designates the individual cassette within the set and a letter indicates side A or B of the cassette; after a diagonal slash, a numeral gives the selection number(s) on that cassette side.

   Following the CD symbol: a numeral indicates whether the reference is to the eight- or three-CD package; after the colon, a number designates the individual CD within the set; after a diagonal slash, a boxed number gives the track or tracks on that CD devoted to the work. (The three-CD package tracks are enclosed in a diamond-shaped box.)

   For an overview of which works appear on the various recording sets, see Appendix D.

The Norton Scores

Seventh Edition

VOLUME II

1. Franz Schubert (1797–1828)   8:5A/1   8:5/ 1 - 7   (MW)

Erlkönig (Erlking), D. 328 (1815)   3:2A/4   3:2/ 20 - 26

Editor's note: In performance, this Lied is often transposed to F minor, and occasionally to E minor.

1

nicht, was Er_len_könig mir lei _ se verspricht?   Sei ru_hig, bleibe

ru_hig, mein Kind;   in dür_ren Blättern säu_selt der Wind.   „Willst,

fei _ ner_Kna_be, du mit mir gehn? mei_ne Töch_ter sol_len dich

war_ten schön; mei_ne Töch_ter_füh_ren den nächt_li_chen Reihn, und

wie_gen und tan_zen und sin_gen dich ein,   sie wie_gen und tan_zen und sin_gen dich ein".

TEXT AND TRANSLATION

Wer reitet so spät durch Nacht und Wind?
Es ist der Vater mit seinem Kind;
er hat den Knaben wohl in dem Arm,
er fasst ihn sicher, er hält ihn warm.

"Mein Sohn, was birgst du so bang dein Gesicht?"
"Siehst, Vater, du den Erlkönig nicht?
den Erlenkönig mit Kron' und Schweif?"
"Mein Sohn, es ist ein Nebelstreif."

"Du liebes Kind, komm, geh mit mir!
gar schöne Spiele spiel' ich mit dir;
manch' bunte Blumen sind an dem Strand;
meine Mutter hat manch' gülden Gewand."

"Mein Vater, mein Vater, und hörest du nicht,
was Erlenkönig mir leise verspricht?"
"Sei ruhig, bleibe ruhig, mein Kind;
in dürren Blättern säuselt der Wind."

"Willst, feiner Knabe, du mit mir geh'n?
meine Töchter sollen dich warten schön;
meine Töchter führen den nächtlichen Reih'n
und wiegen und tanzen und singen dich ein."

"Mein Vater, mein Vater, und siehst du nicht
    dort,
Erlkönigs Töchter am düstern Ort?"

"Mein Sohn, mein Sohn, ich seh' es genau,
es scheinen die alten Weiden so grau."

"Ich liebe dich, mich reizt deine schöne Gestalt,
und bist du nicht willig, so brauch' ich Gewalt."
"Mein Vater, mein Vater, jetzt fasst er mich an!
Erlkönig hat mir ein Leids gethan!"

Dem Vater grauset's, er reitet geschwind,
er hält in Armen das ächzende Kind,
erreicht den Hof mit Müh und Noth:

in seinem Armen das Kind war todt.

JOHANN WOLFGANG VON GOETHE

Who rides so late through night and wind?
It is a father with his child:
he has the boy close in his arm,
he holds him tight, he keeps him warm.

"My son, why do you hide your face in fear?"
"Father, don't you see the Erlking?
The Erlking with his crown and train?"
"My son, it is a streak of mist."

"You dear child, come with me!
I'll play very lovely games with you.
There are lots of colorful flowers by the shore;
my mother has some golden robes."

"My father, my father, and don't you hear
the Erlking whispering promises to me?"
"Be still, stay calm, my child;
it's the wind rustling in the dry leaves."

"My fine lad, do you want to come with me?
My daughters will take care of you;
my daughters lead off the nightly dance,
and they'll rock and dance and sing you to sleep."

"My father, my father, and don't you see

the Erlking's daughters over there in the
    shadows?"
"My son, my son, I see it clearly,
it's the gray sheen of the old willows."

"I love you, your beautiful form delights me!
And if you are not willing, then I'll use force."
"My father, my father, now he's grasping me!
The Erlking has hurt me!"

The father shudders, he rides swiftly,
he holds the moaning child in his arms;
with effort and urgency he reaches the
    courtyard:
in his arms the child was dead.

2. *Hector Berlioz (1803–1869)*

Symphonie fantastique, Fifth Movement (1830)

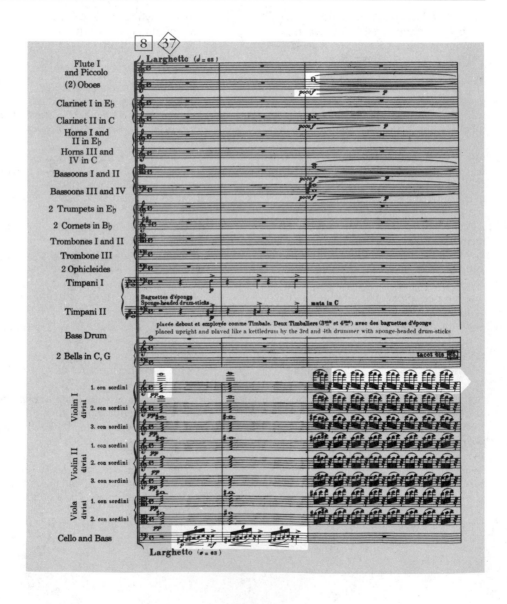

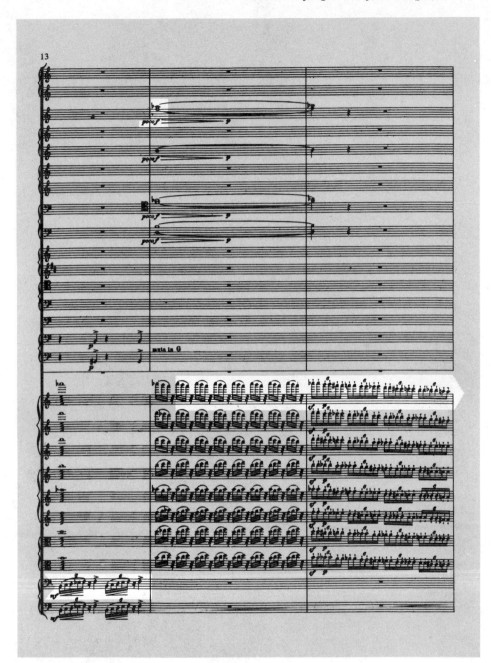

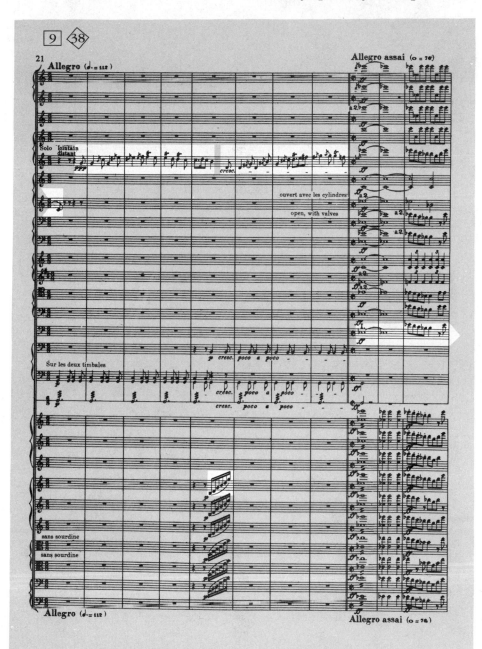

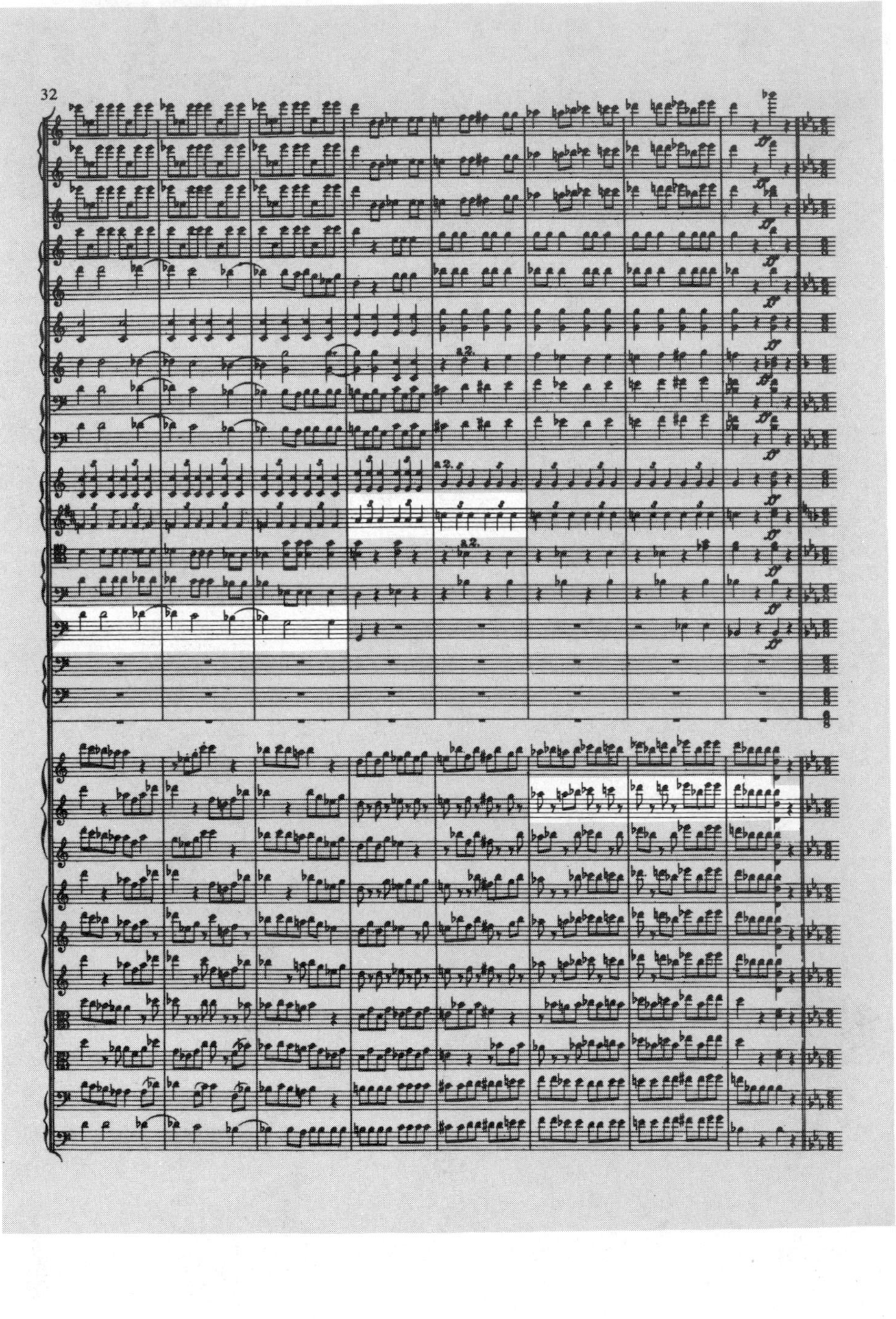
32
a2.
a2.
a2.

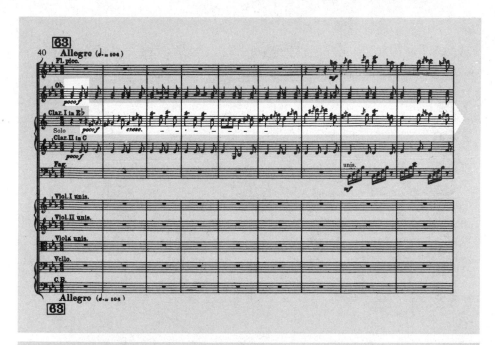

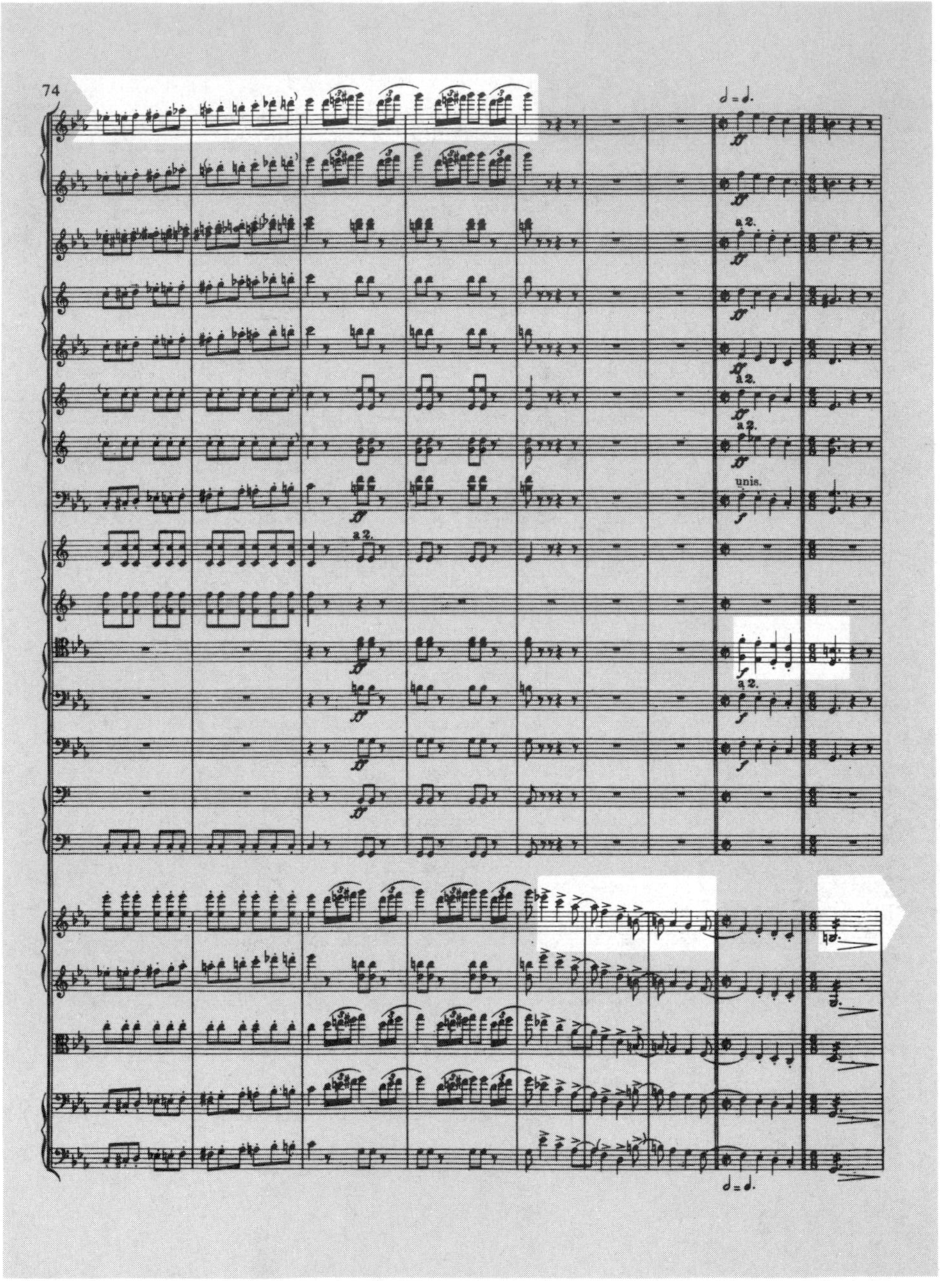
74
a 2.
unis.

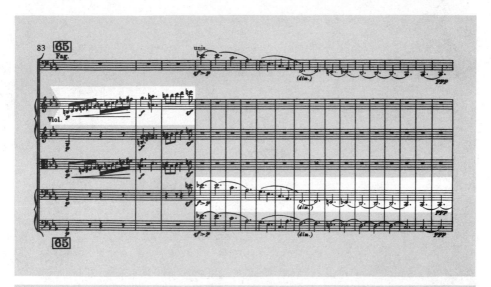

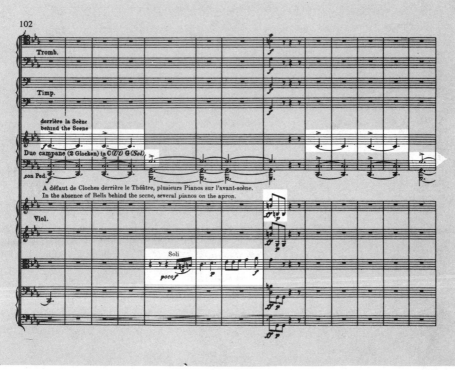

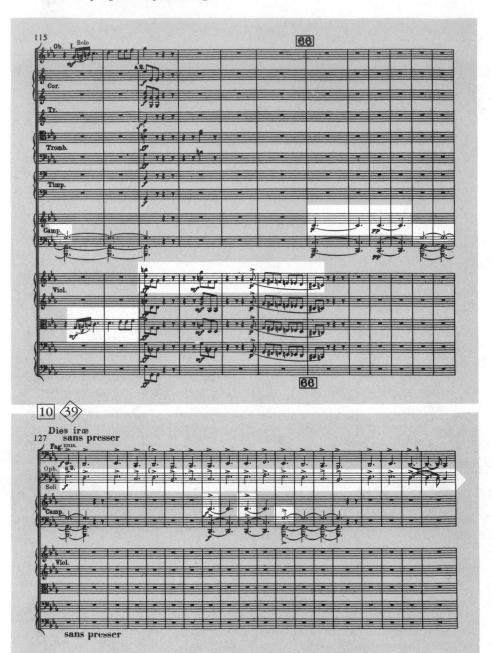

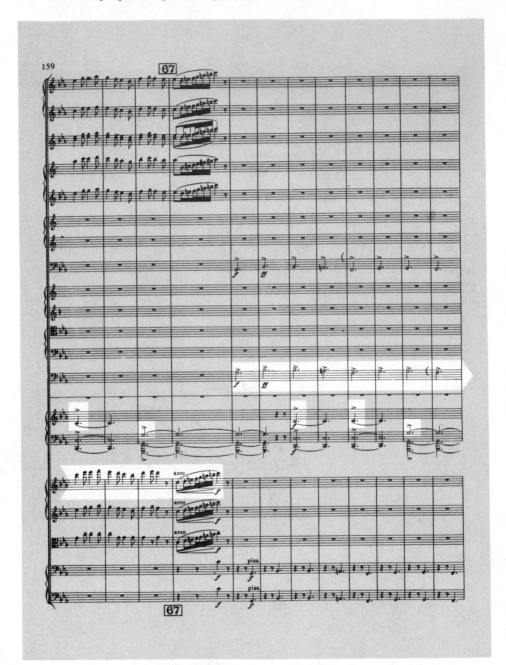

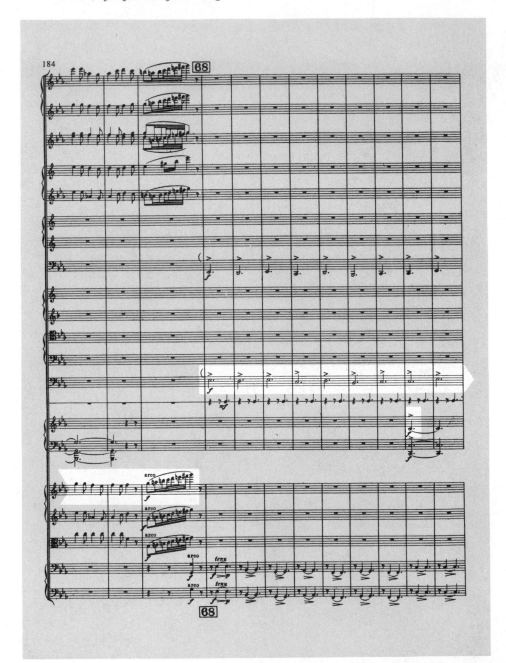

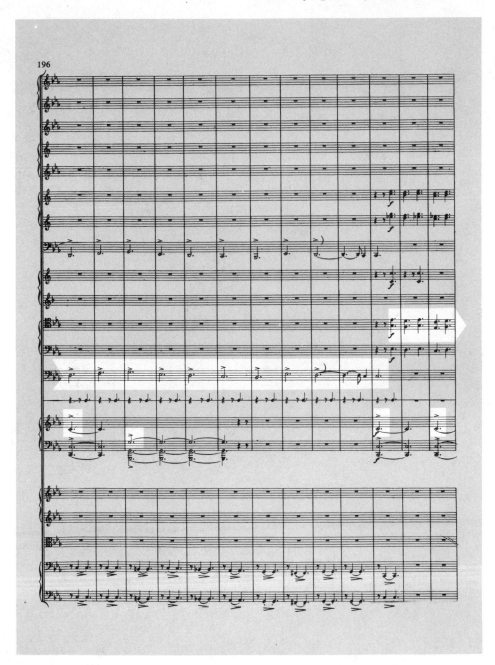

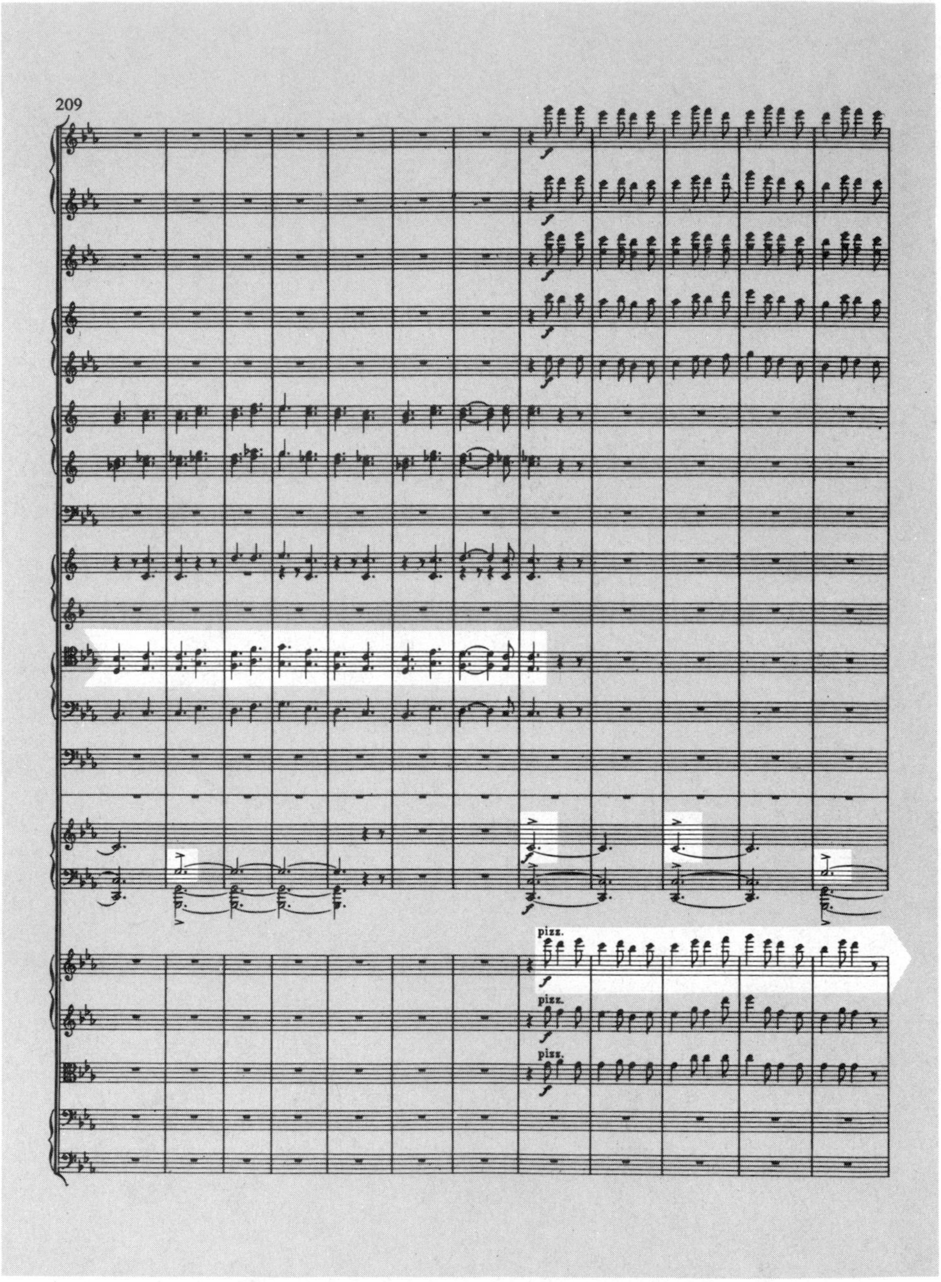
209
pizz.
pizz.
pizz.

11 40

Ronde du Sabbat
Witches' round dance
241 **Un peu retenu**

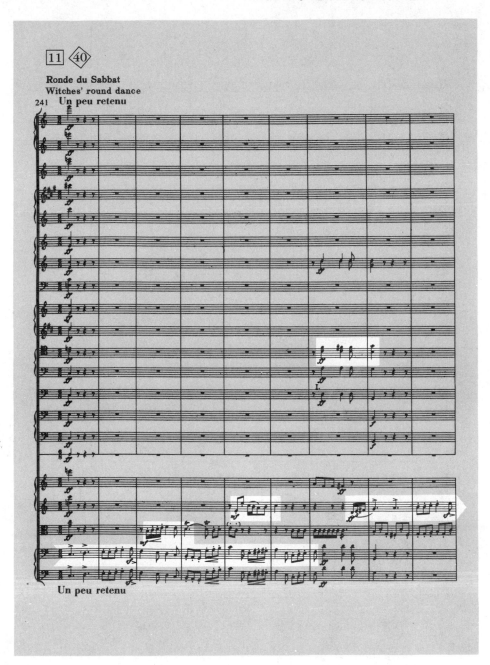

Un peu retenu

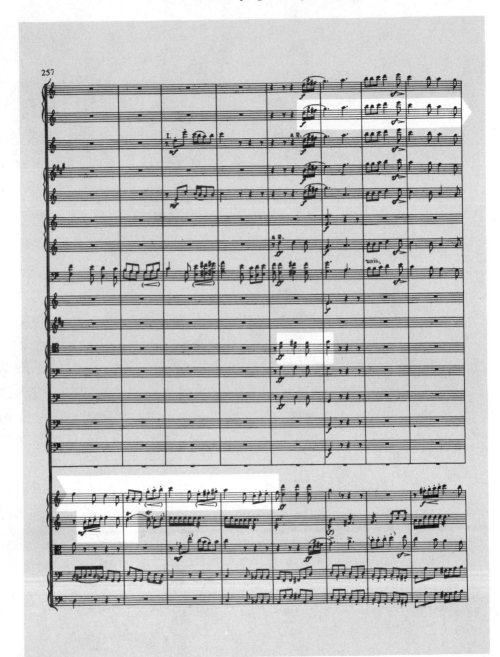

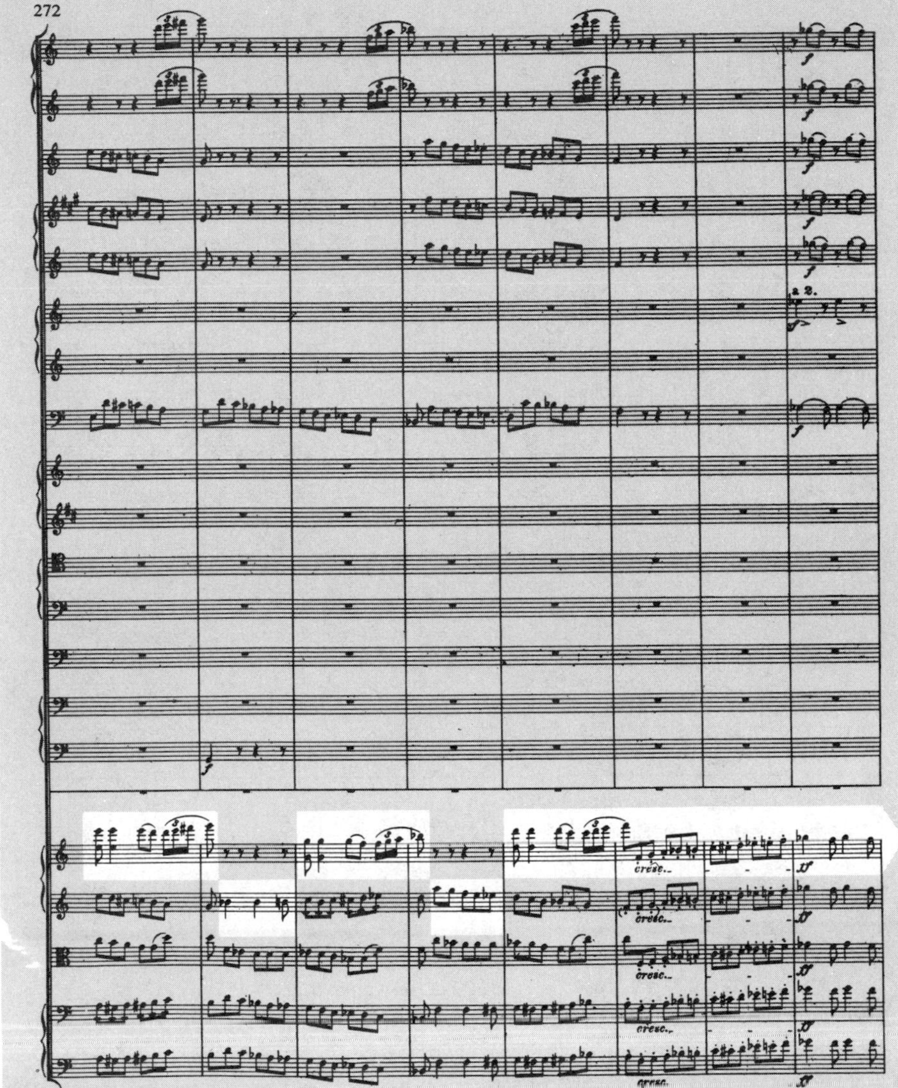
272
f
a 2.
f
f
f
cresc.
ff
cresc.
ff
cresc.
ff
cresc.
ff
cresc.
ff

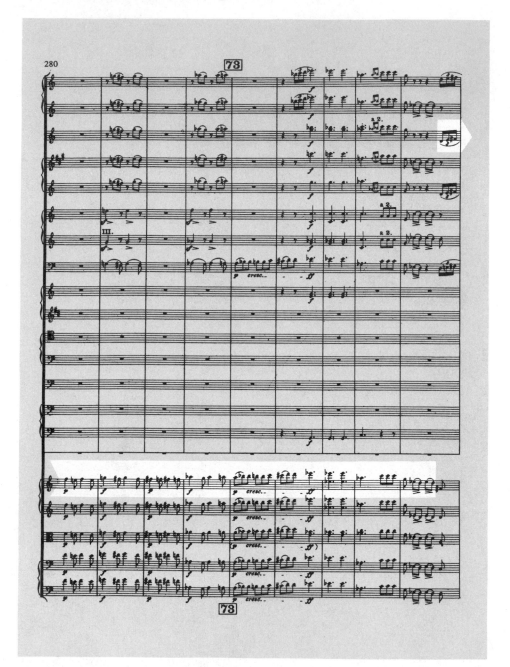

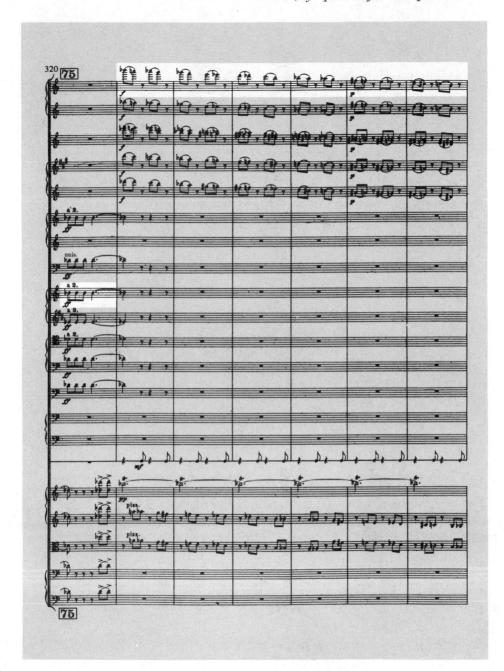

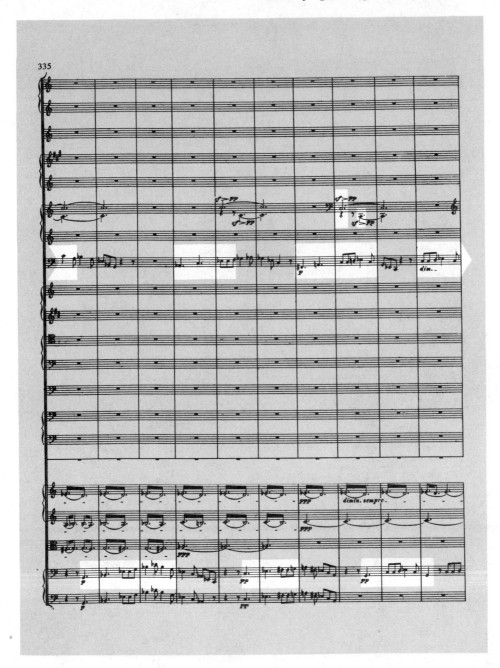

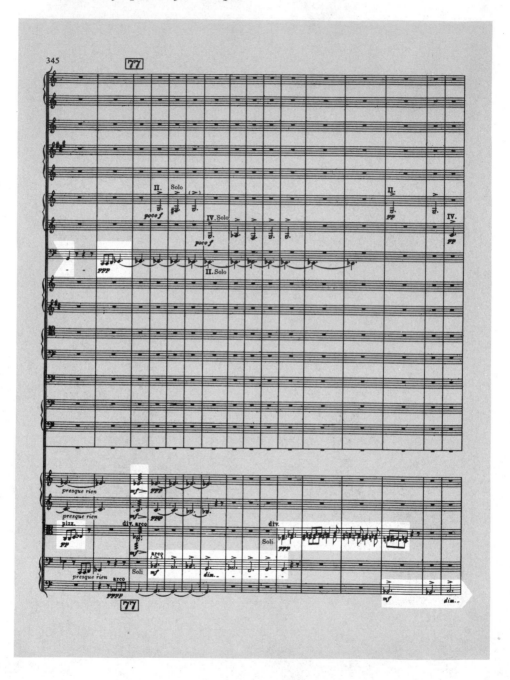

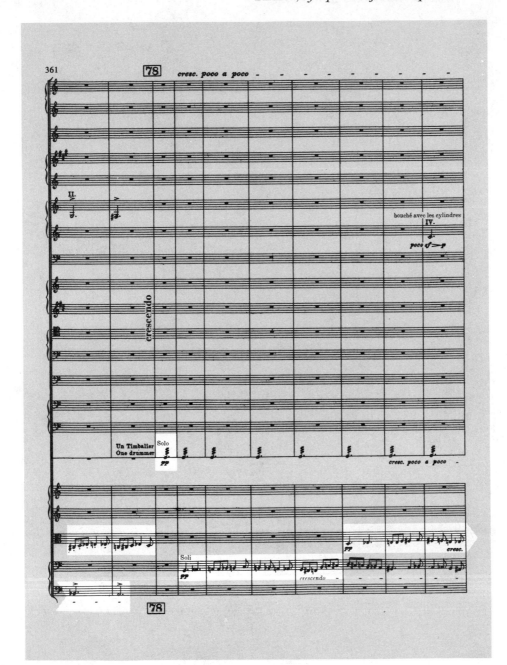

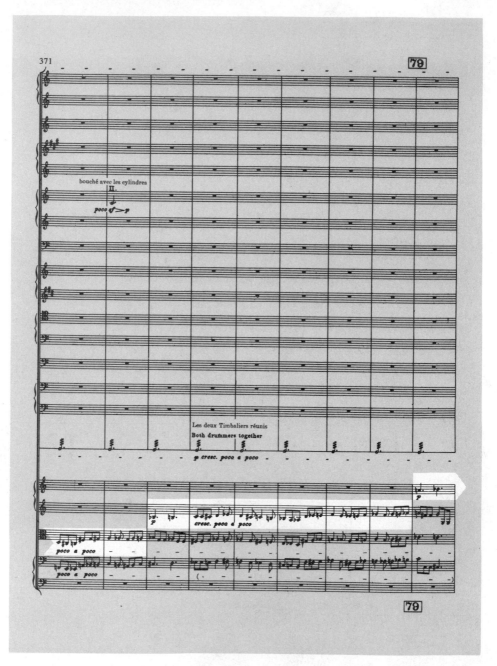

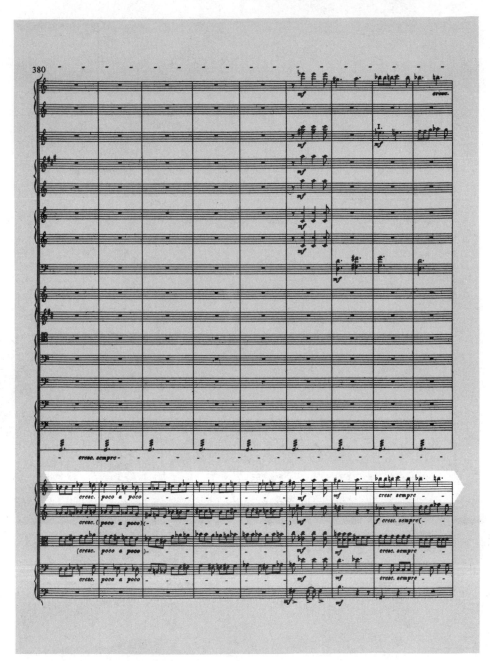

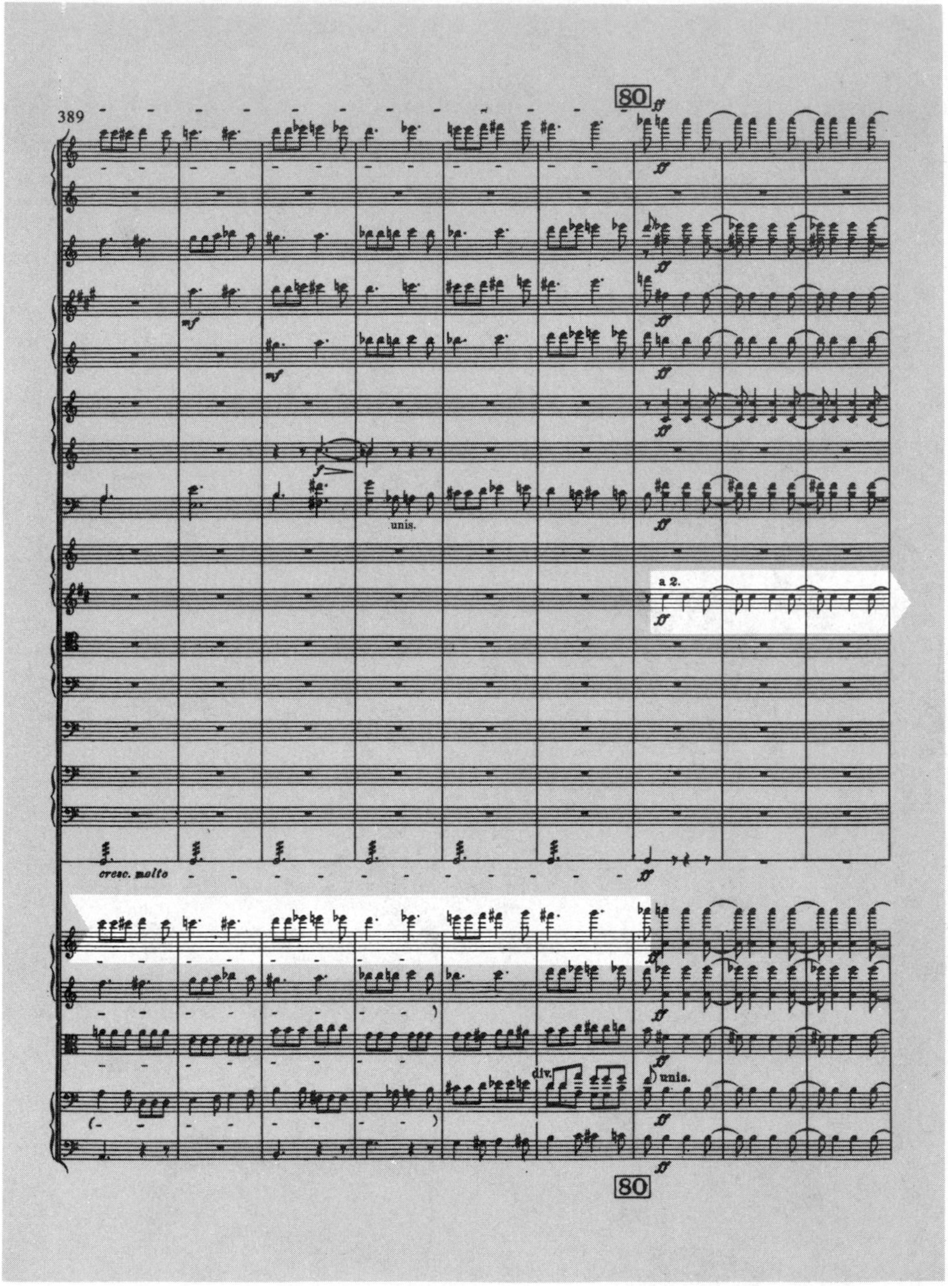
80
389
unis.
a 2.
cresc. molto
div.
unis.
80

12
41
Dies irae et Ronde du Sabbat ensemble
414 Dies irae and witches' round dance together
a 2.
unis.
ff
mf

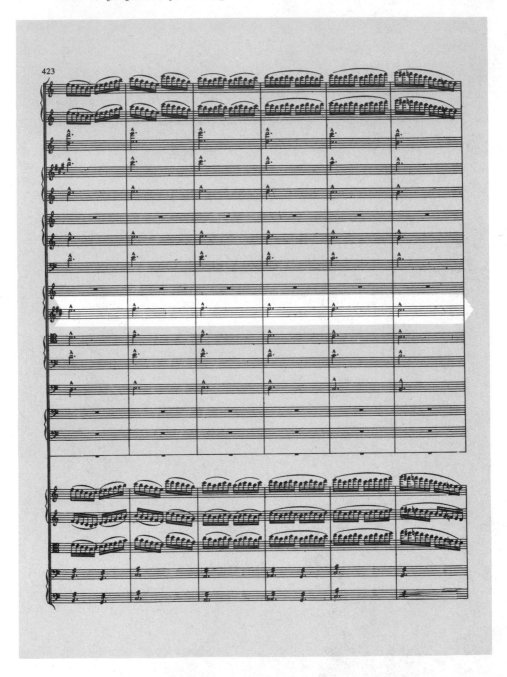

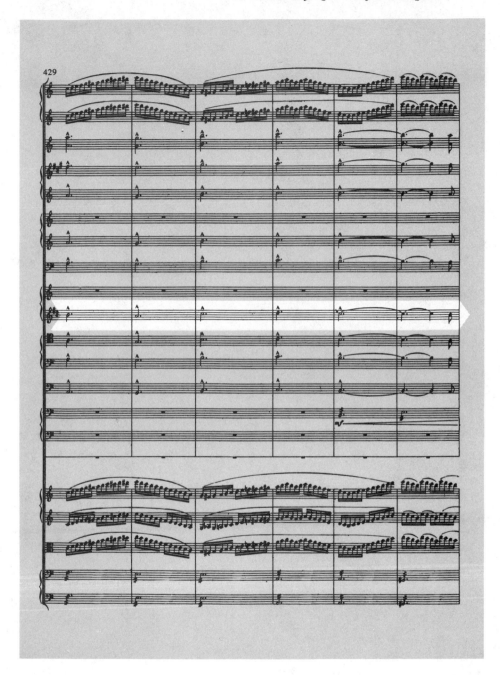

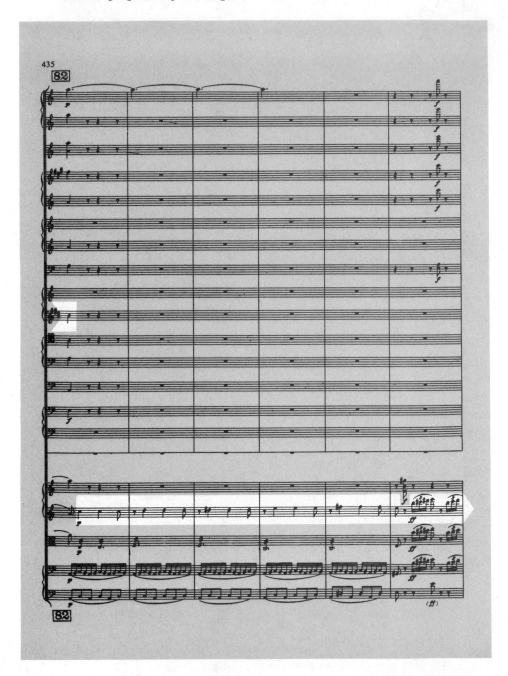

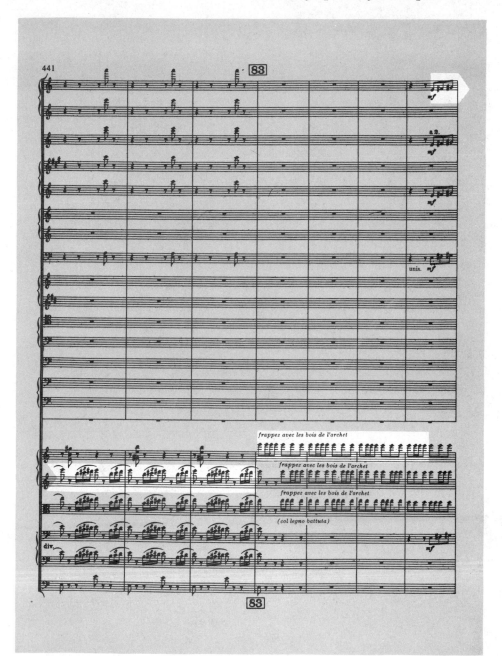

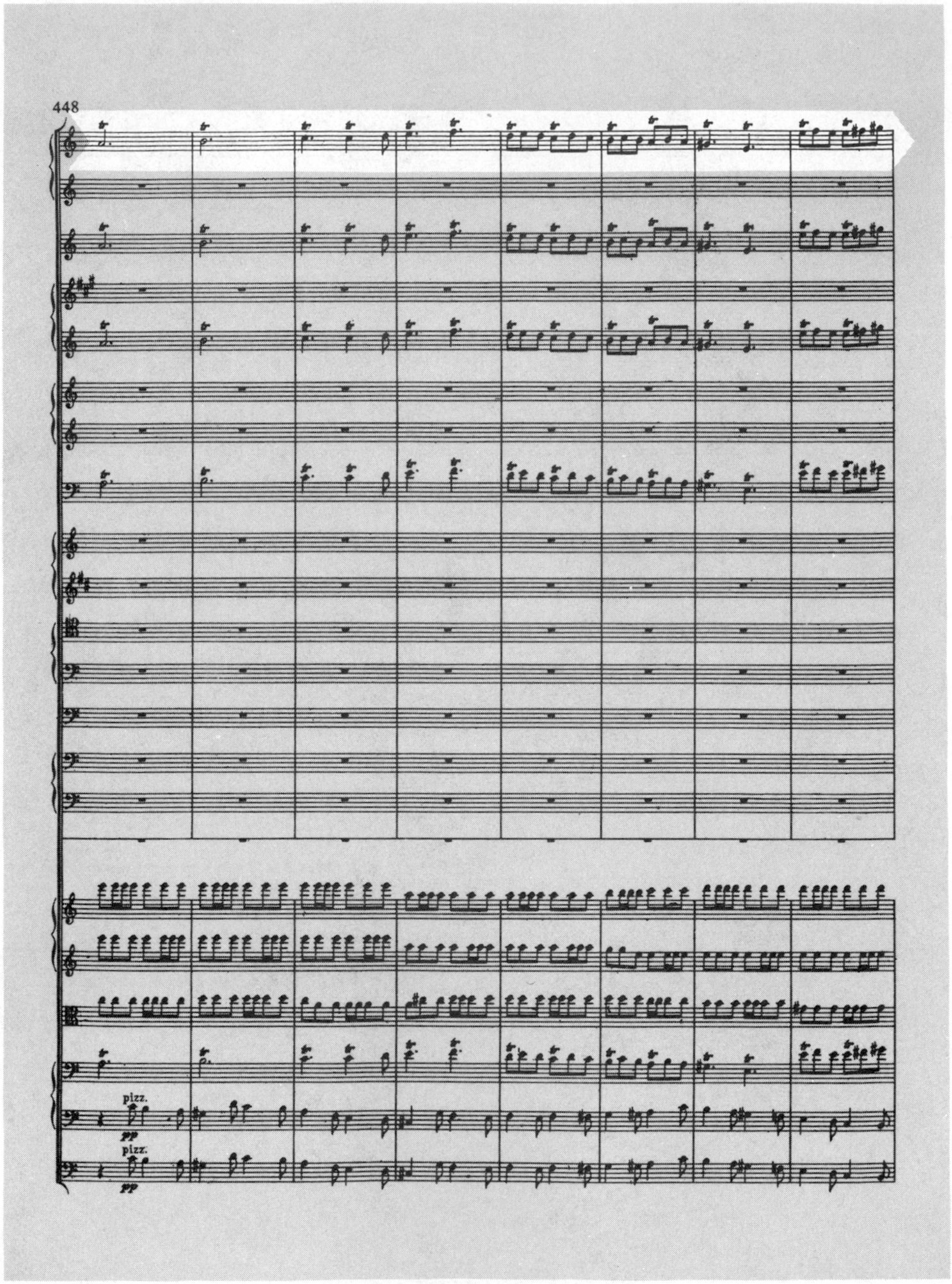
448
pizz.
pp
pizz.
pp

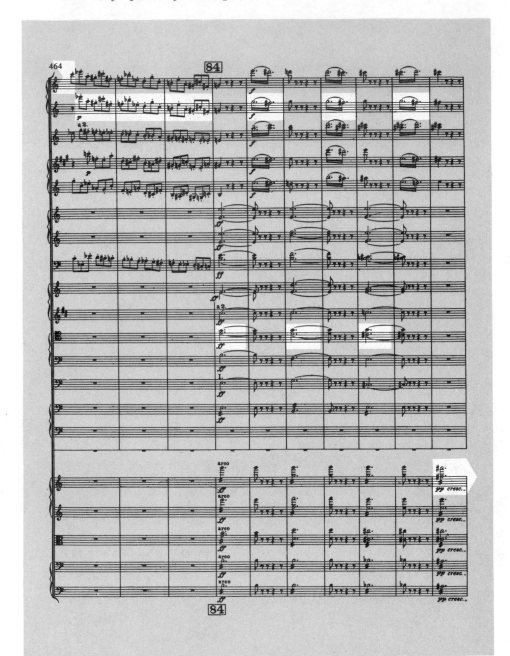

493

animez un peu

3. Felix Mendelssohn (1809–1847)

A Midsummer Night's Dream, Overture (1826)

 8:5A/3   8:5/13 - 21

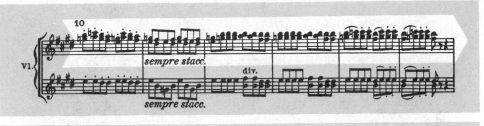

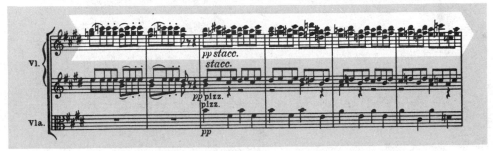

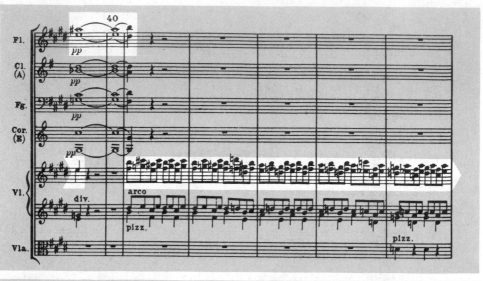

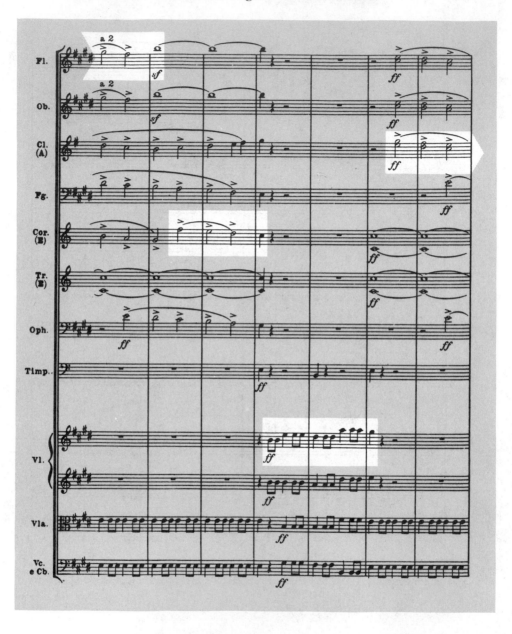

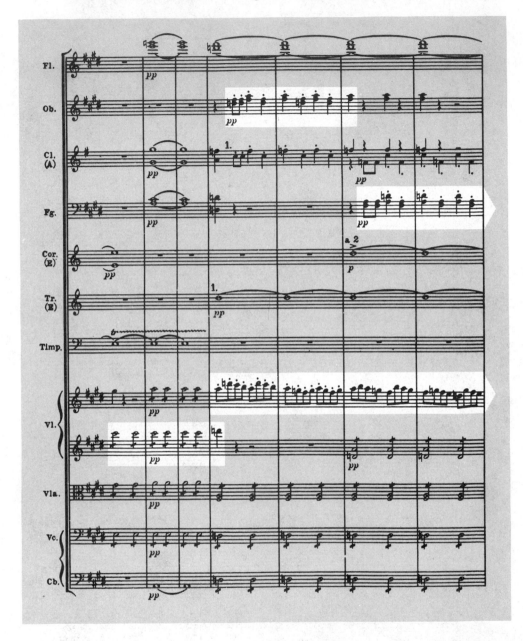

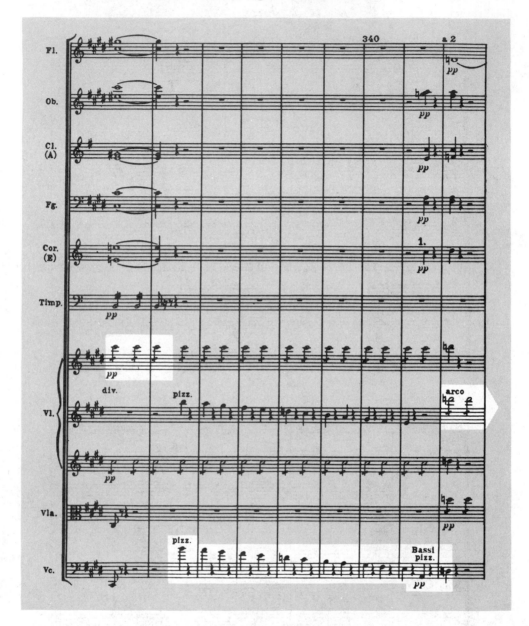

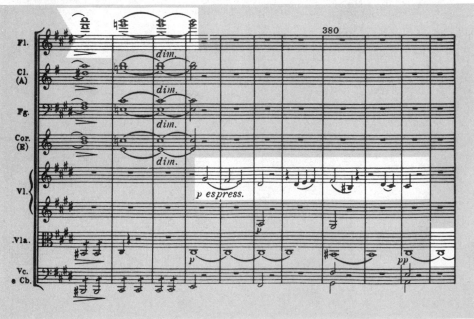

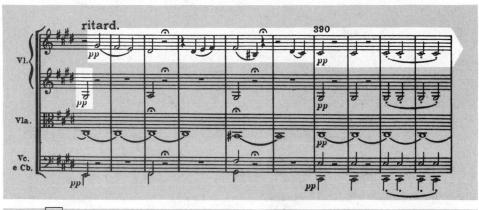

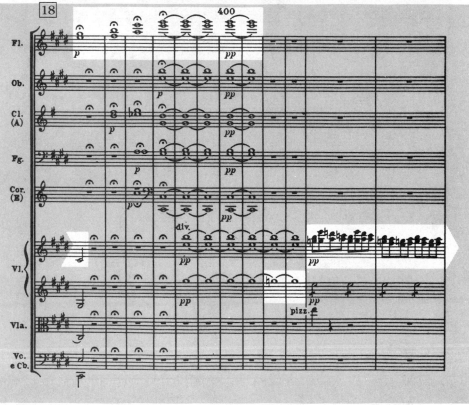

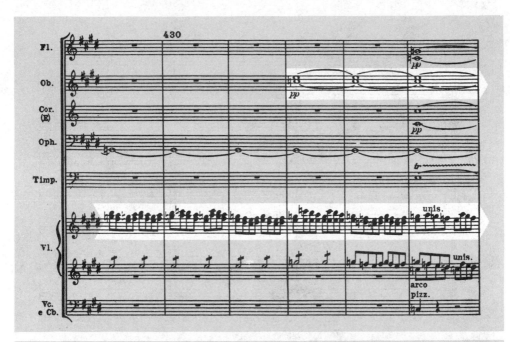

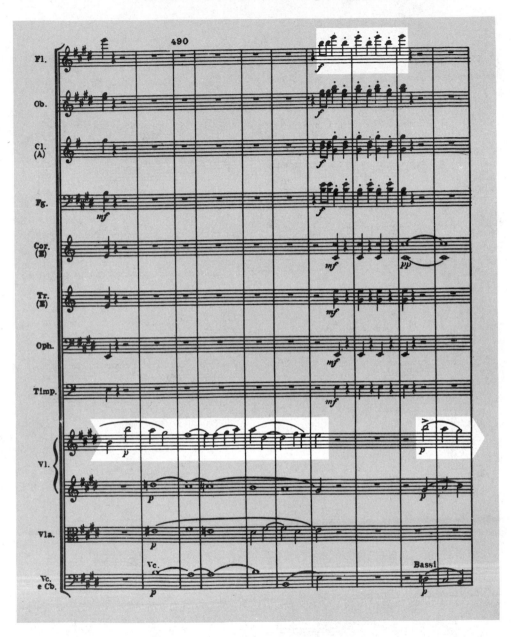

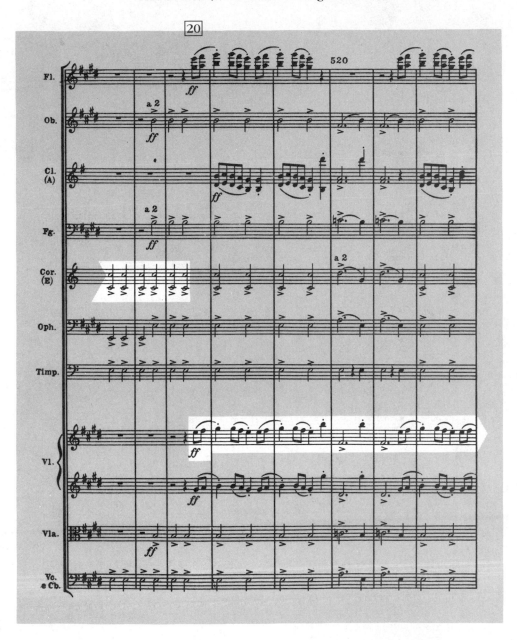

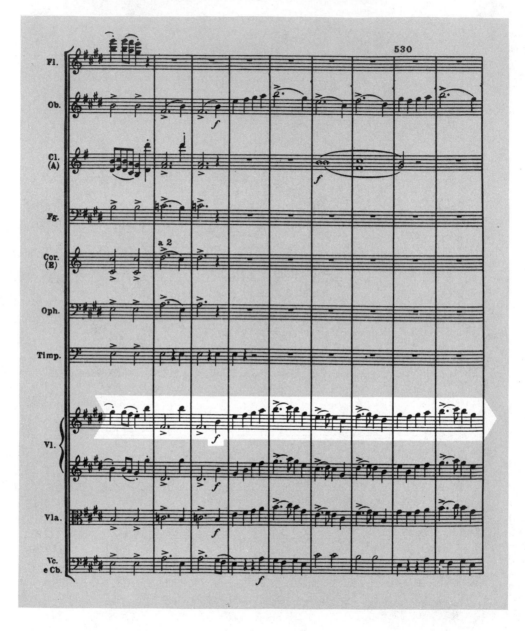

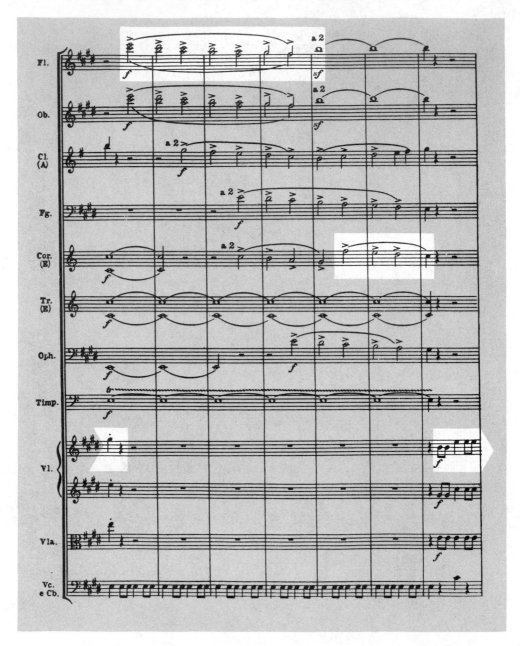

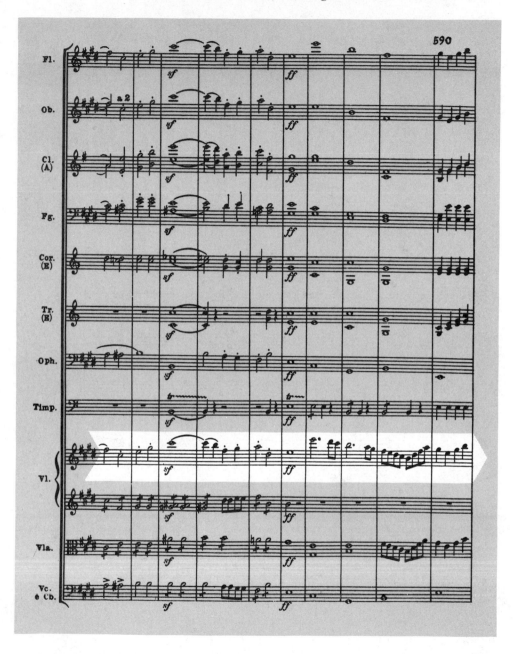

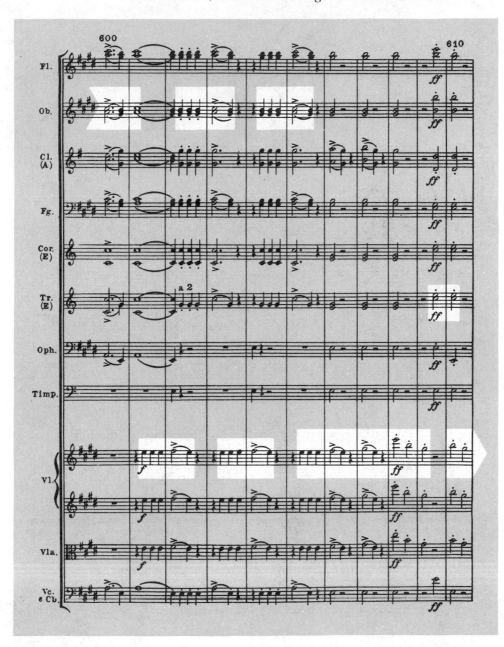

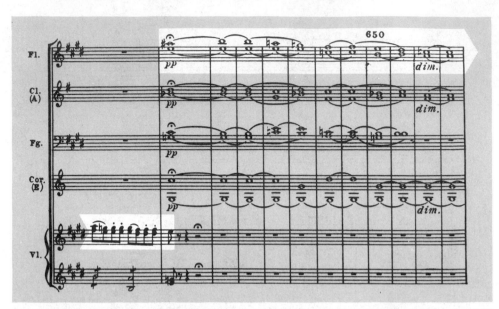

4. Frédéric François Chopin (1810–1849)

Prelude in E minor, Op. 28,
No. 4 (published 1839)

5. Chopin

Polonaise in A-flat major, Op. 53 (1842)

 8:5A/5  8:5/ 24 - 27

 3:2A/5 3:2/ 27 - 30

 MW

117

6. Robert Schumann (1810–1856)

Piano Concerto in A minor, Op. 54,
First Movement (1841)

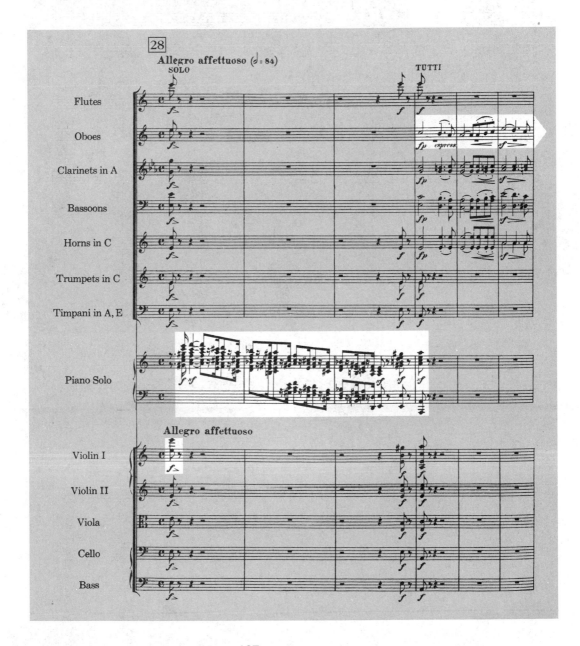

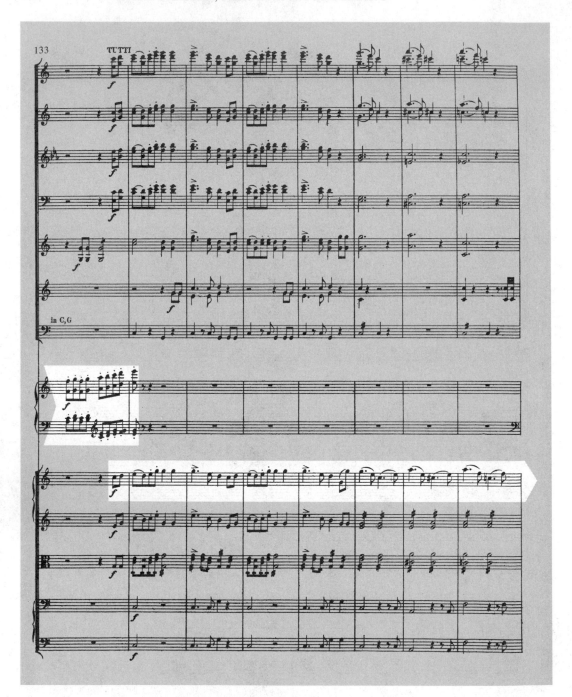

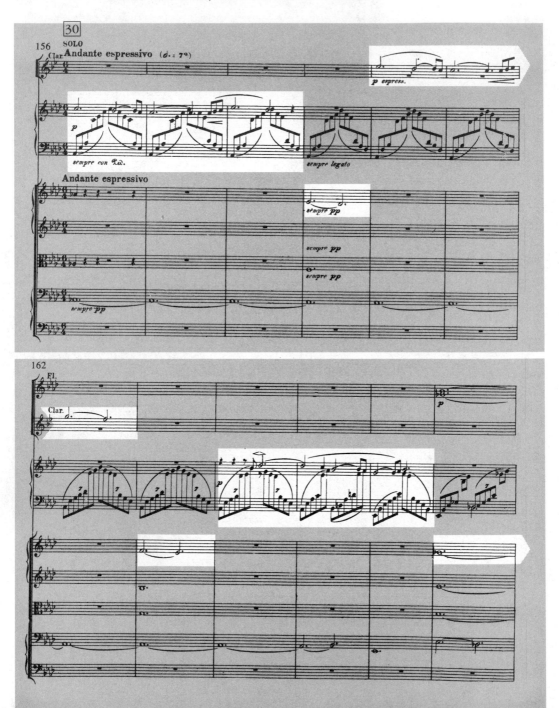

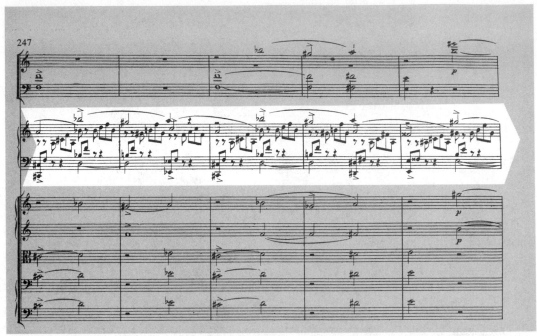

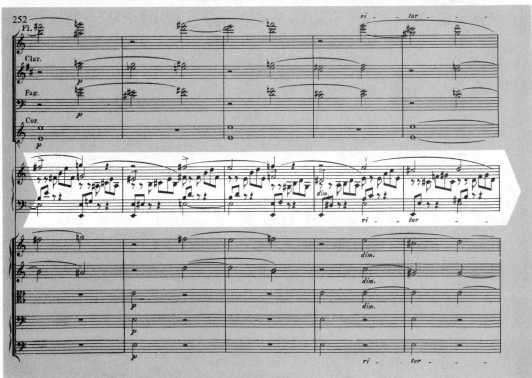

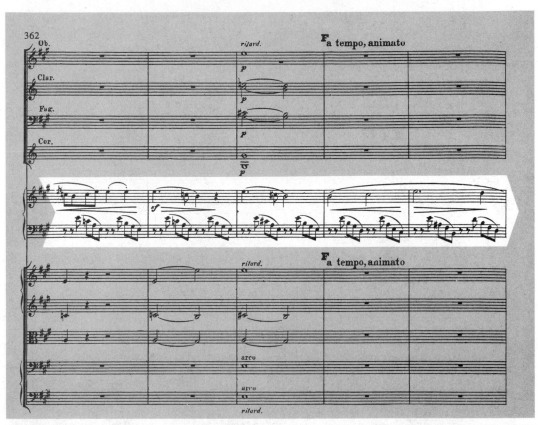

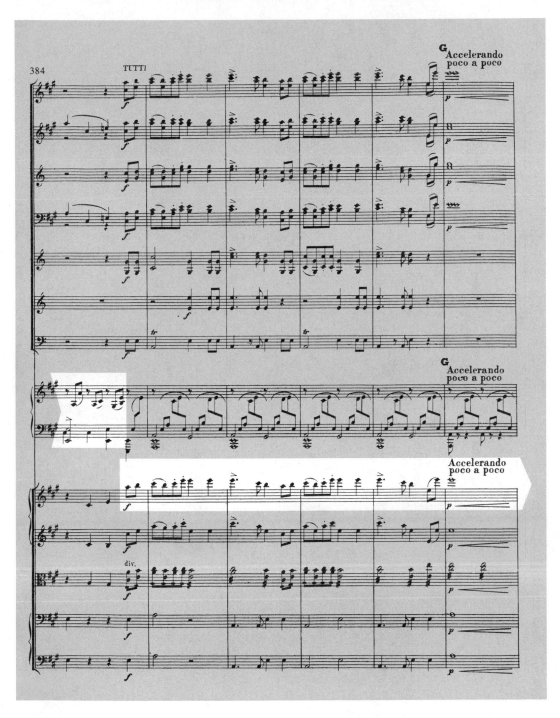

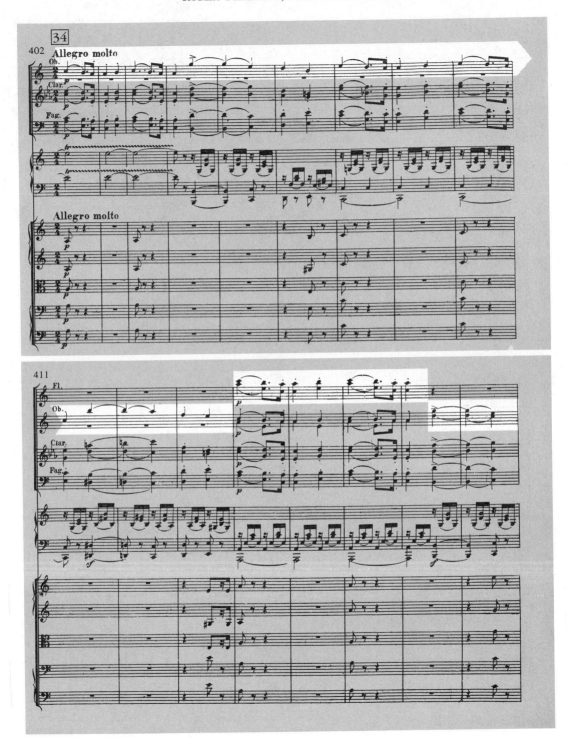

7. Franz Liszt (1811–1886)

8:5A/6   8:5/ 35 – 37

Wilde Jagd (Wild Hunt),
Transcendental Etude No. 8 (1851)

168

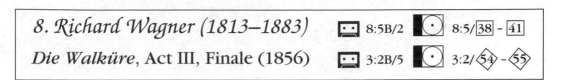

Editor's note: Shorter Norton recording begins on page 183.

WOTAN.

Hel - denLob von hol - den Lippen dir floss: dieser Au - gen strahlendes Paar   das
he - roes'praise from sweetest lips has flowed forth: those gleaming ra - di-ant eyes   that

oft   im Sturm mir ge - glänzt   wenn Hoff - nungsseh-nendasHerz   mir
oft   in storms on me shone,   when hope - less yearning my heart   had

seng - te,   nach Wel - ten-won-ne mein Wunsch ver-langte,   aus wild   we - bendem
wast-ed,   when world's de-lights all   my wish - es wakened, thro'wild   wil - dering

Ban-gen: zum letz - ten Mal   letz' es mich heut'   mit des
sad-ness: once more to - day,   lured by their light,   my

(Sie sinkt mit geschlossenen Augen, sanft ermattend, in seine Arme zurück. Er geleitet sie zart auf einen niedrigen Mooshügel
(*She sinks back with closed eyes, unconscious, in his arms. He gently bears her to a low mossy mound, which is overshadowed*

zu liegen, über den sich eine breitästige Tanne ausstreckt.)　　　　　　　　　　　　　(Er betrachtet sie und schliesst
by a wide-spreading fir tree, and lays her upon it.)　　　　　　　　　　　　　(*He looks upon her and closes*

ihr den Helm: sein Auge weilt dann auf der Gestalt der Schlafenden, die er nun mit dem grossen Stahlschilde der Walküren ganz
her helmet: his eyes then rest on the form of the sleeper, which he now completely covers with the great steel shield of the

zudeckt. ___ Langsam kehrt er sich ab, mit einem schmerzlichen Blicke wendet er sich noch einmal um.)
Valkyrie. ___ He turns slowly away, then again turns round with a sorrowful look.)

9. Giuseppe Verdi (1813–1901)

La traviata, Act II, Finale (1853)

Editor's note: Shorter Norton recording begins on page 200.

No. 15. "Di sprezzo degno se stesso rende"
Continuation of Finale

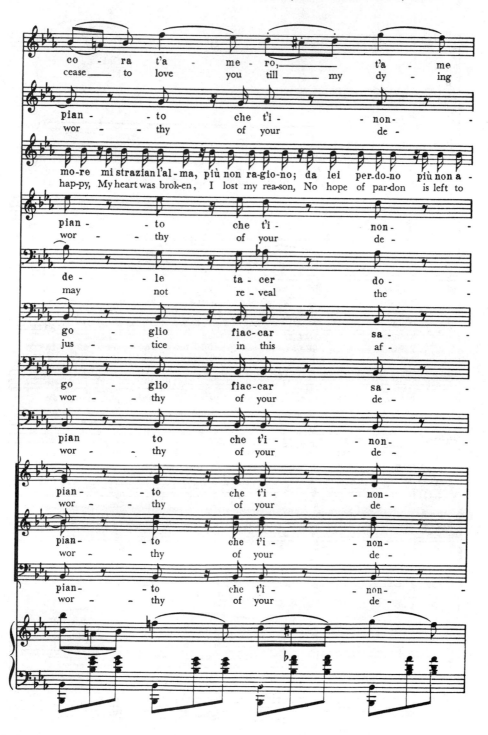

(*Germont draws Alfred with him. The Baron follows him. Violetta is led by Flora into another room. The others disperse.*)

End of the Second Act.

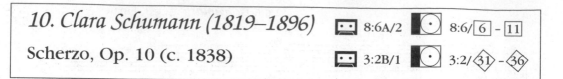

10. Clara Schumann (1819–1896)

Scherzo, Op. 10 (c. 1838)

11. *Johannes Brahms (1833–1897)*

A German Requiem, Fourth Movement (1868)

TEXT AND TRANSLATION

Wie lieblich sind deine
Wohnungen, Herr Zebaoth!
Meine Seele verlanget und sehnet
sich nach den Vorhöfen des Herrn:
mein Leib und Seele freuen sich
in dem lebendigen Gott.
Wie lieblich . . .
Wohl denen, die in deinem
Hause wohnen, die loben
dich immerdar!
Wie lieblich . . .

How lovely is Thy dwelling
place, O Lord of hosts!
My soul longs and even
faints for the courts of the Lord;
my flesh and soul rejoice
in the living God.
How lovely . . .
Blessed are they that live in
Thy house, that praise
Thee evermore!
How lovely . . .

Vergebliches Ständchen
(Futile Serenade), Op. 84, No. 4 (1881)

Lebhaft und gut gelaunt. (Er.)

Gu - ten A - bend, mein Schatz, gu - ten

A - bend, mein Kind, gu - ten A - bend, mein

Kind! Ich komm' aus Lieb' zu dir, ach, mach' mir auf die Tür,

mach' mir auf die Tür, mach' mir auf, mach' mir auf, mach' mir auf die Tür!

TEXT AND TRANSLATION

Er (He)

Guten Abend, mein Schatz,	Good evening, my love,
Guten Abend, mein Kind!	Good evening, my child!
Ich komm' aus Lieb' zu dir,	I come out of love for you,
Ach, mach' mir auf die Tür!	Ah, open the door for me!
Mach' mir auf die Tür!	Open the door for me!

Sie (She)

Mein Tür ist verschlossen,	My door is locked,
Ich lass' dich nicht ein;	I will not let you in.
Mutter, die rät mir klug,	Mother warned me
Wär'st du herein mit Fug,	That if I let you in willingly,
Wär's mit mir vorbei!	All would be over with me!

Er (He)

So kalt ist die Nacht,	The night is so cold,
So eisig der Wind,	The wind is so icy,
Dass mir das Herz erfriert,	That my heart is freezing.
Mein' Lieb' erlöschen wird;	My love will be extinguished;
Öffne mir, mein Kind!	Open up for me, child!

Sie (She)

Löschet dein Lieb',	If your love is extinguished,
Lass sie löschen nur!	Just let it go out!
Löschet sie immer zu,	Just keep on extinguishing it;
Geh' heim zu Bett, zur Ruh',	Go home to bed, to rest!
Gute Nacht, mein Knab'!	Good night, my boy!

Translated by *Philip Miller*

TRADITIONAL

13. Brahms

Symphony No. 4 in E minor, Fourth Movement (1885)

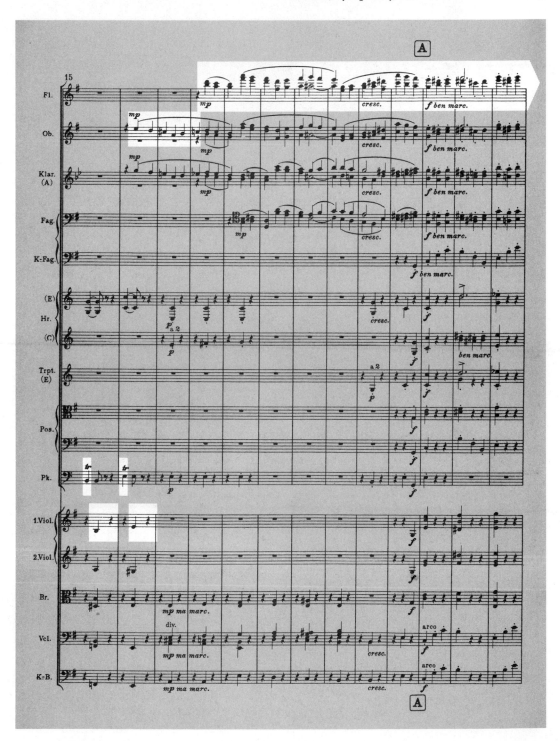

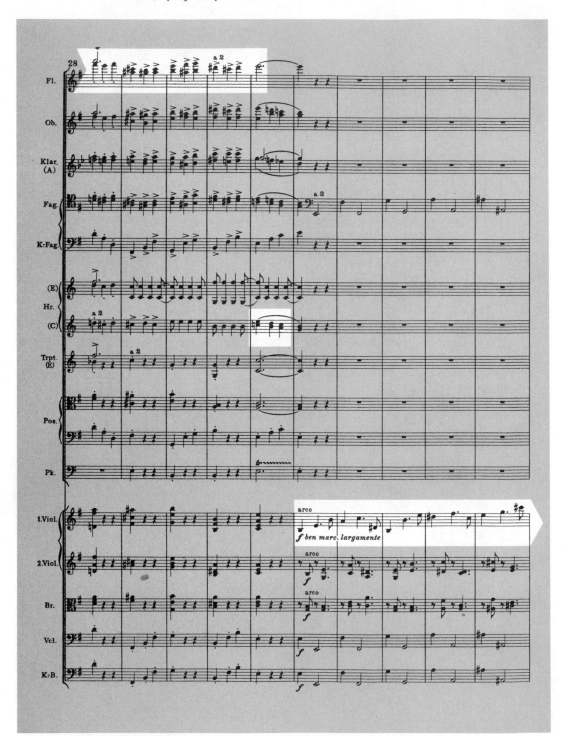

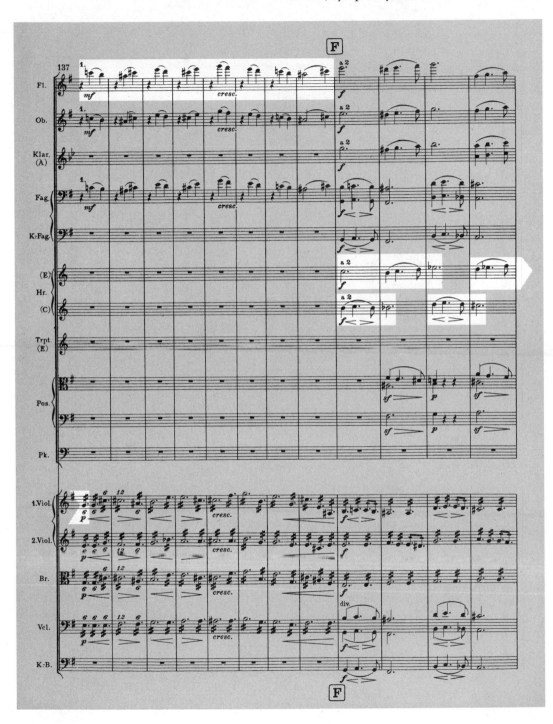

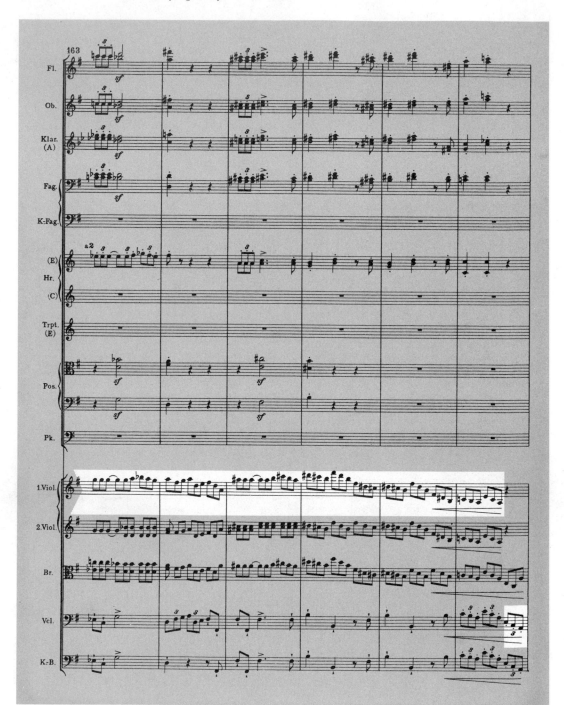

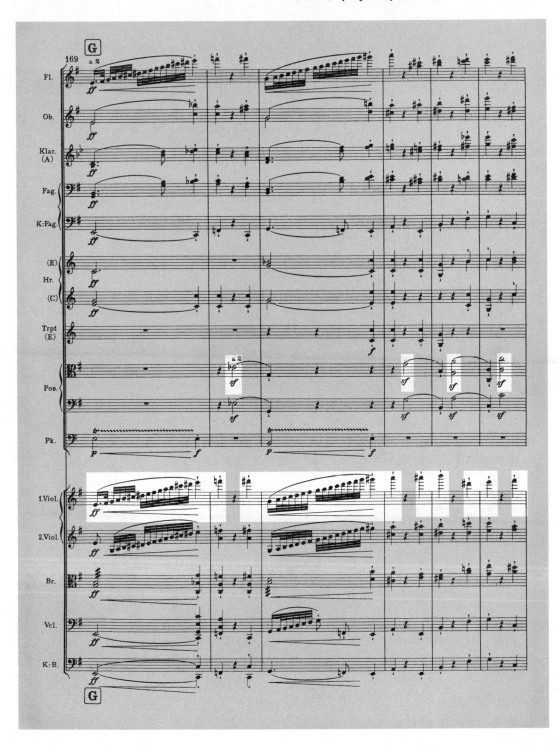

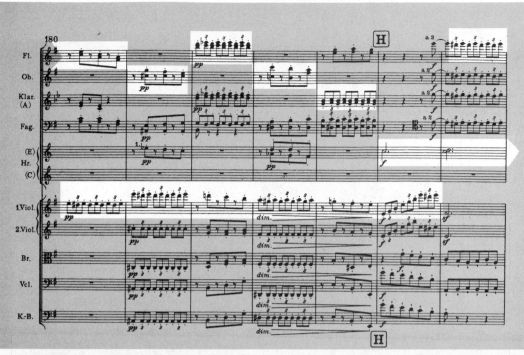

193
Fl.
Ob.
a 2
Klar. (A)
Fag.
K.-Fag.
(E)
Hr.
(C)
Trpt. (E)
Pos.
Pk.
1.Viol.
2.Viol.
Br.
div.
Vcl.
K.-B.
ff marc.

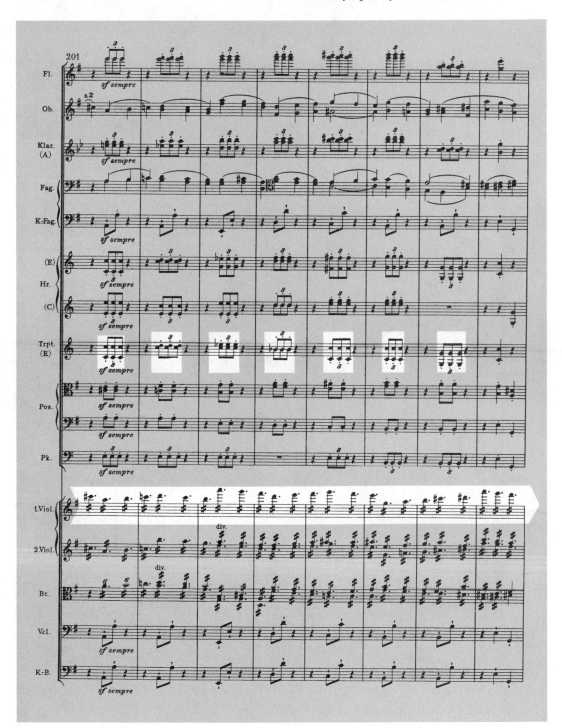

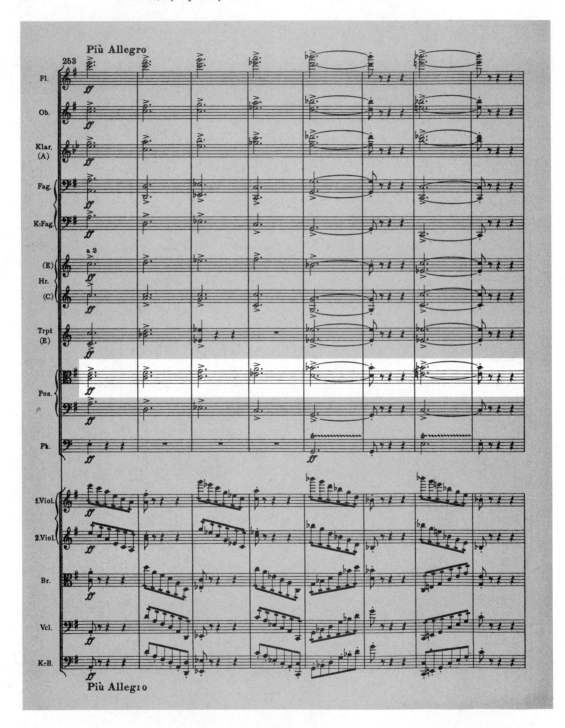

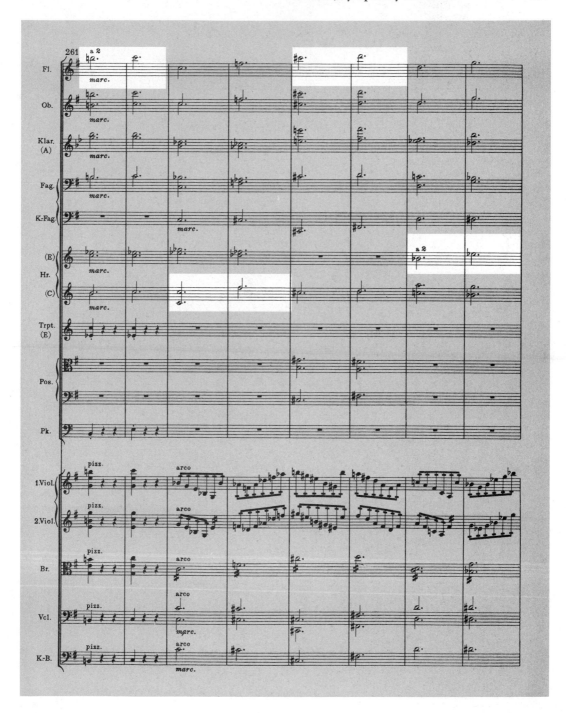

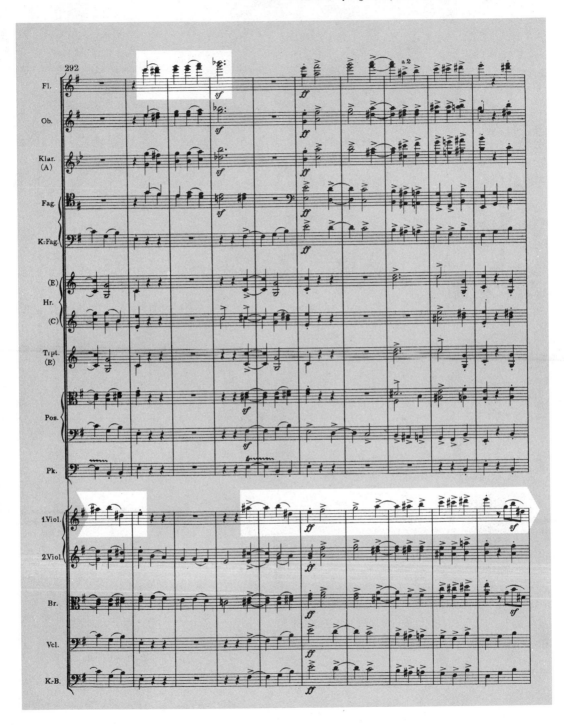

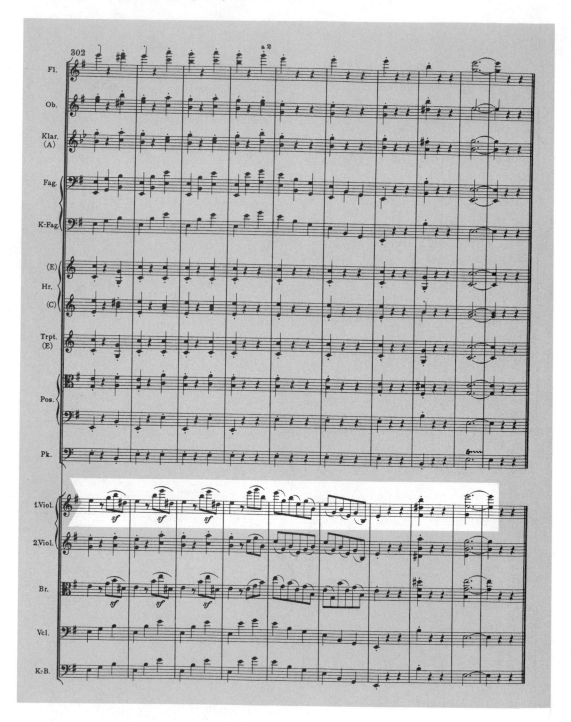

14. Georges Bizet (1838–1875)

Carmen, Act I, excerpt (1875)

Scene No. 3

BIZET, *Carmen*: Act I, excerpt

(The relief appears:

poco a poco cresc.

first a bugler and fifer, then a crowd of street-boys. — Following the latter, Lieutenant Zuniga and

Corporal Don José, then the dragoons. — During Street-boys' Chorus, the relief forms in front of the

guard going off duty.)

Don José.

ban - te. / Ce doit ê - tre Mi - ca - é - la!
braids. / I am sure that was Mi - ca - e - la.

17 (Exeunt guard going off duty. — Street-boys march off behind bugler and fifer of the retiring guard, in the same manner as they followed those of the relief.)

Et la gar - de des - cendan - te / Ren - tre chez elle
We are sol - diers march-ing proud - ly, / Leav-ing with the

et s'en va. / Son - ne, trom - pette é - cla - tan - te! / Ta ra ta ta ta
chang-ing guard. / Boys, blow your bu - gles loud - ly! /

ra ta ta. / Nous mar - chons la tê - te hau - te / Com - me de pe -
See us march in per - fect man - ner, / We are nev - er

Recitative

Ju - pe bleue   et nat - te tom - ban - te.
"Light blue skirt   and ver - y   long   braids!"

Don José.

Tu ne ré - ponds rien __ à ce - la? Je ré - ponds que c'est
Well,   am I   right __ a - bout that? I ad - mit   you are

vrai, je ré - ponds que je l'ai - - me!
right. I con - fess, she's the girl   I love.

Recit.

Quant aux ou - vri - è - res d'i - ci, Quant __ à leur beau-
And   as for the fac - to - ry   girls, When __ you hear the

té,   les voi - ci! Et vous pou - vez ju - ger vous - mê - me.
bell,   they'll be here. Then you can judge their looks quite well.

attacca subito.

Scene No. 4

Carmen.

Sopranos I & II.
(*Cigarette-girls*).

(The factory-bell is ringing.)

Chorus.

Tenors.
(*Young men*).

Basses.
(*Townspeople*)

(*Don José sits down and pays no attention to the shifting scenes. He repairs the*

Allegro. (♩. = 104.)

Piano.

pp

chain of his saber.)

(the bell stops.)   *cresc. molto.*

ff

Allegretto moderato. (♩ = 104.)

pp

Scene No. 5

*)Imitated from a Spanish song.

15. Modest Petrovich Musorgsky (1839–1881)

Pictures at an Exhibition, Three Movements (1874; orchestrated by Ravel, 1922)

8:6B/1–2   8:6/ 23 – 33

3:2B/3   3:2/ 42 – 48

Promenade

Editor's note: The pianoforte part at the bottom of each score system shows the original piano version; it is not part of the orchestral score.

9. *The Hut on Fowl's Legs (Baba-Yaga)*

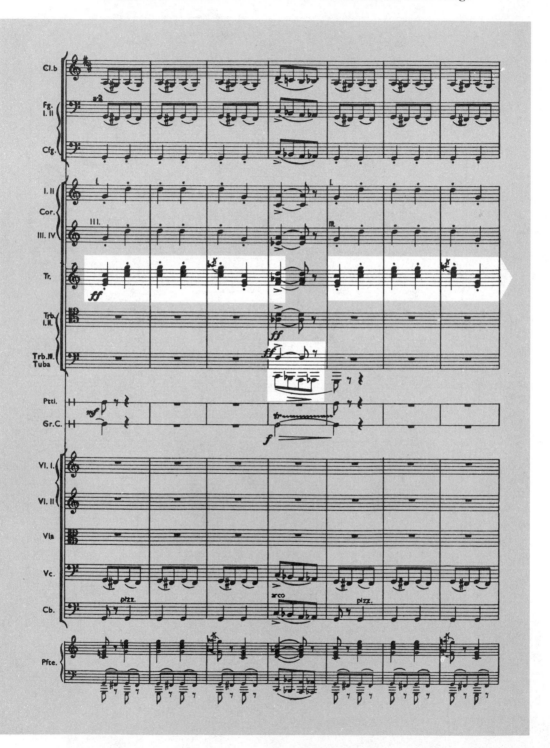

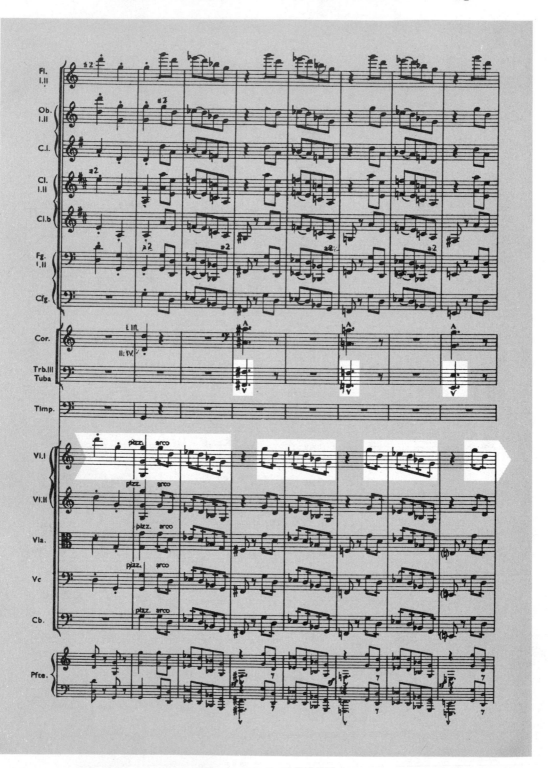

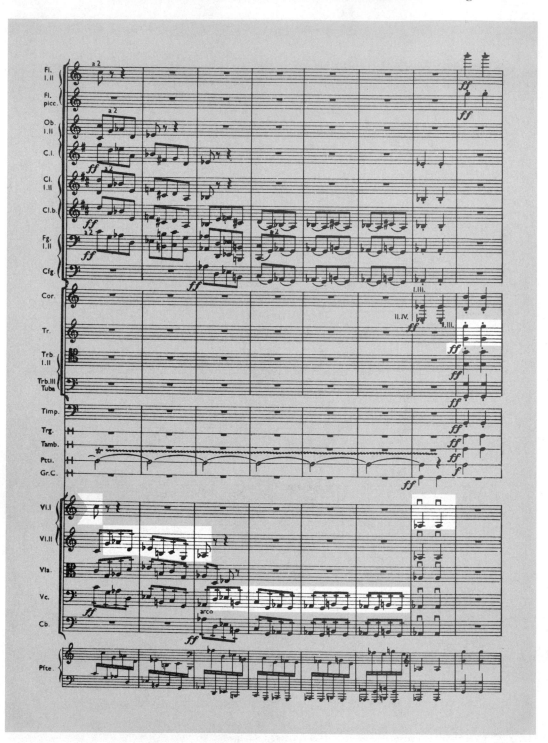

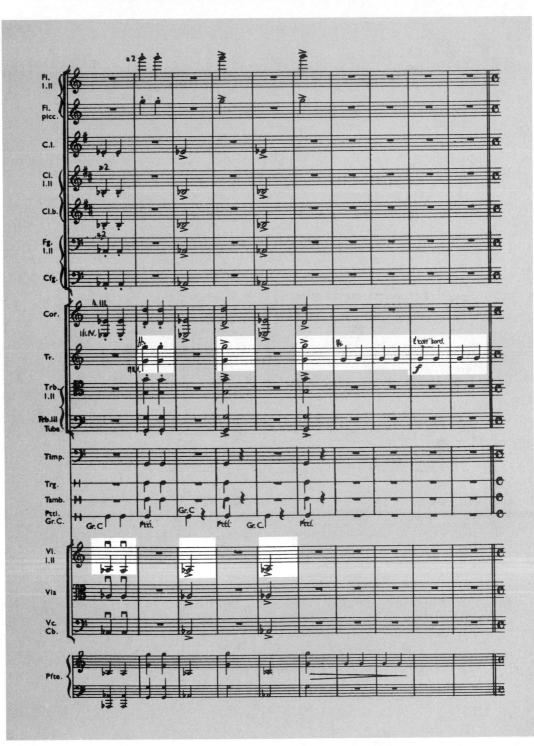

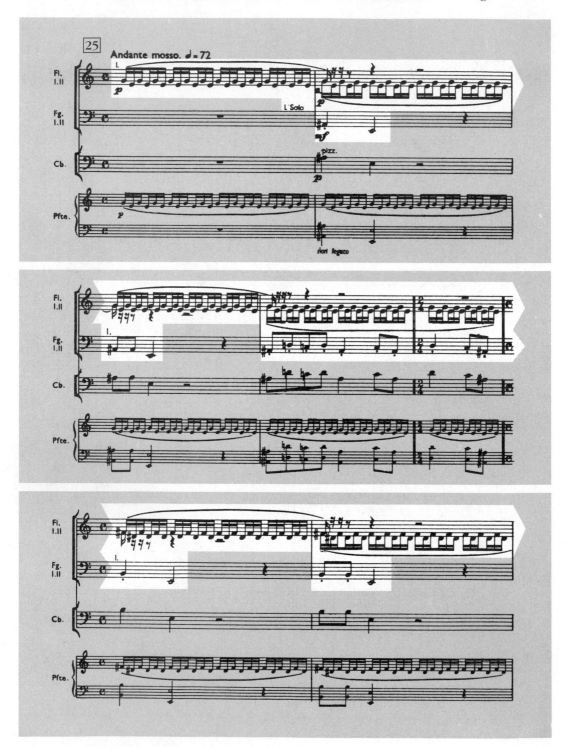

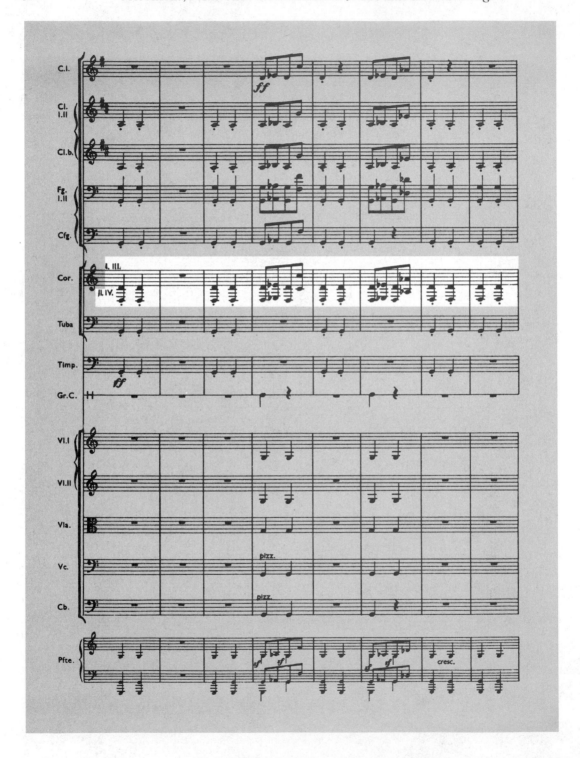

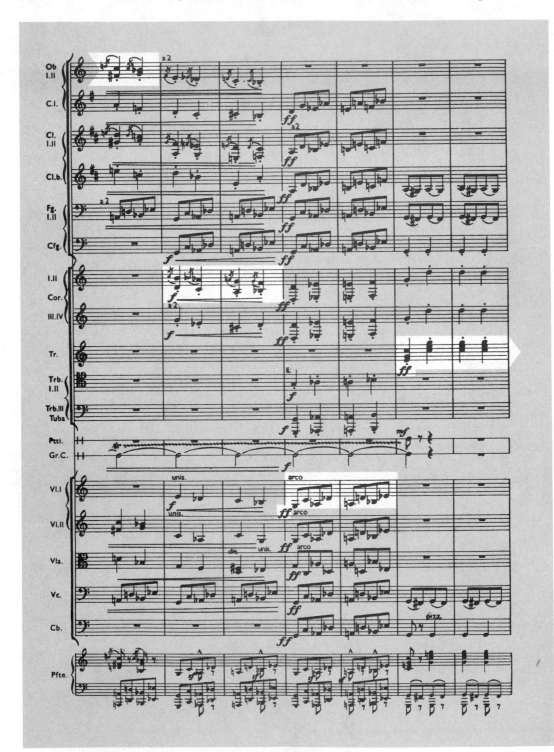

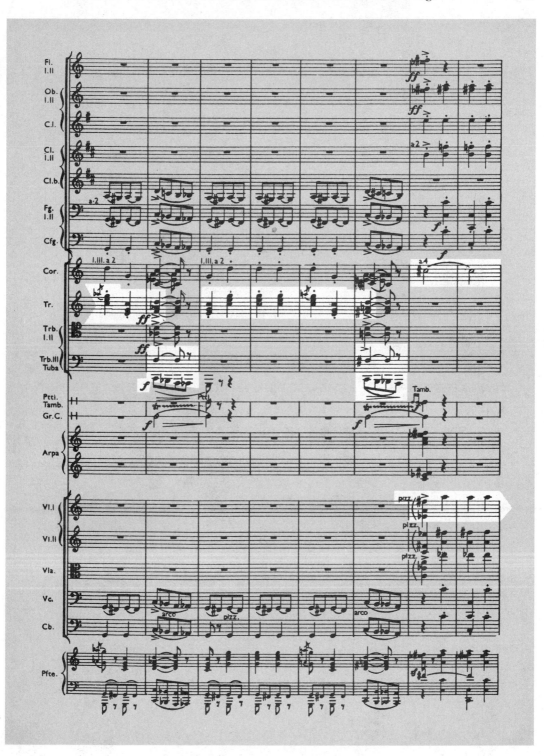

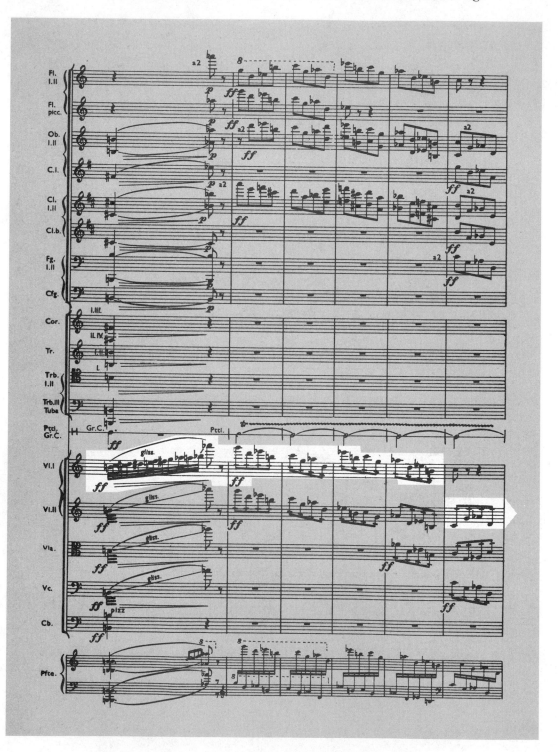

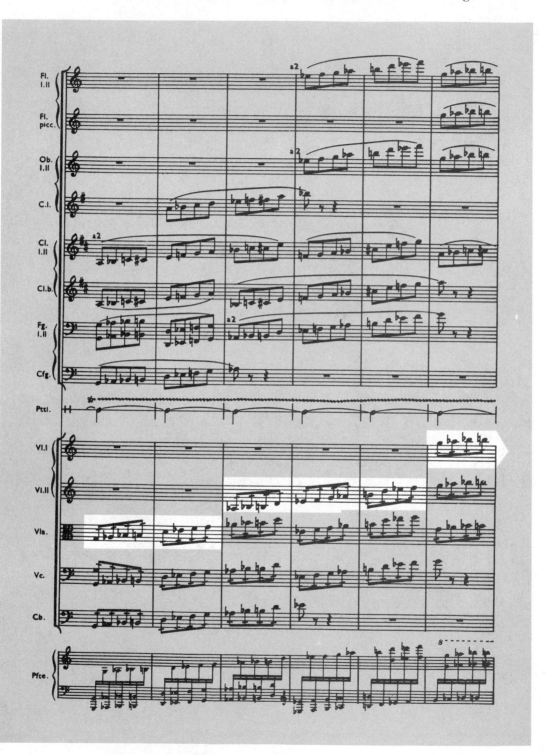

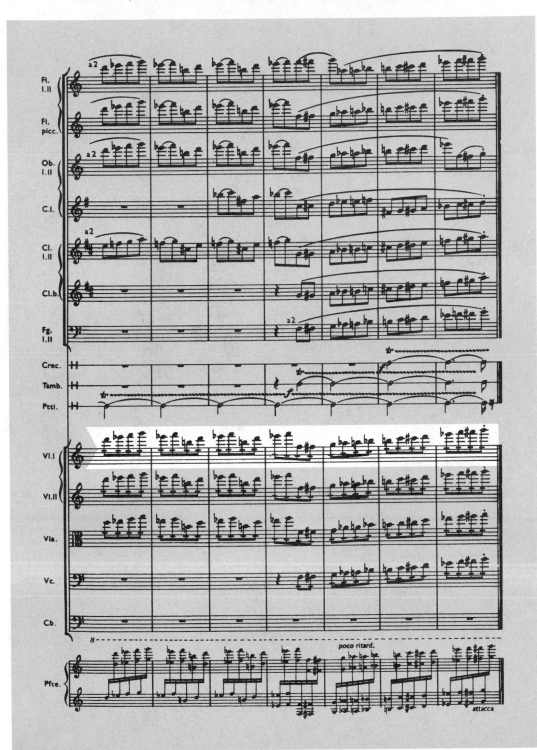

10. *The Great Gate of Kiev*

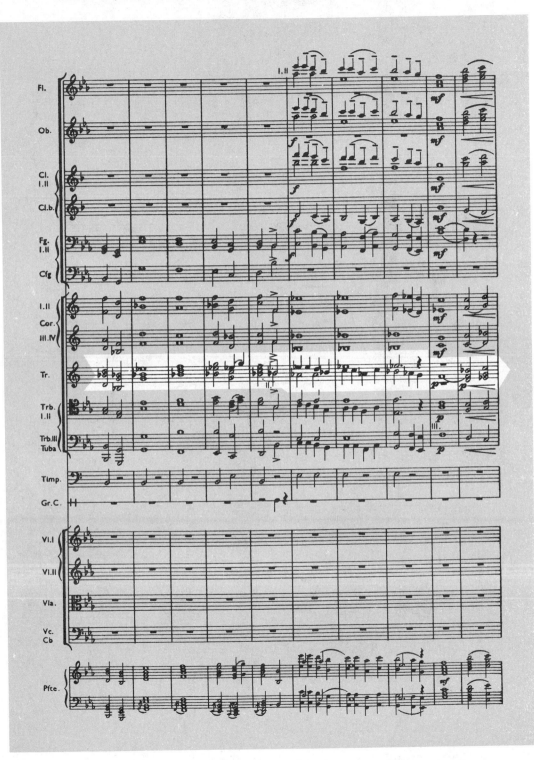

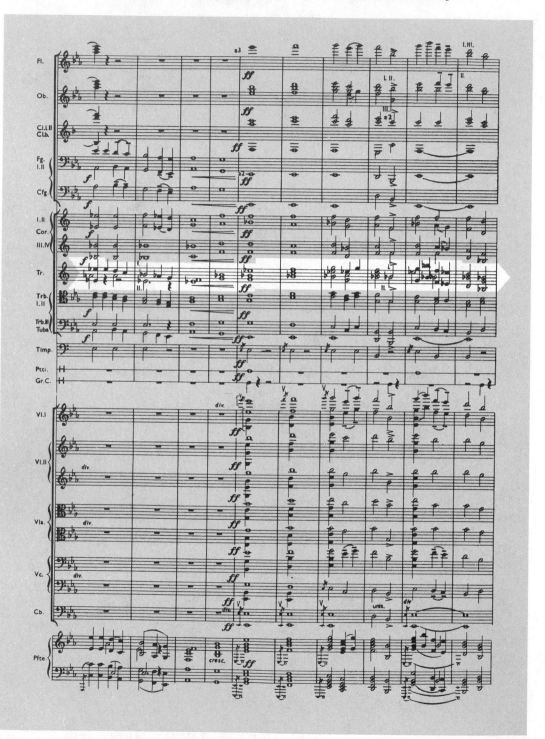

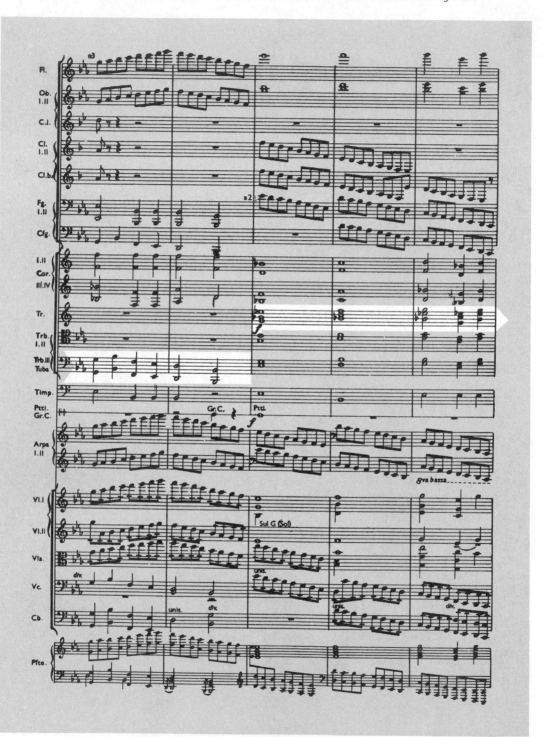

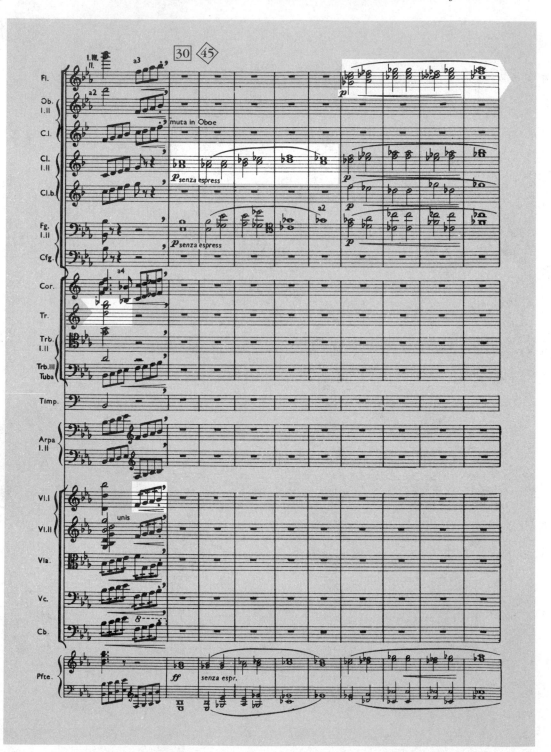

16. Peter Ilyich Tchaikovsky (1840–1893)

The Nutcracker, Three Dances from Act II (1892)

March

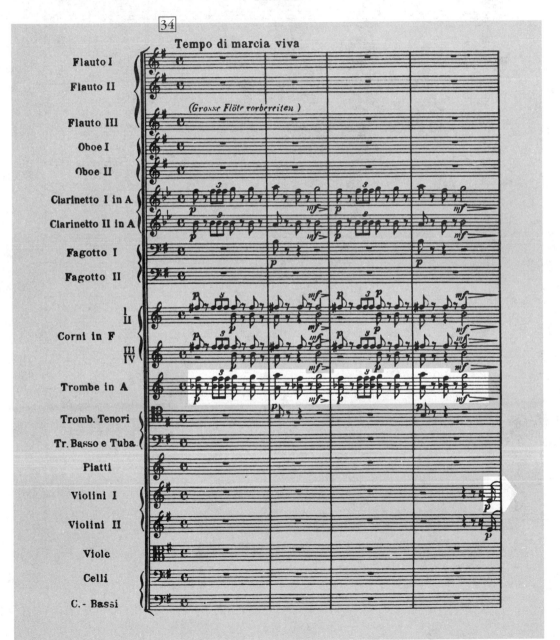

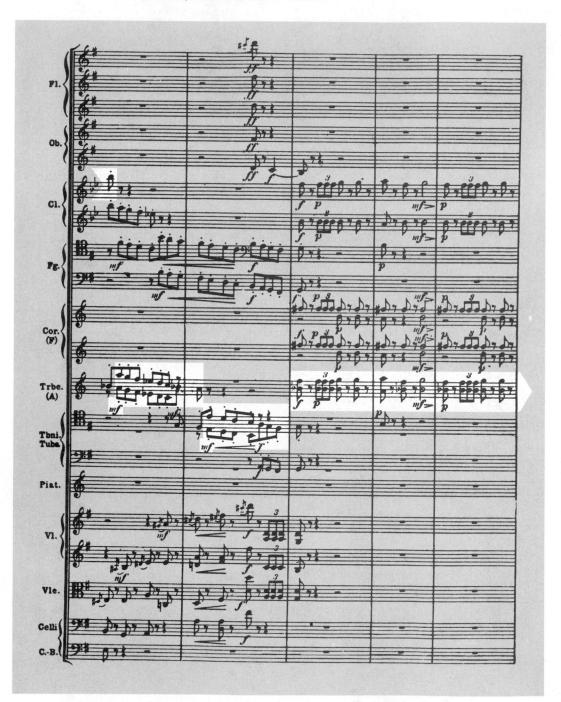

Fl.
Ob.
Cl.
Fg.
Cor. (F)
Trbe. (A)
Tbni. Tuba
Mit Paukenschlägel.
Piat.
Vl.
Vle.
Celli
C.-B.

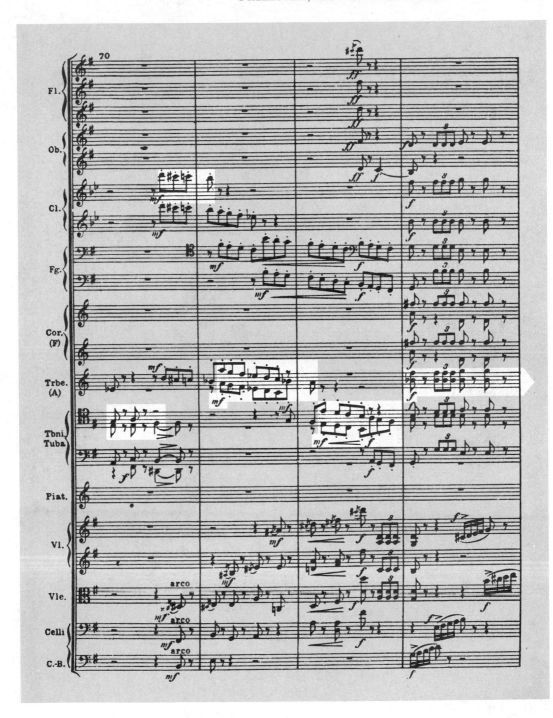

Dance of the Sugar Plum Fairy

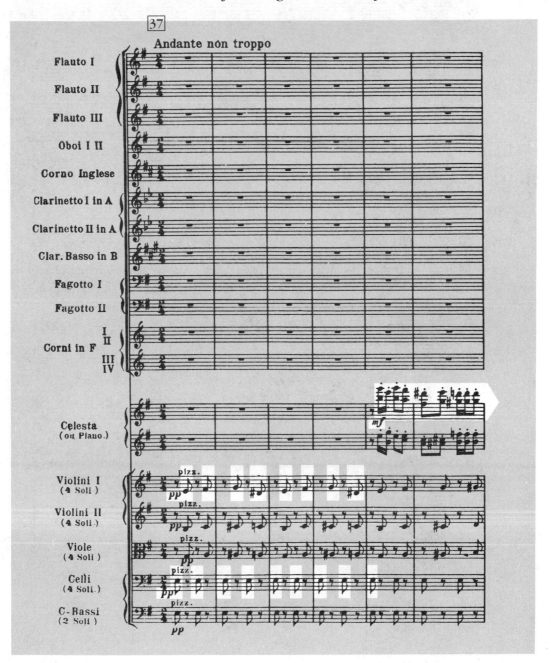

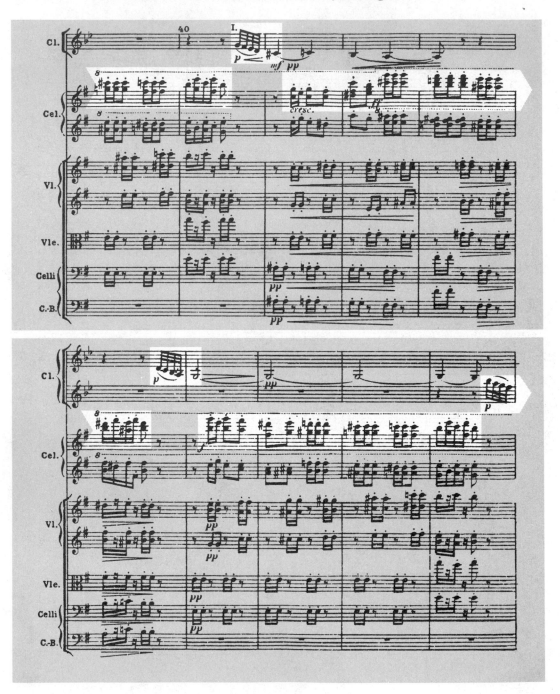

Trepak (Russian Dance)

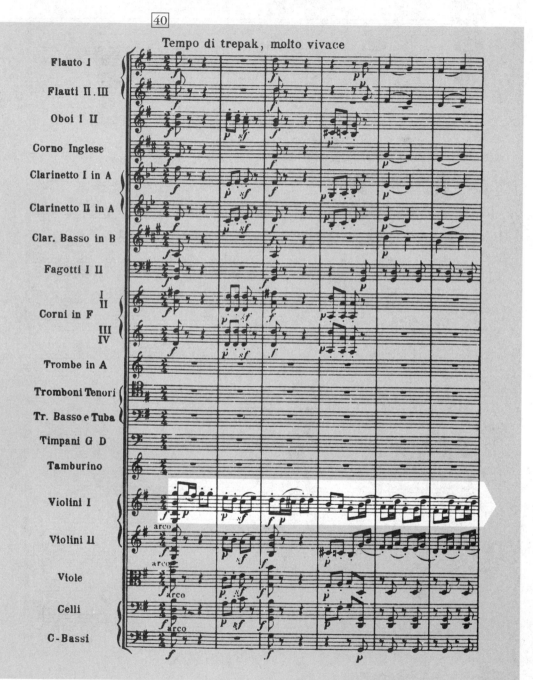

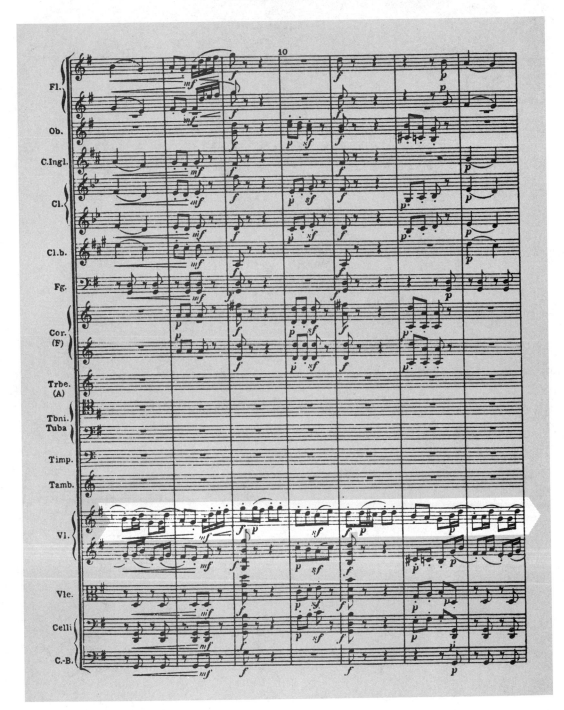

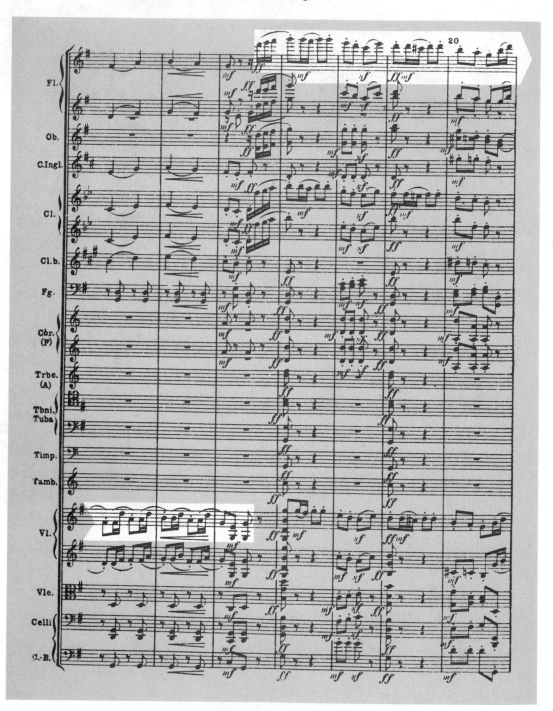

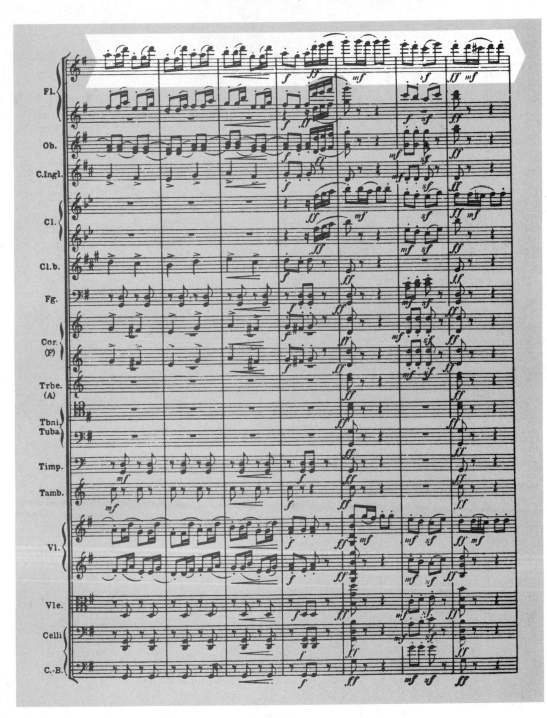

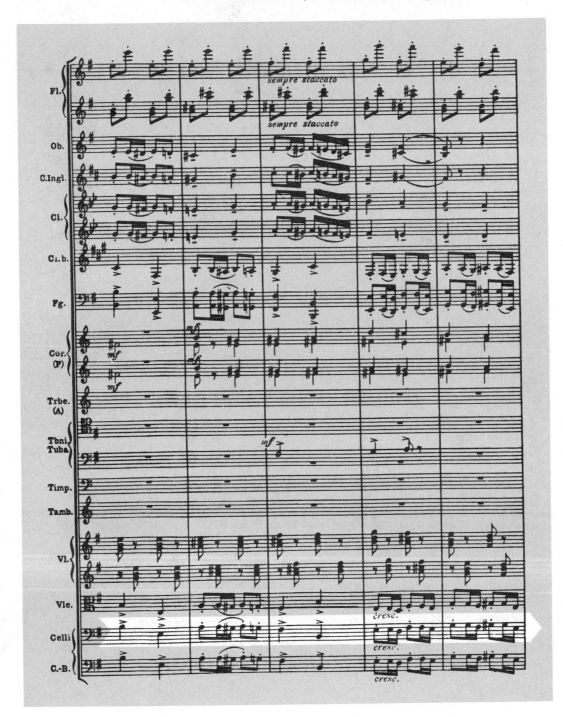

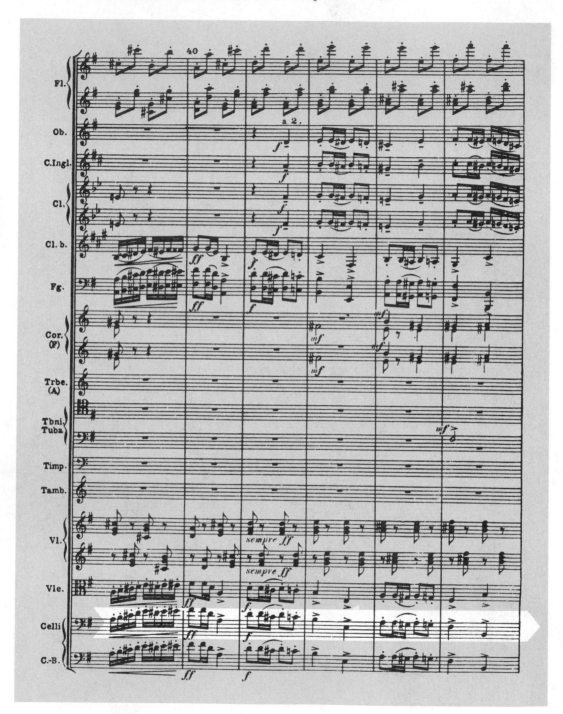

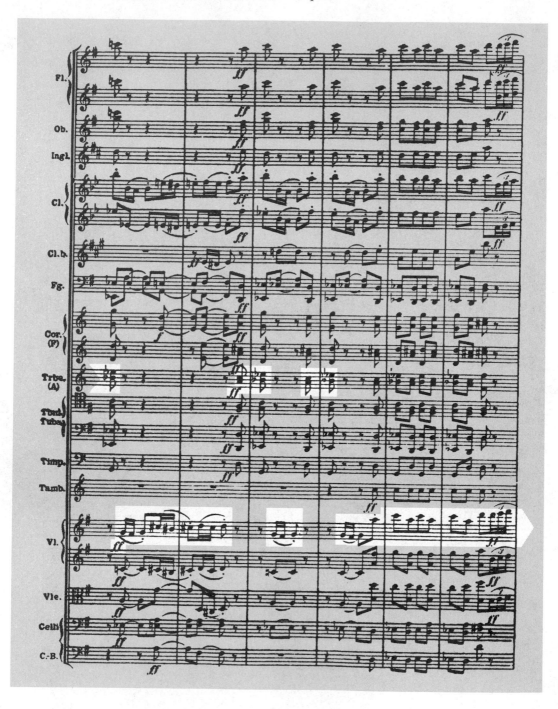

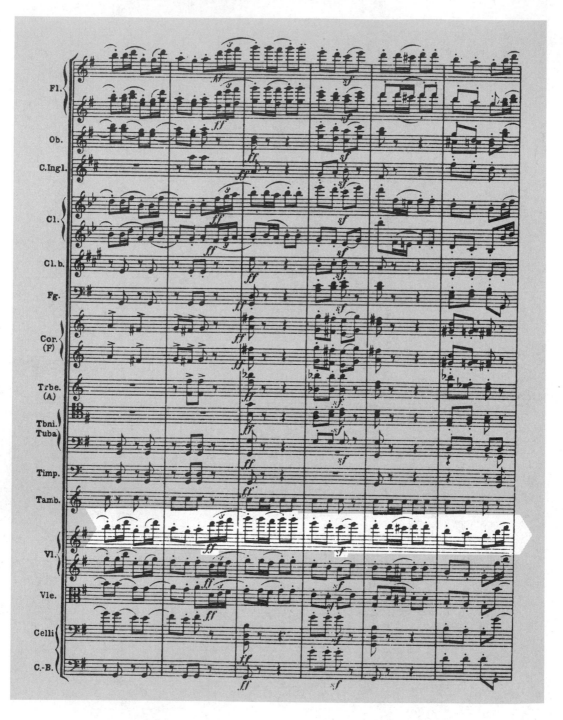

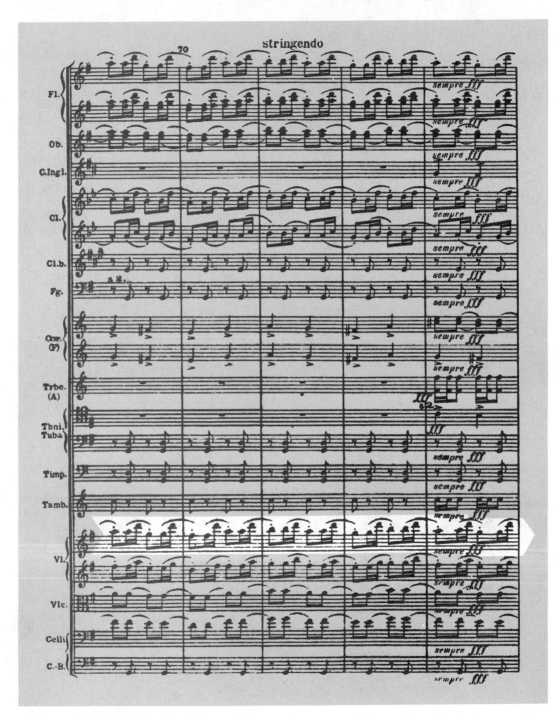

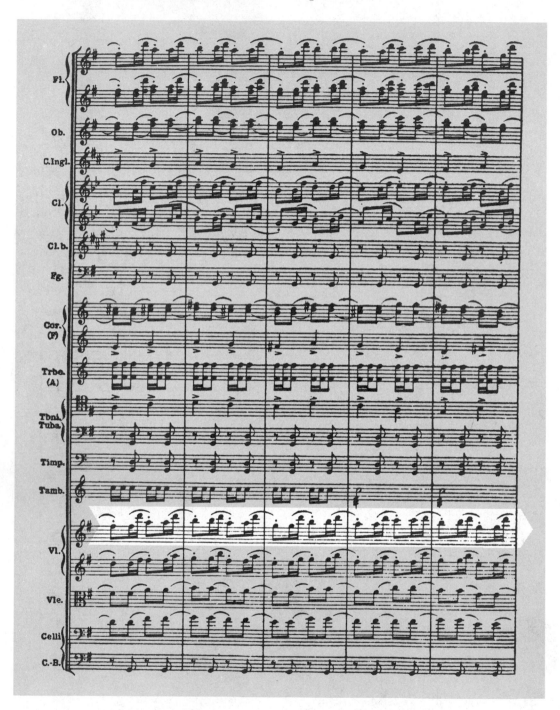

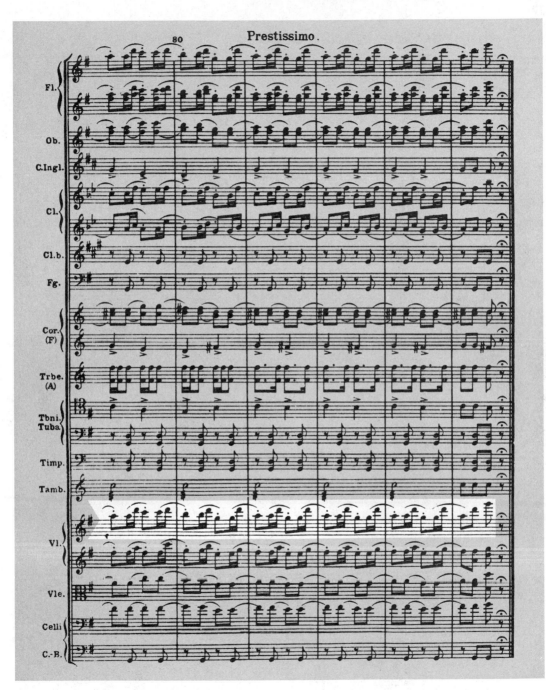

17. Antonín Dvořák (1841–1904)

Symphony No. 9 in E minor,
From the New World,
Second Movement (1893)

 8:6B/6   8:6/ 43 - 45

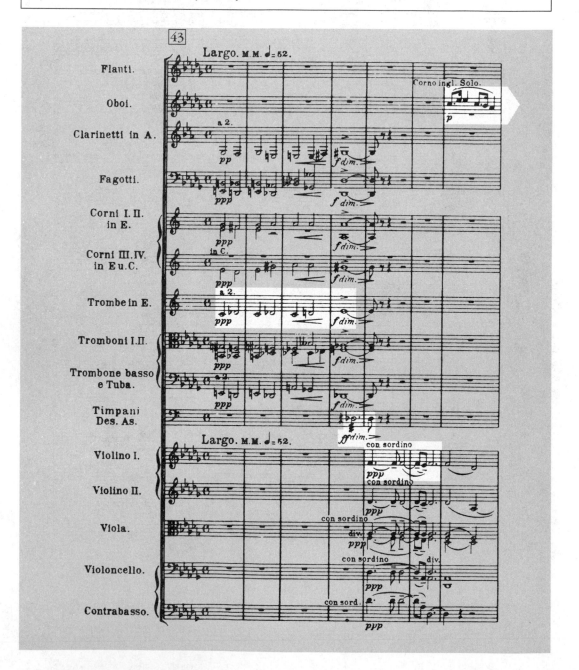

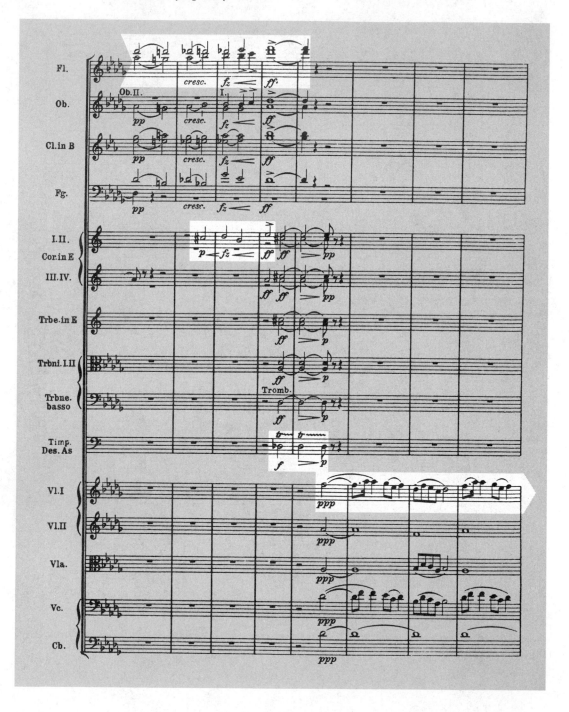

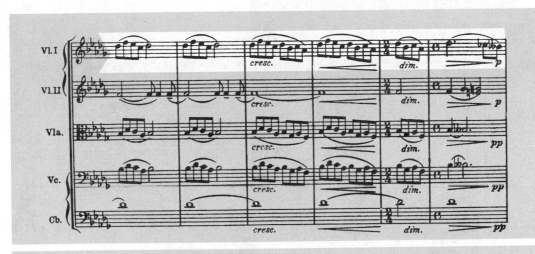

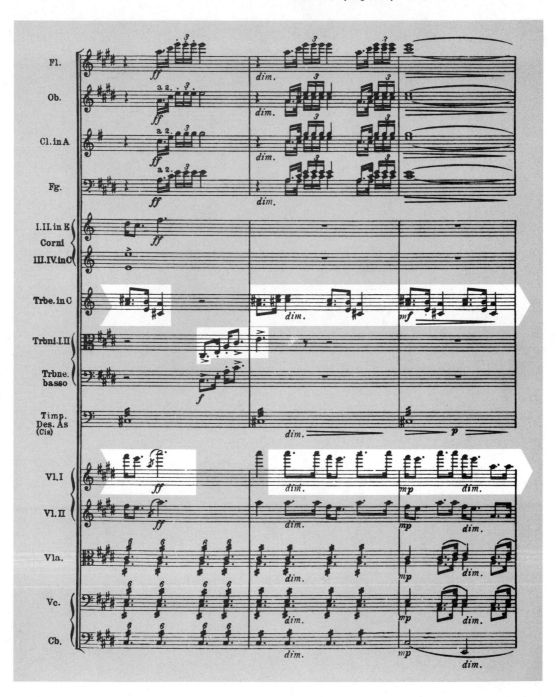

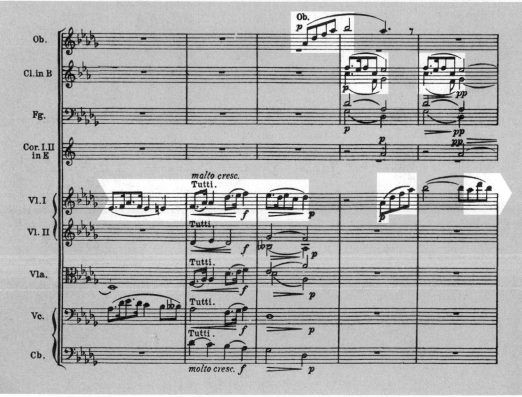

18. Ruggero Leoncavallo (1857–1919)

Pagliacci, Act I,
Canio's Aria (1892)

Recitar! Mentre pre - so dal de-li-
To per-form! When my head's whir-ling with an-

rio non so più quel che di-co e quel che fac-cio! Ep-pur è
guish, not know-ing what I'm say-ing or what I'm do-ing! And yet I'll

End of Act I

Das Lied von der Erde (The Song of the Earth), Third Movement (1908–9)

3. "Von der Jugend" ("Of Youth")

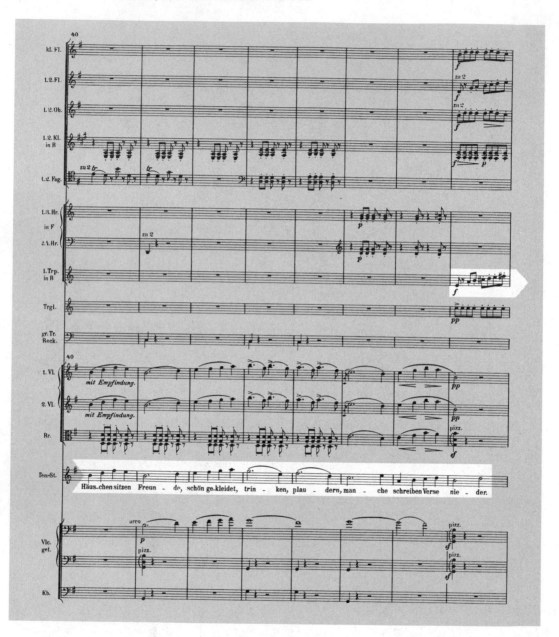

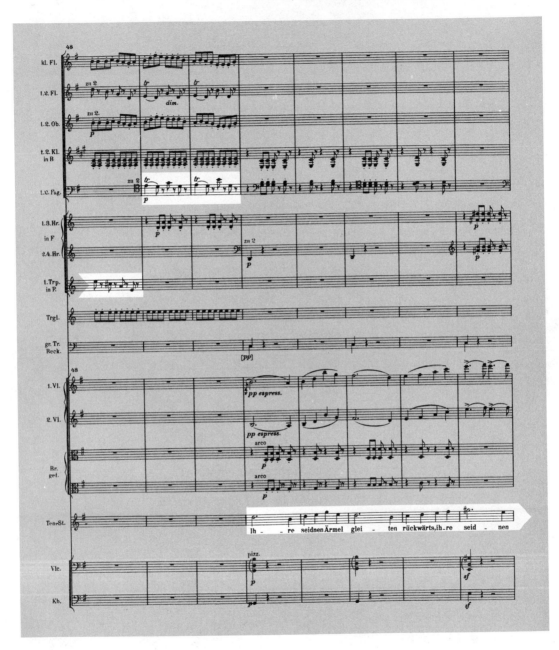

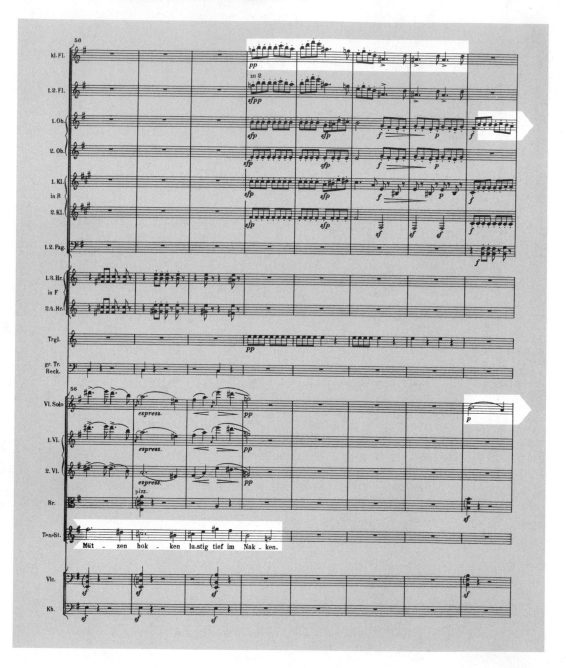

Al - les auf dem Kop - fe ste - hend in dem Pa - vil - lon aus grü - nem und aus wei - ßem

TEXT AND TRANSLATION

Mitten in dem kleinen Teiche steht ein Pavillon aus grünem und aus weissem Porzellan.	In the middle of the little pool stands a pavilion of green and of white porcelain.
Wie der Rücken eines Tigers wölbt die Brücke sich aus Jade zu dem Pavillon hinüber.	Like the back of a tiger arches the bridge of jade over to the pavilion.
In dem Häuschen sitzen Freunde, schön gekleidet, trinken, plaudern, manche schreiben Verse nieder.	In the little house, friends are sitting beautifully dressed, drinking, chatting; several are writing verses.
Ihre seidnen Ärmel gleiten rückwärts, ihre seidnen Mützen hokken lustig tief im Nakken.	Their silken sleeves slip backwards, their silken caps perch gaily on the back of their necks.
Auf des kleinen Teiches stiller Wasserfläche zeigt sich alles wunderlich im Spiegelbilde.	On the little pool's still surface everything appears fantastically in a mirror image.
Alles auf dem Kopfe stehend in dem Pavillon aus grünem und aus weissem Porzellan;	Everything is standing on its head in the pavilion of green and of white porcelain;

wie ein Halbmond scheint die Brükke
umgekehrt der Bogen.
Freunde, schön gekleidet,
   trinken, plaudern.
	like a half-moon stands the bridge,
	upside-down its arch.
	Friends, beautifully dressed, are
	   drinking, chatting.

20. Claude Debussy (1862–1918) 📼 8:7A/1 💿 8:7/ 1 - 4

Prélude à "L'après-midi d'un faune" 📼 3:3A/2 💿 3:3/ ◇3 - ◇6
(Prelude to "The Afternoon of a
Faun") (1894)

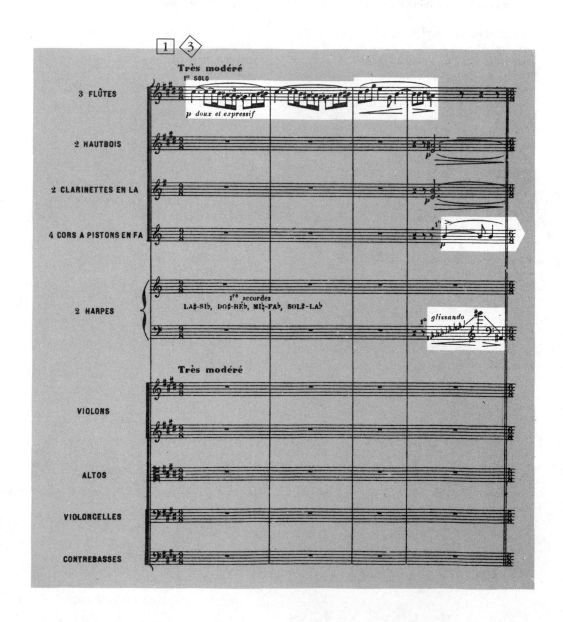

458

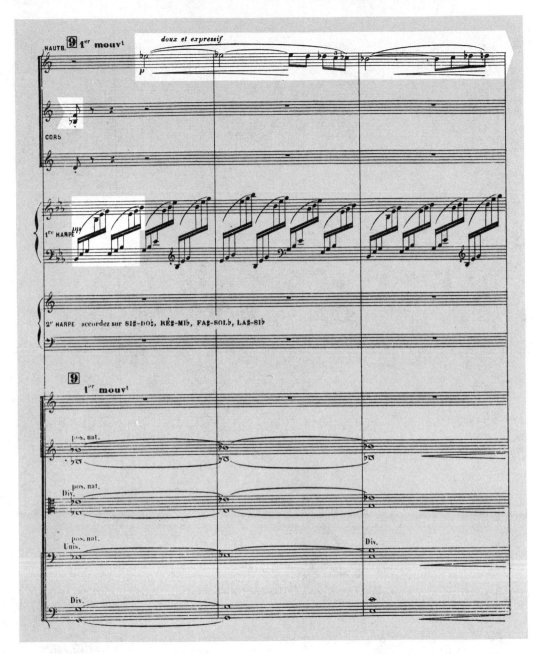

21. Richard Strauss (1864–1949) 8:7A/2 8:7/ 5 - 6

Der Rosenkavalier (The Cavalier of the Rose), Act III, Trio (1909–10)

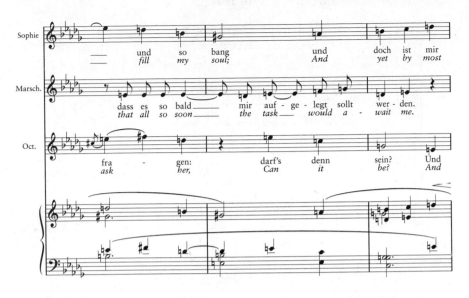

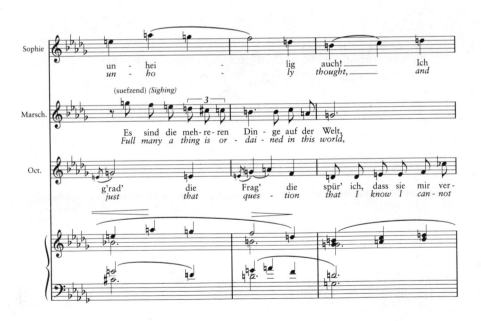

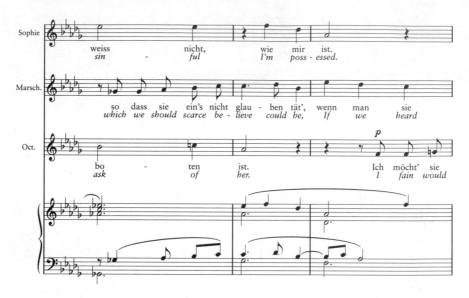

(Die Marschallin geht leise links hinein,
die Beiden bemerken es gar nicht.)
*(The Princess goes quietly into the room on the left;
the two others do not notice her.)*

22. Arnold Schoenberg (1874–1951)

Pierrot lunaire, Op. 21,
Nos. 18 and 21 (1912)

8:7A/3-4   8:7/ 7 - 10

3:3A/4-5   3:3/ 16 - 19   (MW)

No. 18. "Der Mondfleck"

ohne größere Pause, bloß
aushalten, folgt:

Serenade.
Klavier, Violoncell

Übergang zu Heimfahrt kommen dazu
Flöte, Klarinette in A, Geige

TEXT AND TRANSLATION

Einen weissen Fleck des hellen Mondes

Auf dem Rücken seines schwarzen Rockes,
So spaziert Pierrot im lauen Abend,
Aufzusuchen Glück und Abenteuer.

Plötzlich stört ihn was an seinem Anzug,
Er besieht sich rings und findet richtig—
Einen weissen Fleck des hellen Mondes
Auf dem Rücken seines schwarzen Rockes.

Warte! denkt er: das ist so ein Gipsfleck!
Wischt und wischt, doch—bringt ihn nicht
    herunter!
Und so geht er, giftgeschwollen, weiter,
Reibt und reibt bis an den frühen Morgen—
Einen weissen Fleck des hellen Mondes.

With a fleck of white—from the bright
    moon—
On the back of his black jacket,
Pierrot strolls about in the mild evening
Seeking his fortune and adventure.

Suddenly something strikes him as wrong,
He checks his clothes and sure enough finds
A fleck of white—from the bright moon—
On the back of his black jacket.

Damn! he thinks: that's a spot of plaster!
Wipes and wipes, but—he can't get it off.

And so goes on his way, his pleasure poisoned,
Rubs and rubs till the early morning—
A fleck of white—from the bright moon.

No. 21. "O alter Duft"

TEXT AND TRANSLATION

O alter Duft aus Märchenzeit,
Berauschest wieder meine Sinne!
Ein närrisch Heer von Schelmerein
Durchschwirrt die leichte Luft.

Ein glückhaft Wünschen macht mich froh
Nach Freuden, die ich lang verachtet:
O alter Duft aus Märchenzeit,
Berauschest wieder mich!

All meinen Unmut geb ich preis:
Aus meinem sonnumrahmten Fenster
Beschau ich frei die liebe Welt
Und träum hinaus in selge Weiten . . .
O alter Duft aus Märchenzeit!

O scent of fabled yesteryear,
Intoxicating my senses once again!
A foolish swarm of idle fancies
Pervades the gentle air.

A happy desire makes me yearn for
Joys that I have long scorned:
O scent of fabled yesteryear,
Intoxicating me again.

All my ill humor is dispelled:
From my sun-drenched window
I look out freely on the lovely world
And dream of beyond the horizon . . .
O scent of fabled yesteryear!

23. Charles Ives (1874–1954)

 8:7A/5   8:7 |11| - |18|

The Fourth of July, from *A Symphony: New England Holidays* (1911–13)

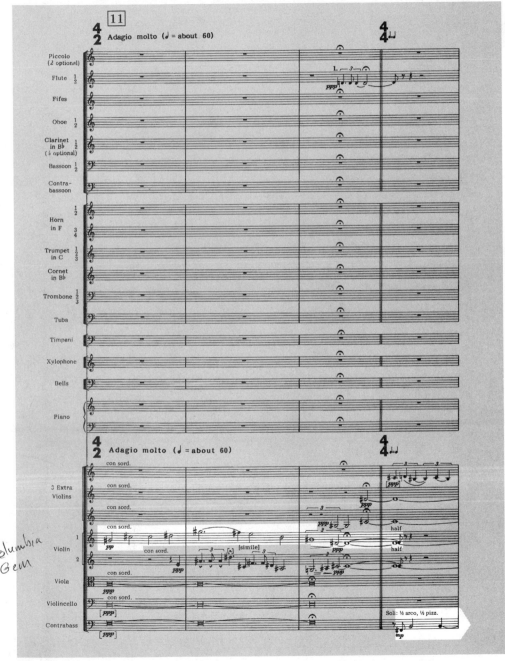

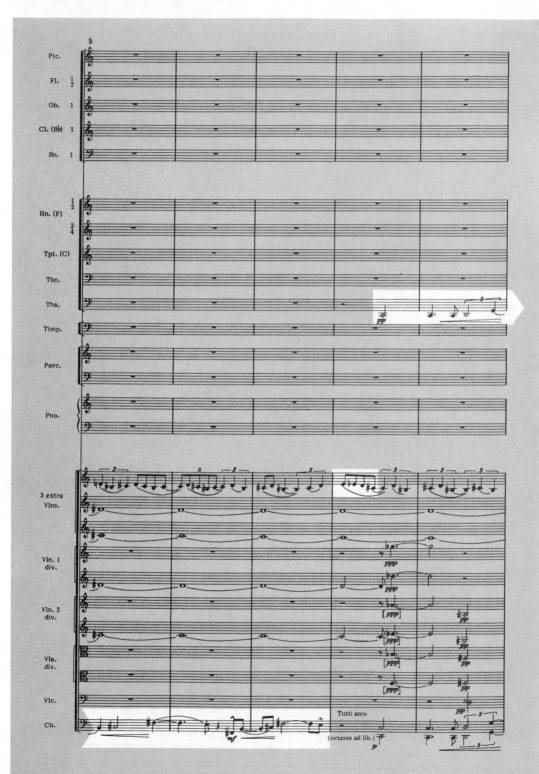

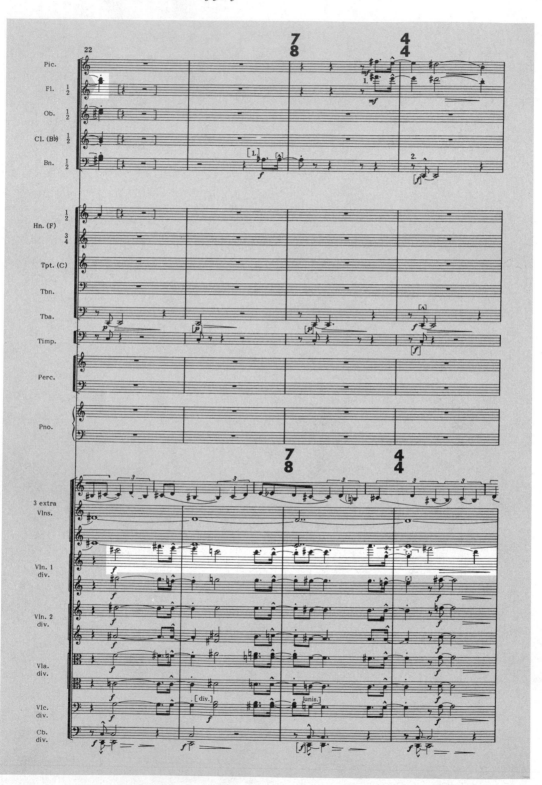

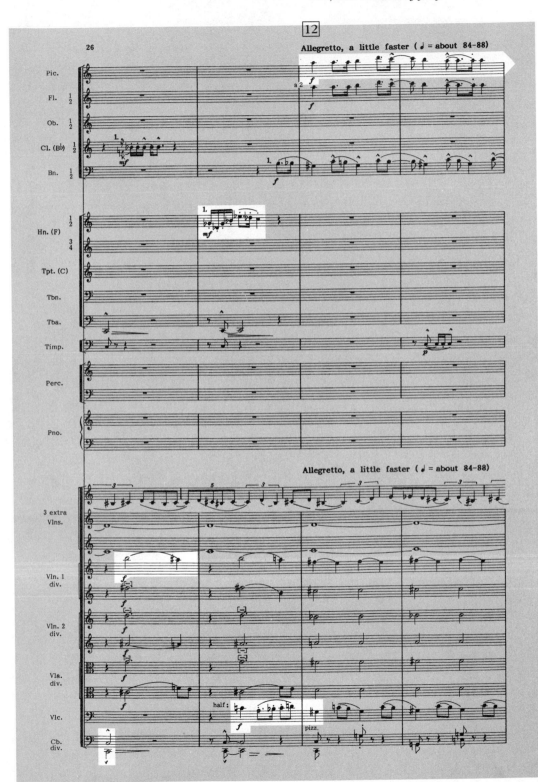

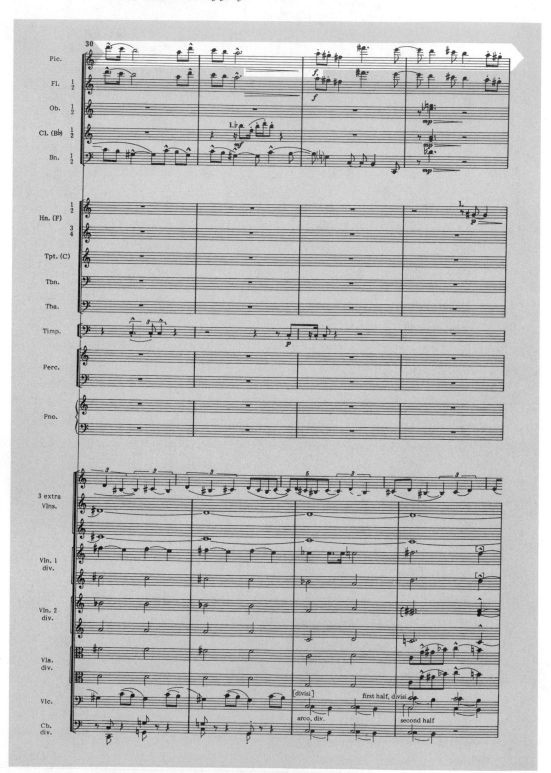

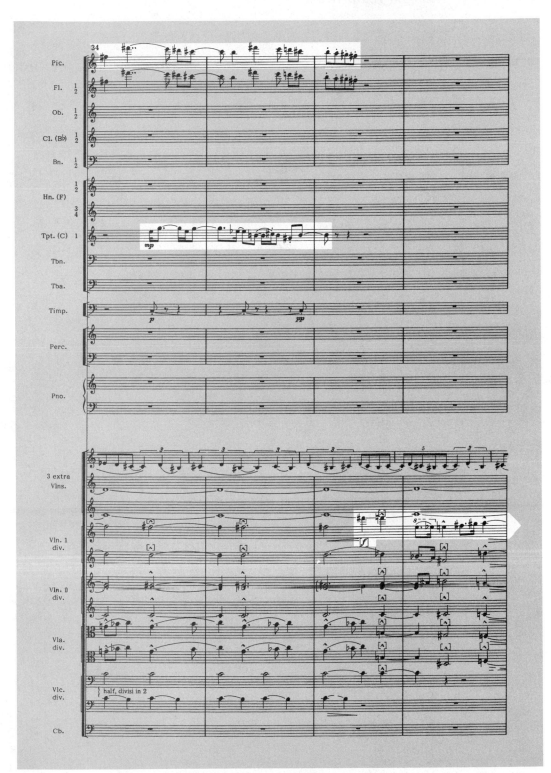

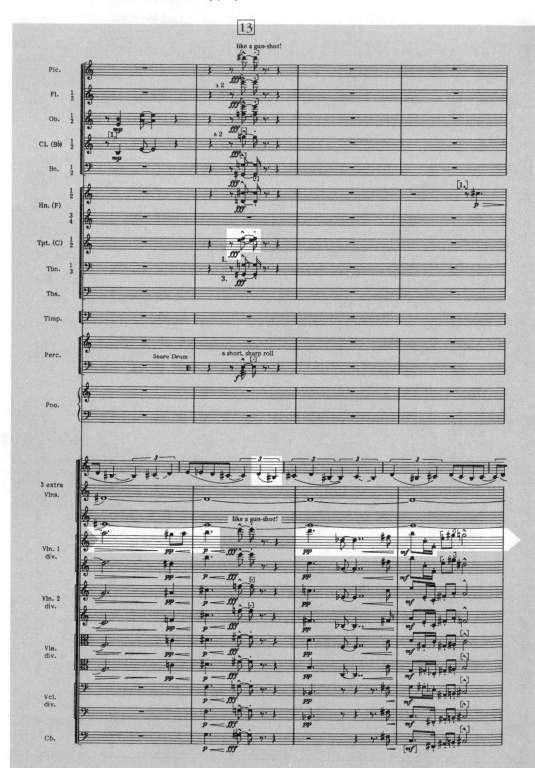

* From this point on, Ives seems to think of the Timpani as high, medium, and low,
rather than of definite pitches. This score reproduces the pitches Ives wrote. –Ed.

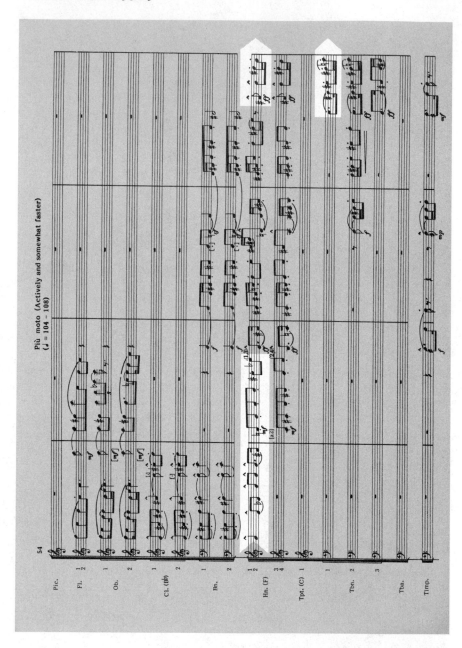

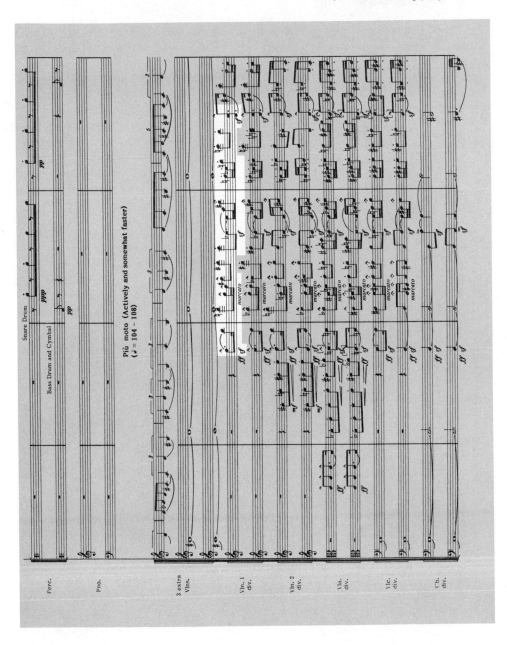

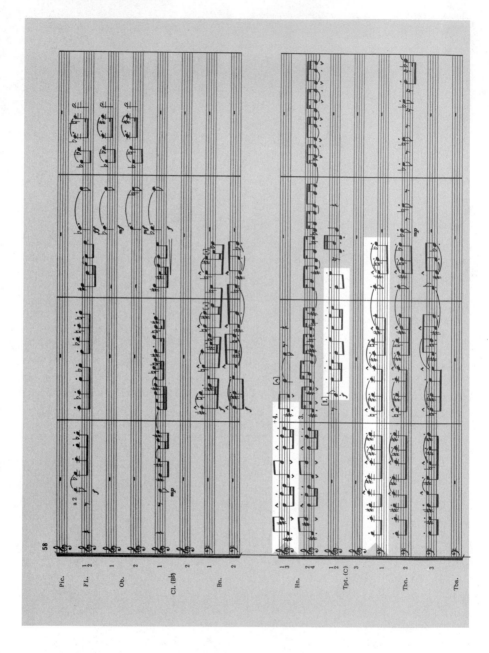

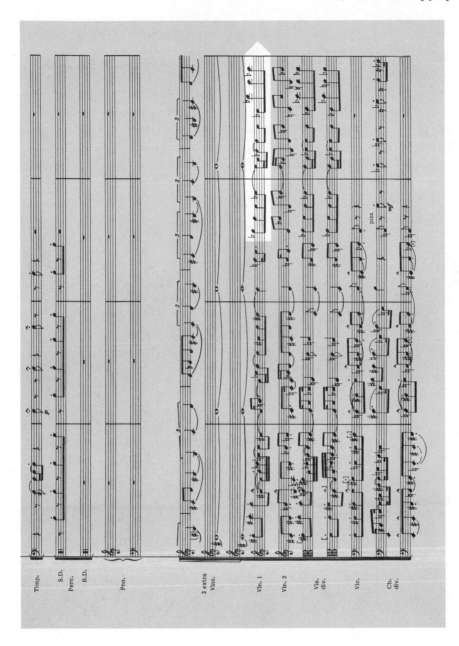

Timp.

S.D.

Perc.

B.D.

Pno.

3 extra
Vlns.

Vln. 1

Vln. 2

Vla.
div.

Vlc.

Cb.
div.

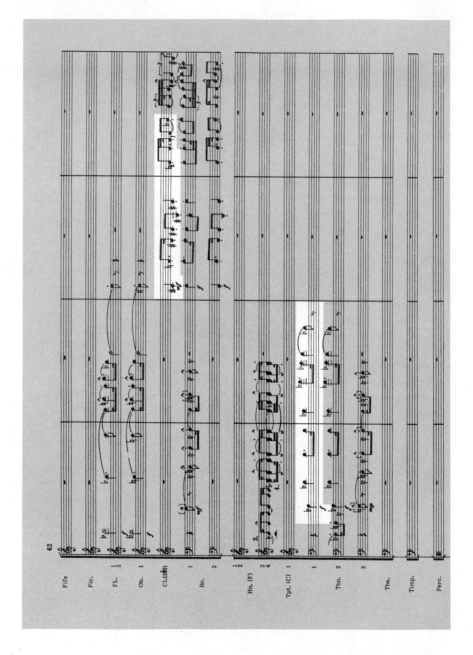

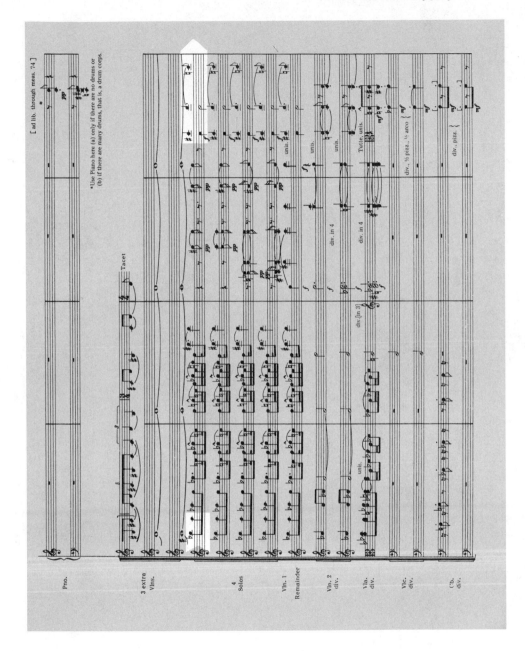

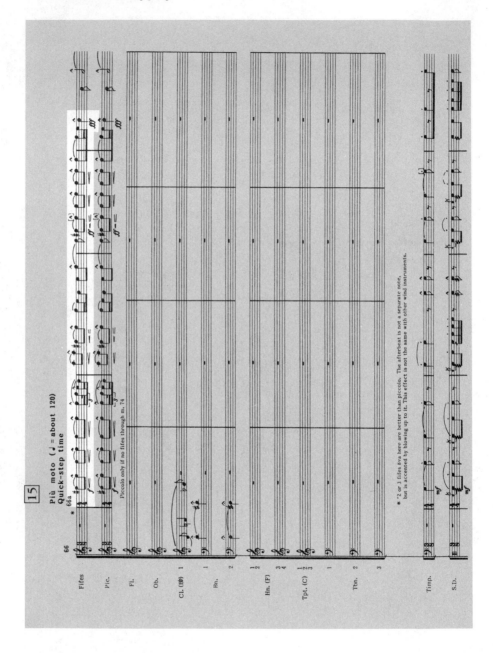

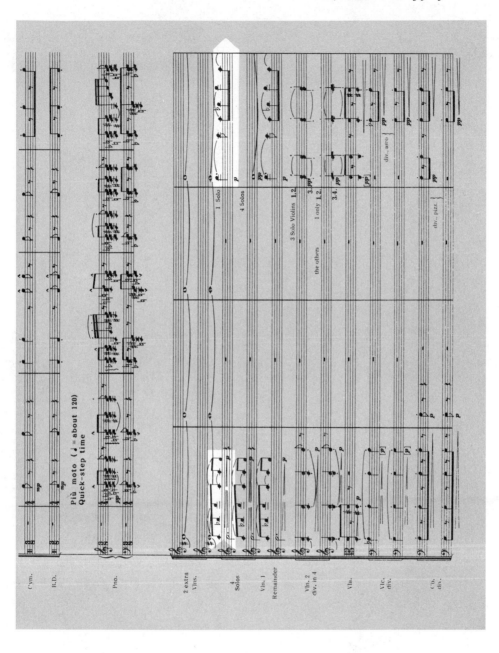

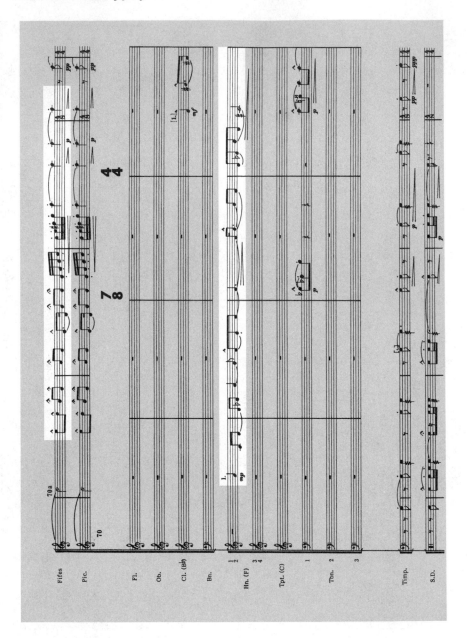

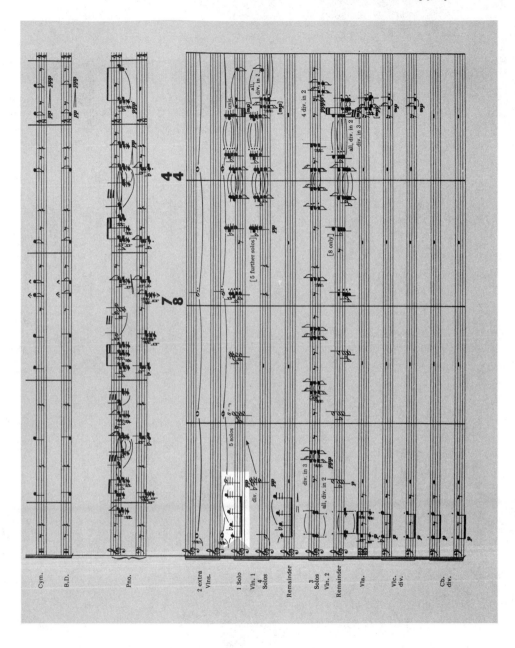

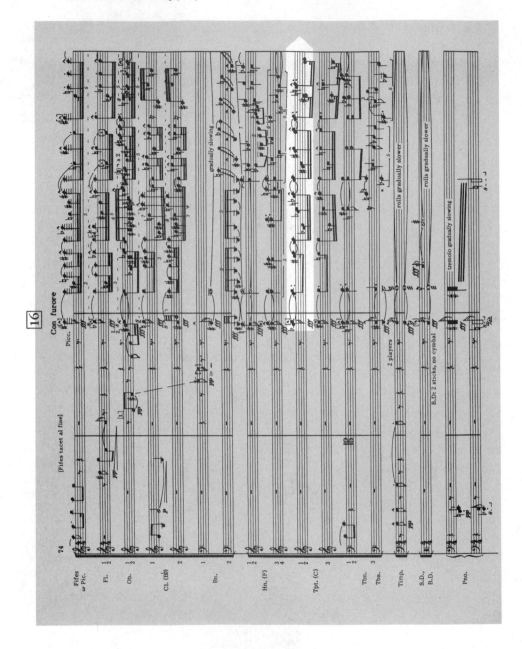

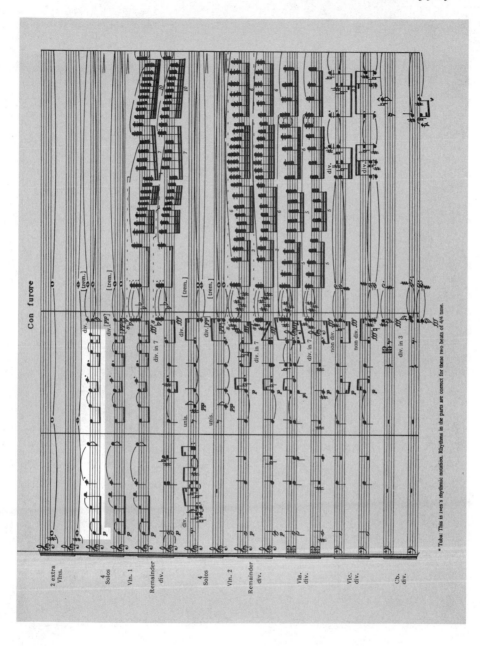

* Tuba: This is Ives's rhythmic notation. Rhythms in the parts are correct for these two beats of 4/4 time.

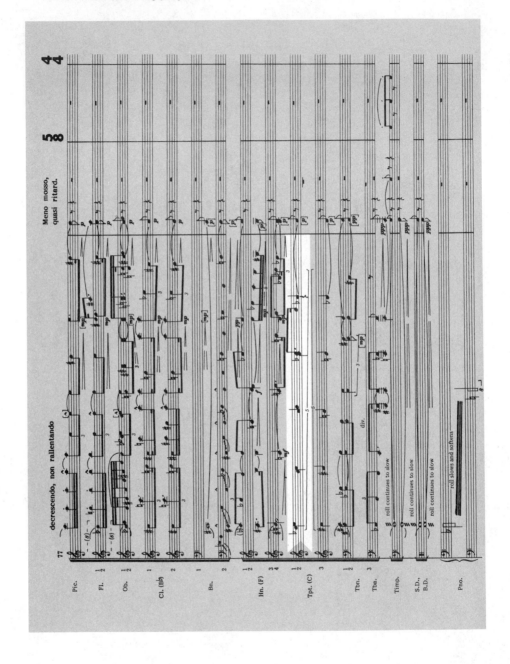

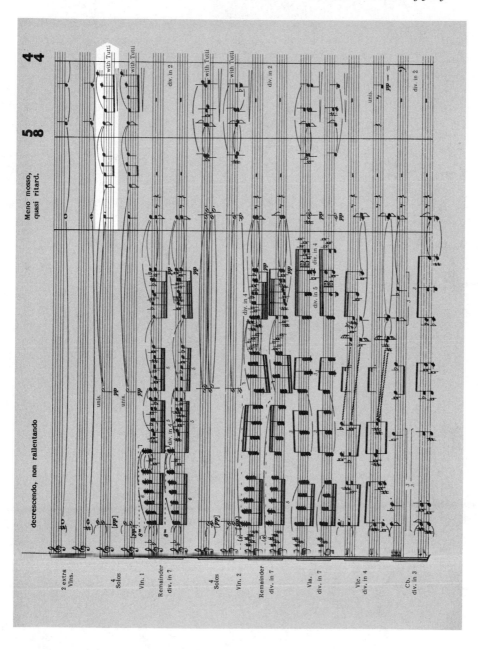

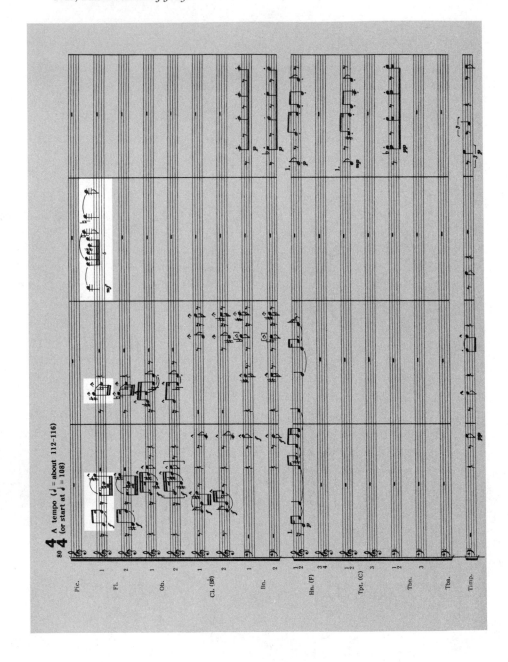

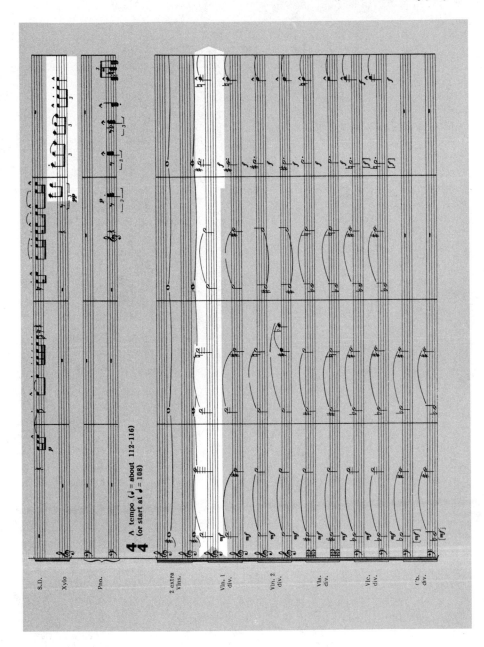

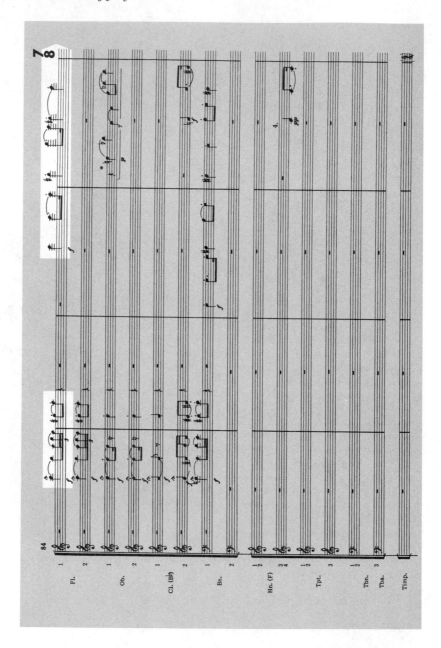

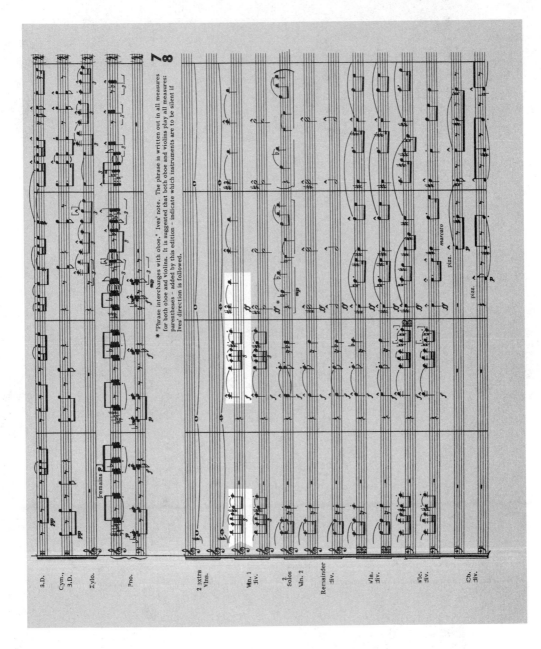

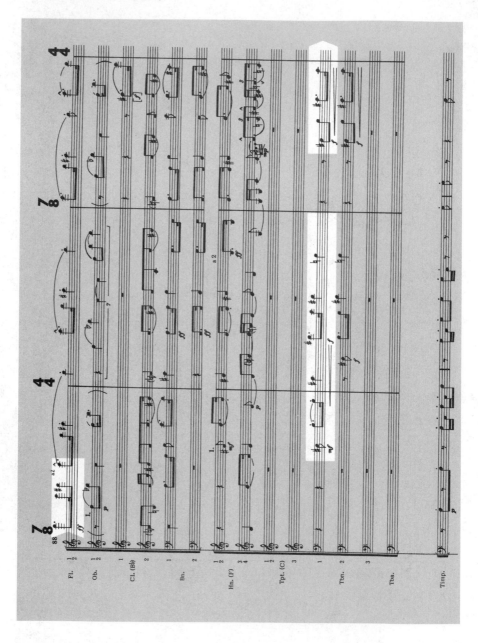

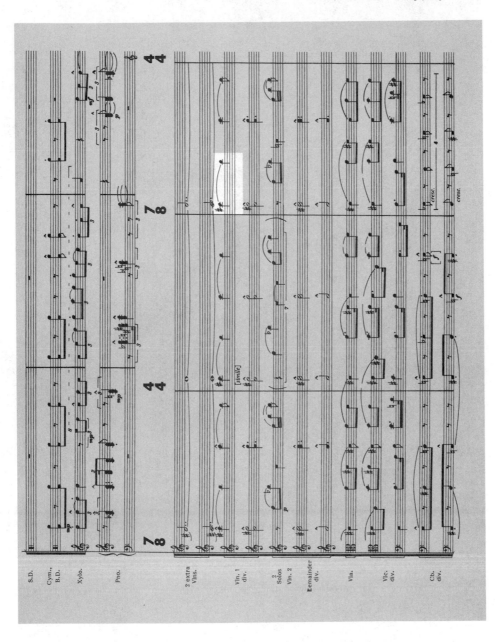

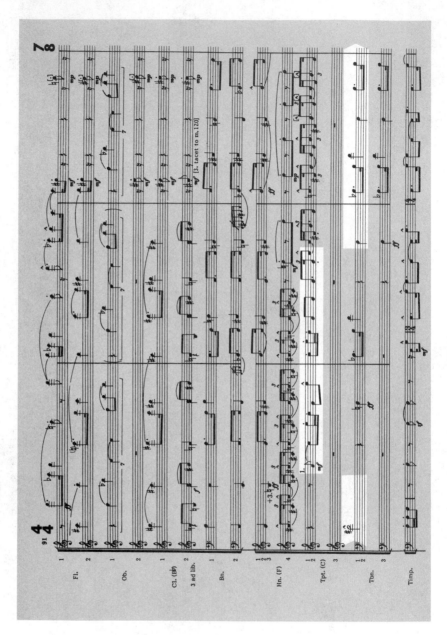

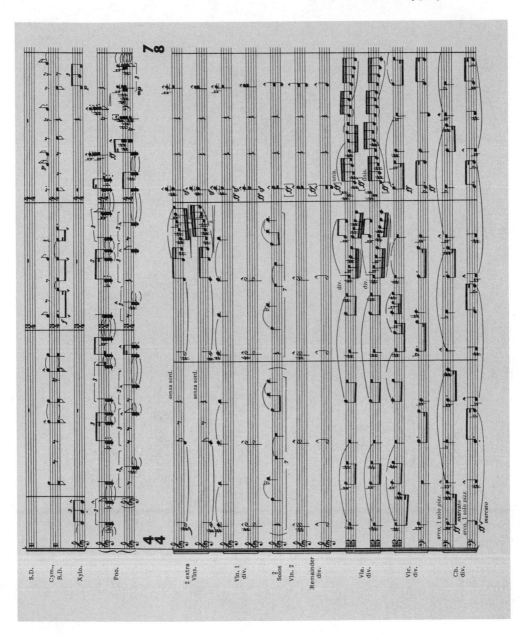

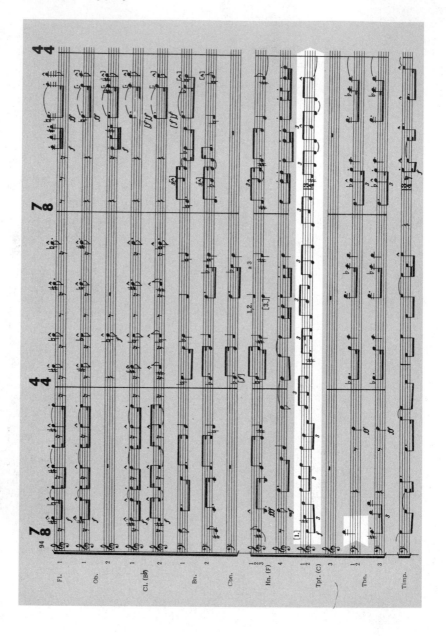

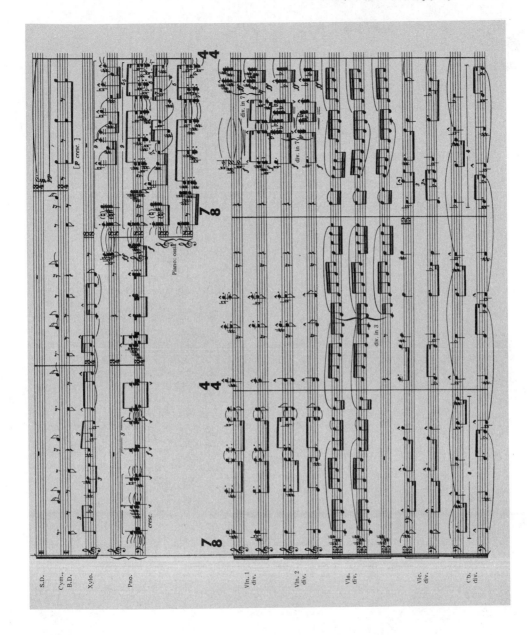

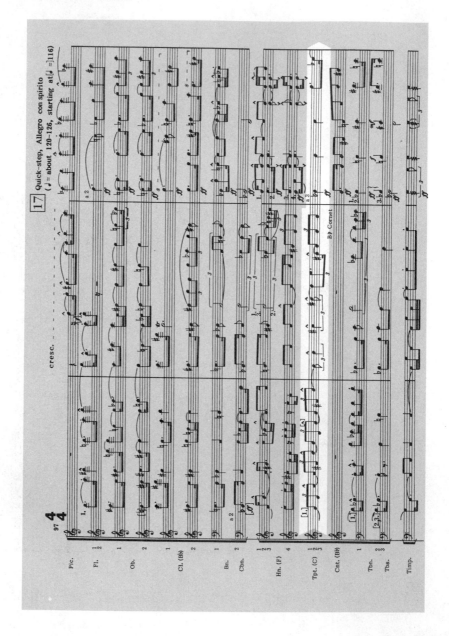

Yankee Doodle

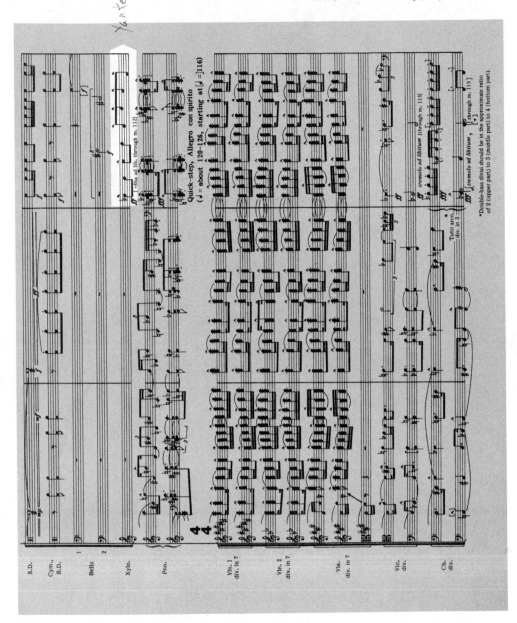

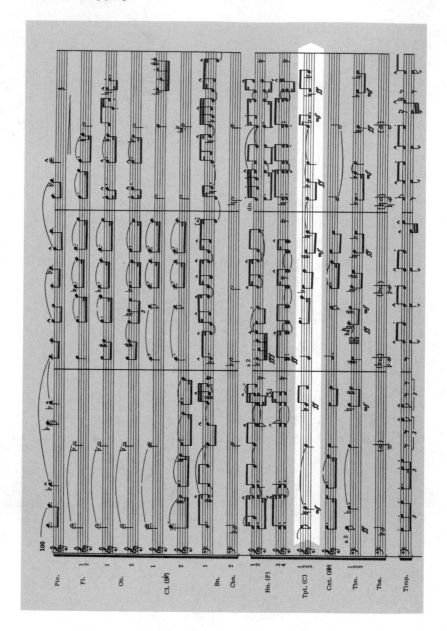

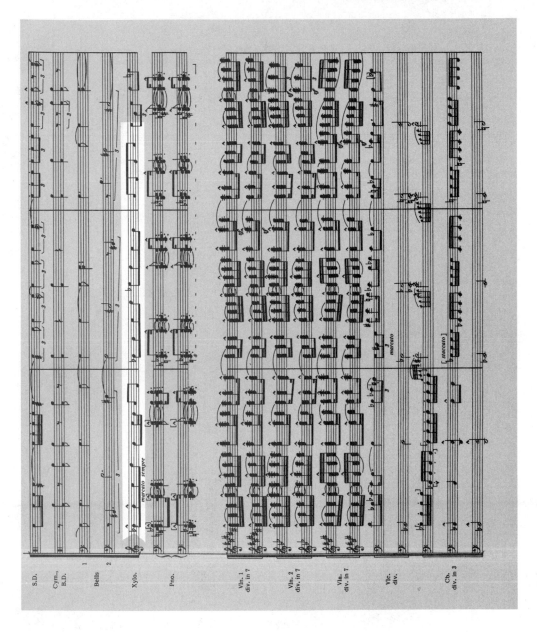

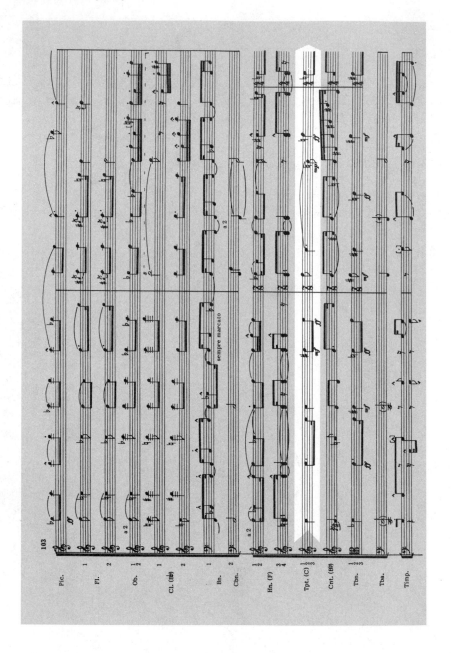

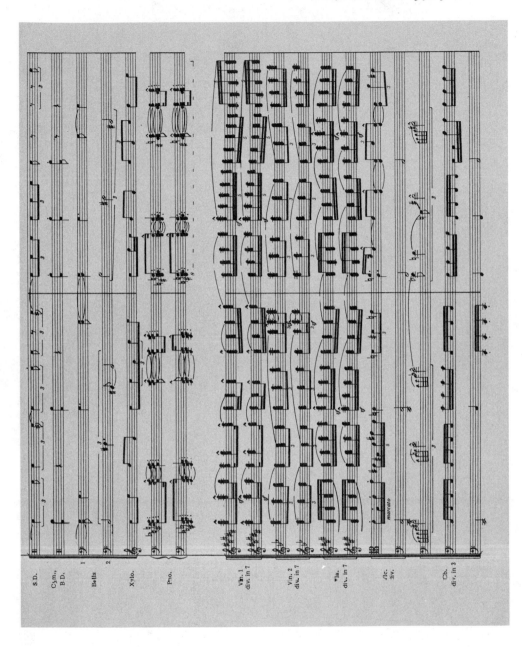

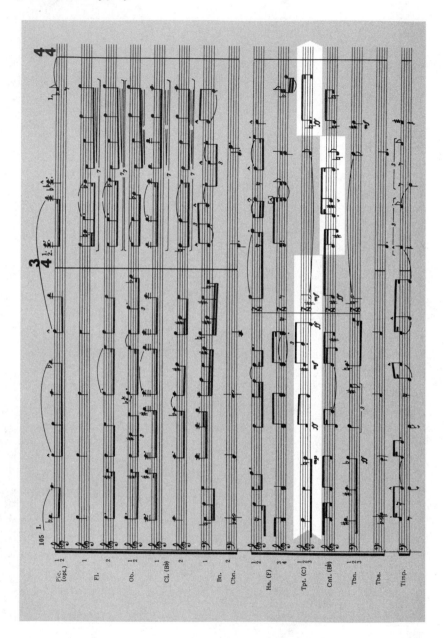

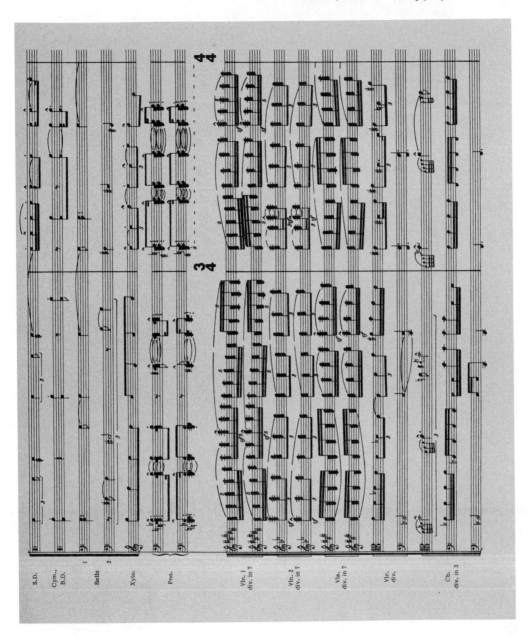

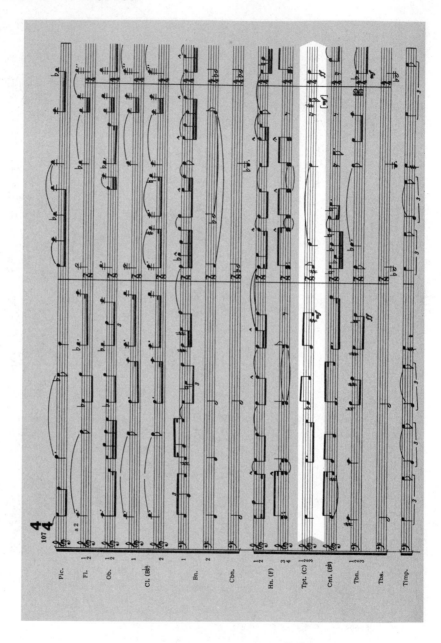

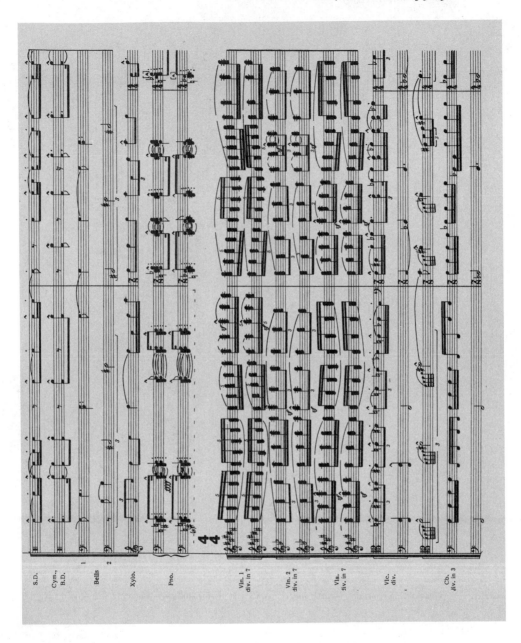

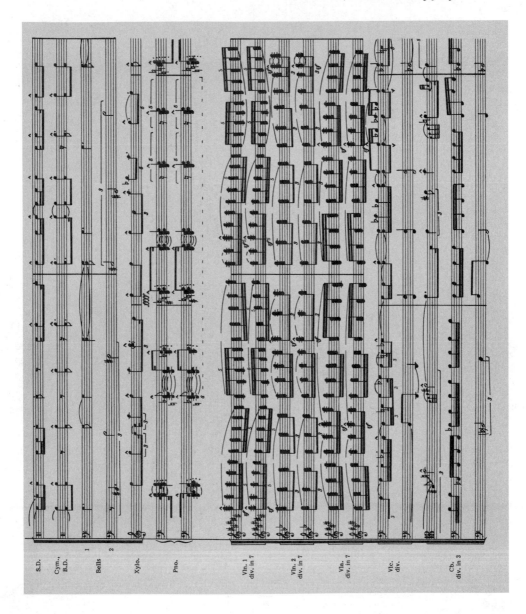

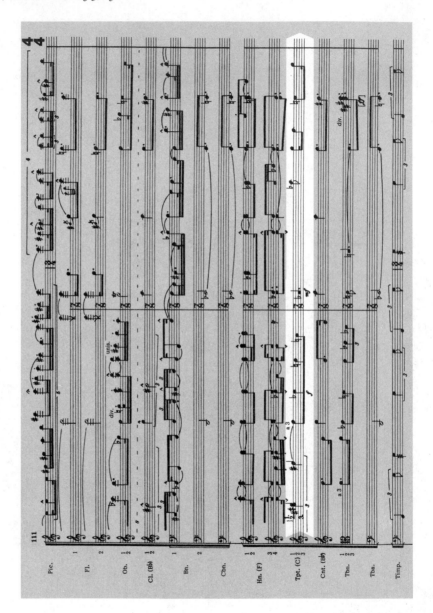

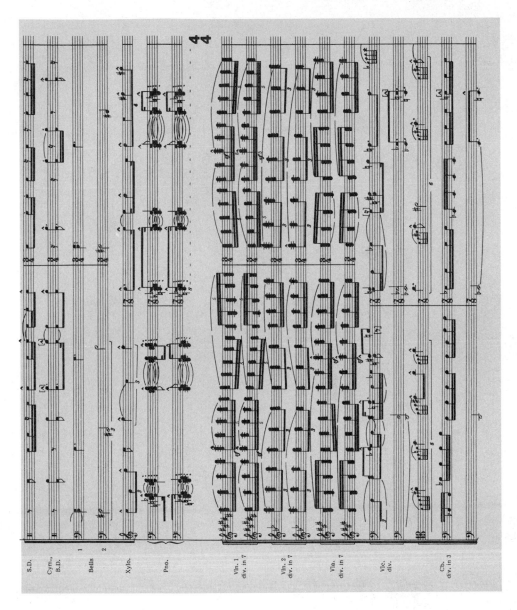

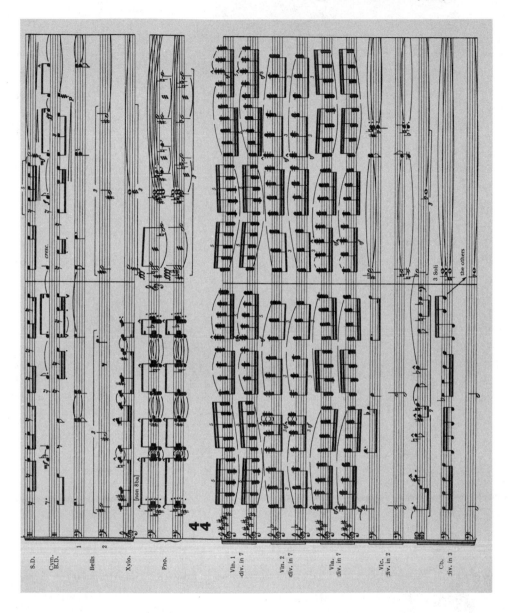

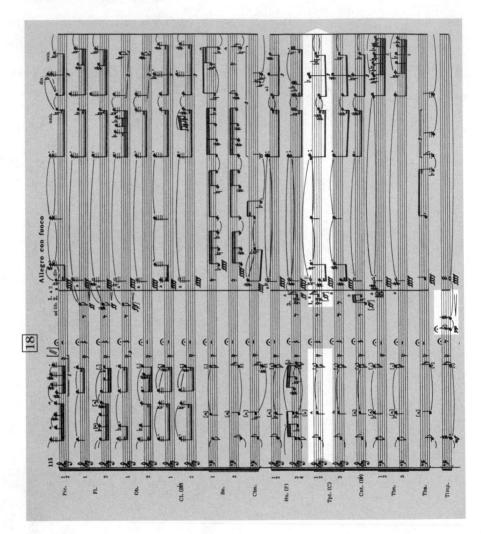

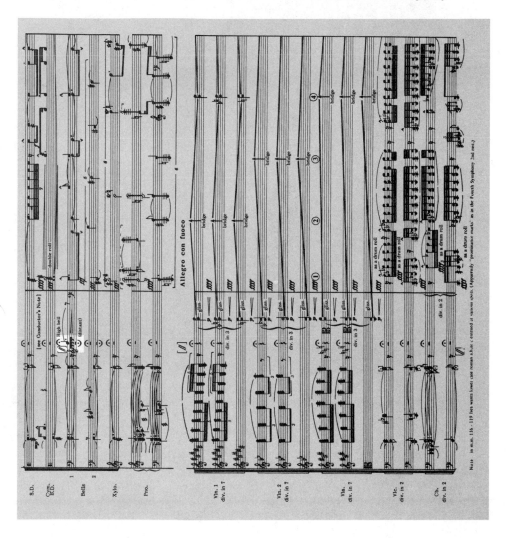

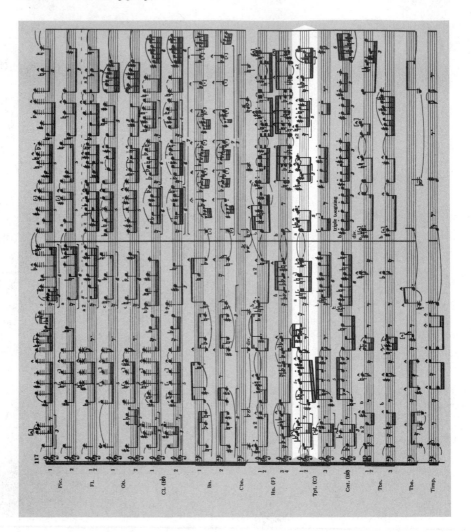

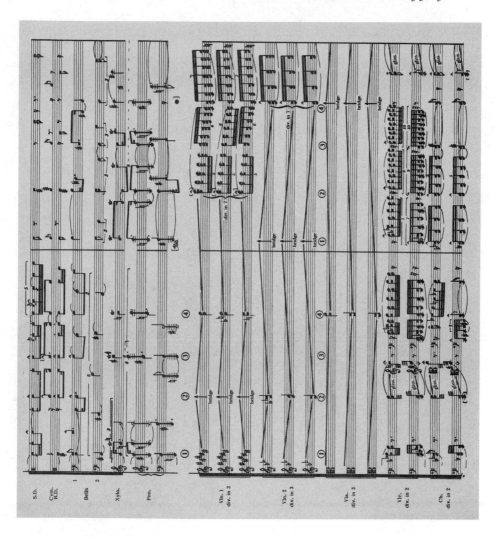

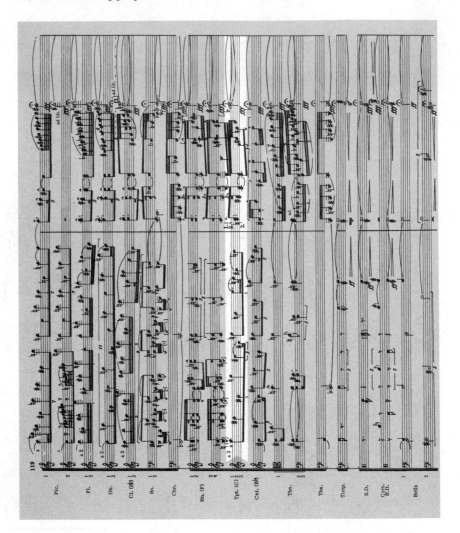

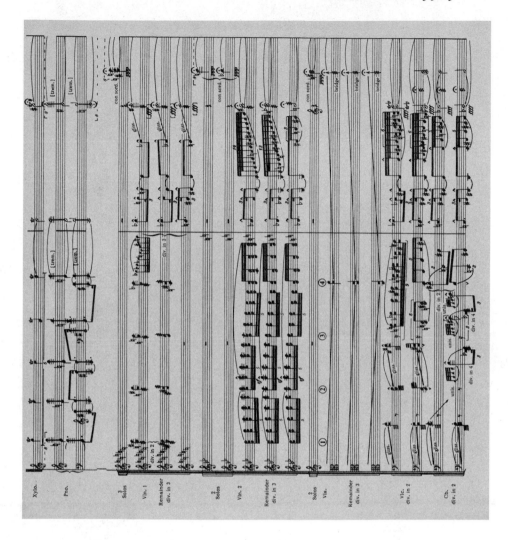

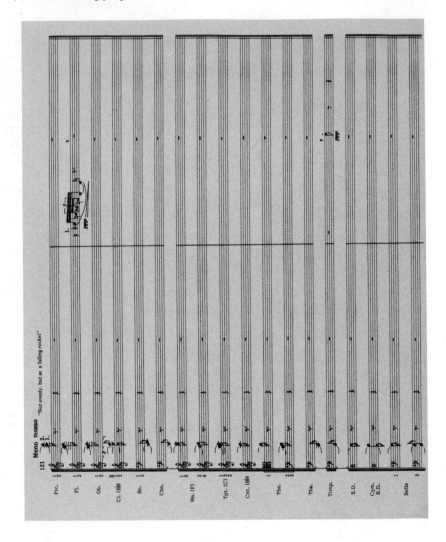

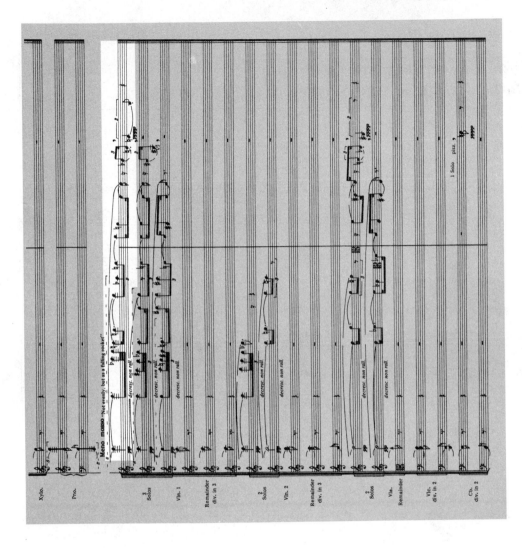

24. Maurice Ravel (1875–1937) 8:7A/6 ▣ 8:7/⑲ – ⑳

Chansons madécasses (Songs of Madagascar), Second Movement (1925–26)

TEXT AND TRANSLATION

Aoua! Aoua! Méfiez-vous des blancs,
    habitans du rivage.
Du temps de nos pères, des blancs
    descendirent dans cette île;
on leur dit: Voilà des terres; que
    vos femmes les cultivent.
Soyez justes, soyez bons, et devenez nos
    frères.
Les blancs promirent, et cependant
    ils faisaient des retranchements.
Un fort mençant s'éleva; le tonnerre
    fut renfermé dans des bouches d'airain;
leurs prêtres voulurent nous donner
    un Dieu que nous ne connaissons pas;
ils parlèrent enfin d'obéissance et
    d'esclavage; plûtot la mort!
Le carnage fut long et terrible; mais,
    malgré la foudre qu'ils vomissaient,
et qui écrasait des armées entières,
    ils furent tous exterminés.
Aoua! Aoua! Méfiez-vous des blancs!
Nous avons vu de nouveaux tyrans,
    plus forts et plus nombreux,
planter leur pavillon sur le rivage;
    le ciel a combattu pour nous;
il a fait tomber sur eux les pluies,
    les tempêtes, et les vents empoisonnés.
Ils ne sont plus, et nous vivons, et
    nous vivons libres.
Aoua! Aoua! Méfiez-vous des blancs,
    habitans du rivage.

Aoua! Aoua! Do not trust the white men,
    those who live on these shores.
From our father's time, white men
    have descended upon this island;
they said: "Here is the soil; have
    your women cultivate it.
Be fair, be kind, and become our
    brothers."
The white men promised, and yet
    they built entrenchments.
A menacing fort was erected;
    thunder was enclosed in brass mouths;
their priests wished to give us a
    God we did not know;
they finally spoke of obedience and
    slavery; what's more, of death!
The carnage was long and terrible; but,
    in spite of the lightning they belched forth,
annihilating whole armies, they
    were all destroyed.
Aoua! Aoua! Do not trust the white men!
We have seen new tyrants,
    stronger and more numerous,
raise their tents on the shore; the
    heavens waged war for us,
unleashing rains, storms, and
    poisonous winds.
They are gone, and we live, and
    we live freely.
Aoua! Aoua! Do not trust the white men,
    those who live on these shores.

25. Béla Bartók (1881–1945)

Music for Strings, Percussion, and Celesta, Fourth Movement (1936)

 8:7A/7   7/ 21 – 24

 3:3A/6   3/ 20 – 23

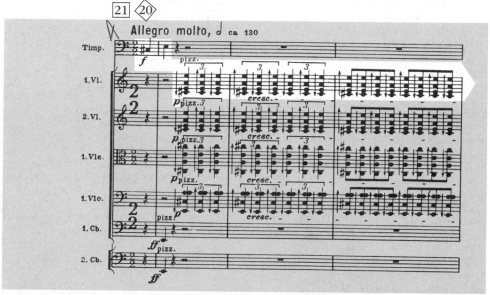

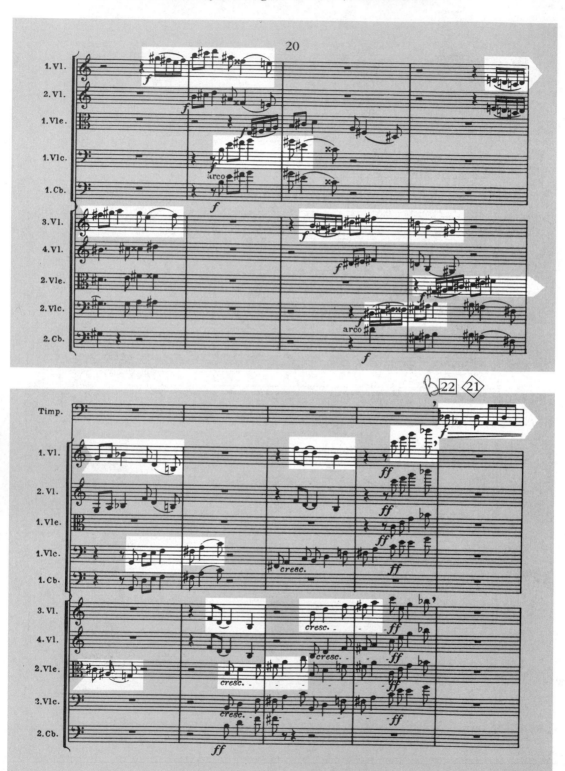

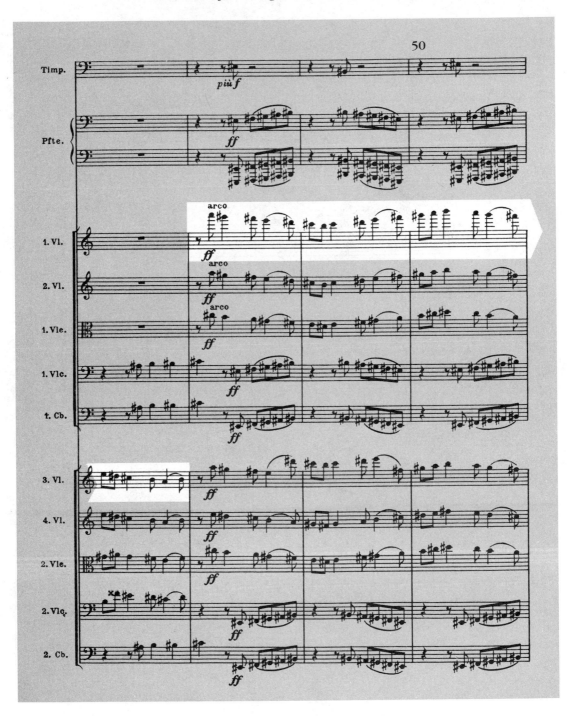

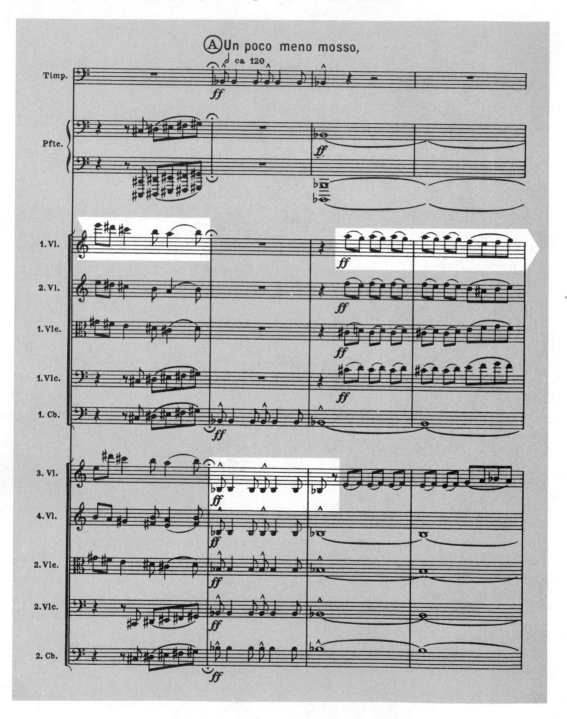

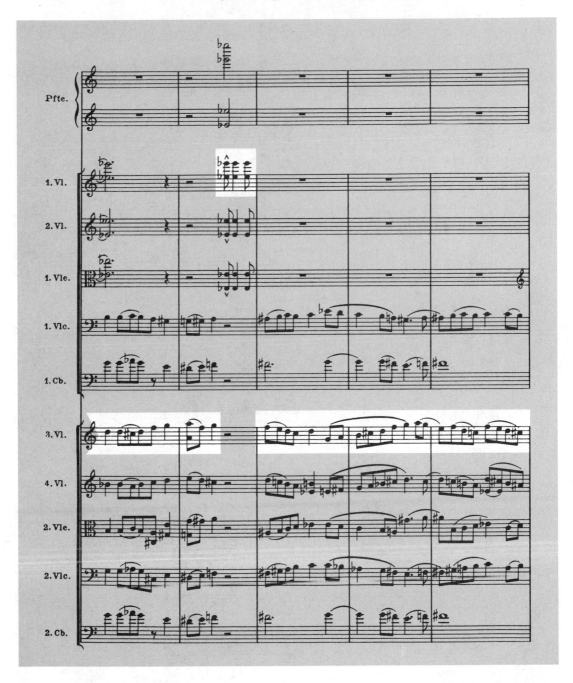

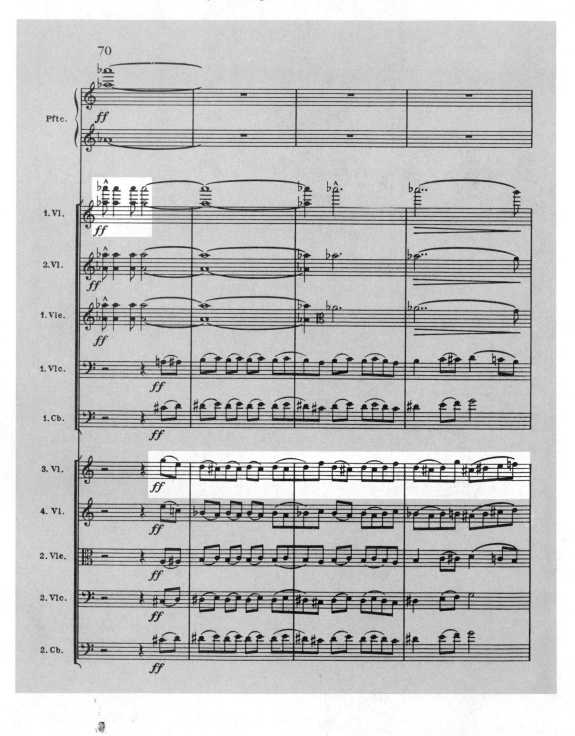

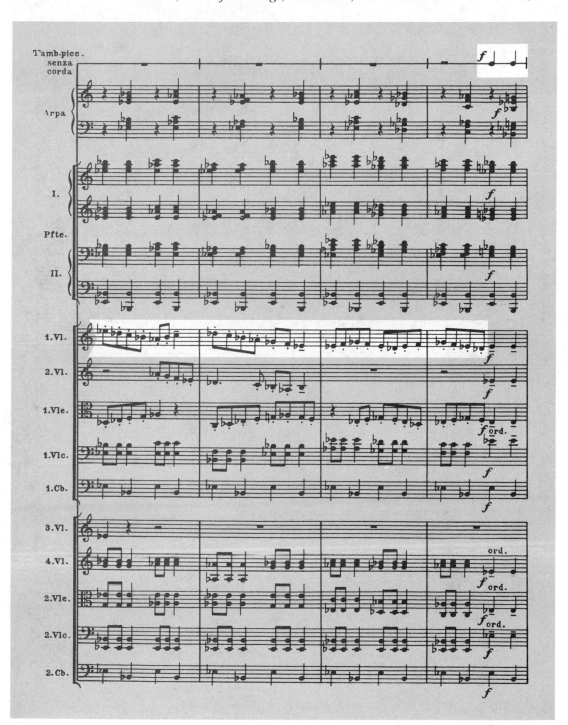

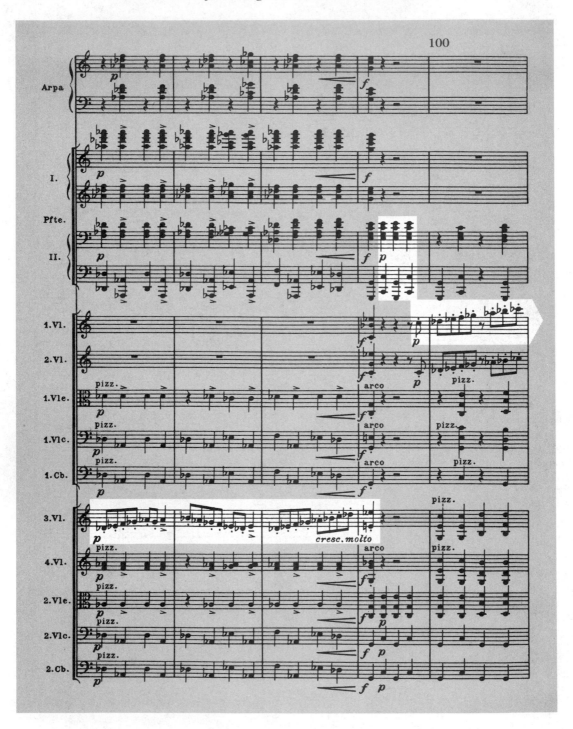

100

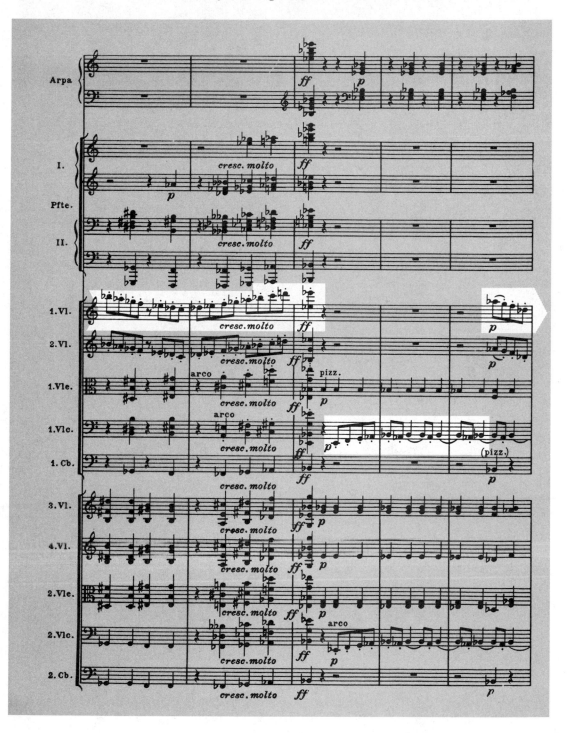

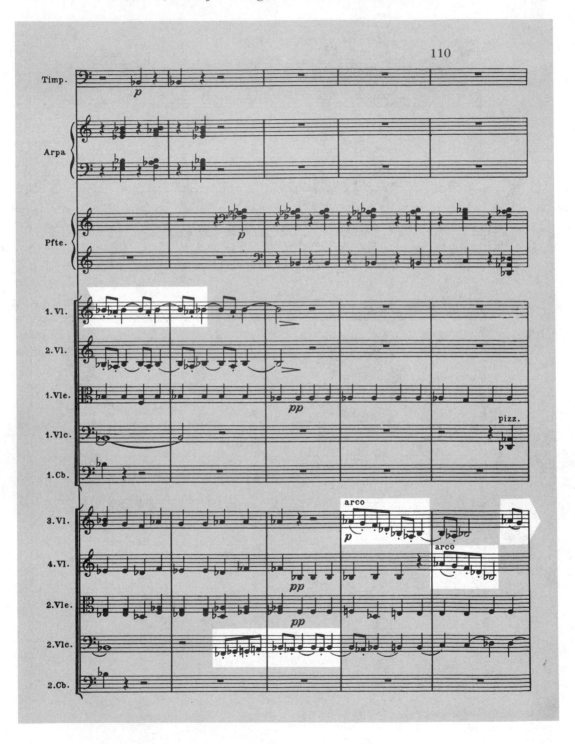

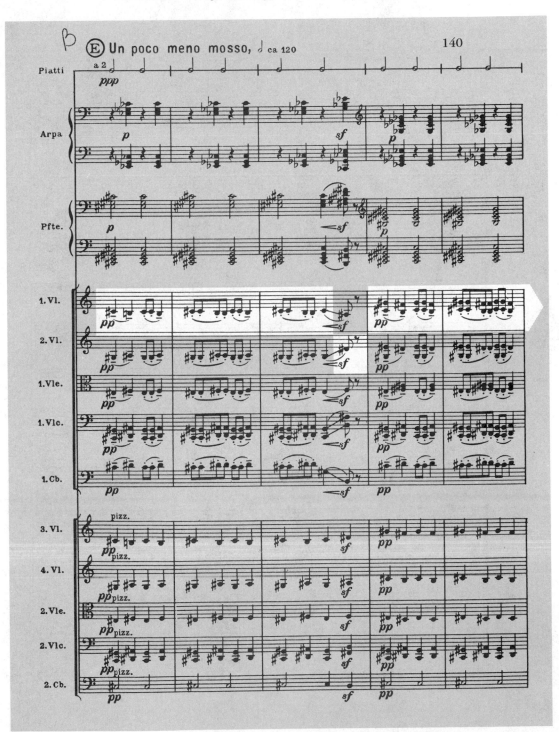

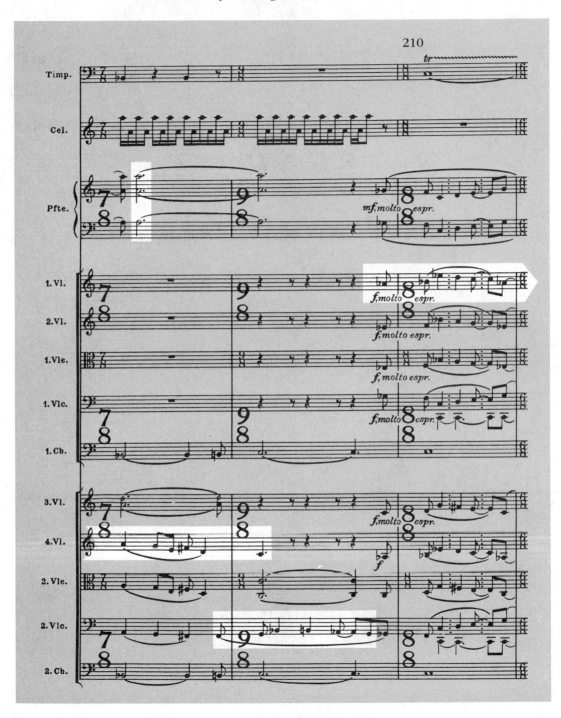

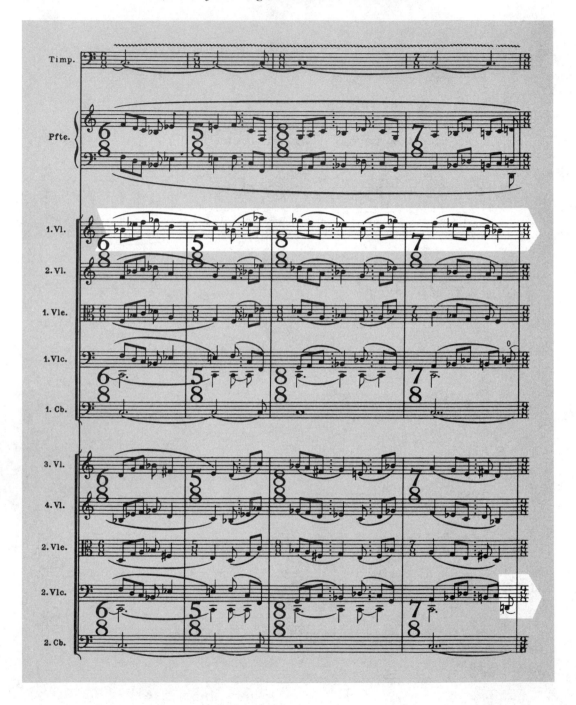

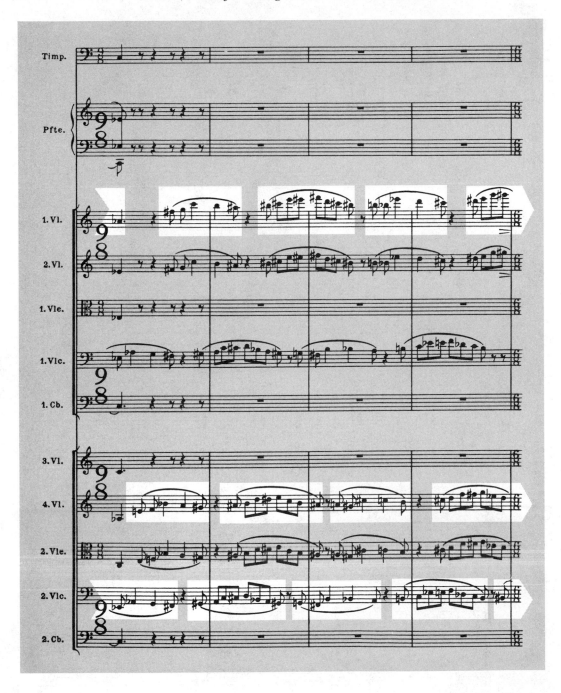

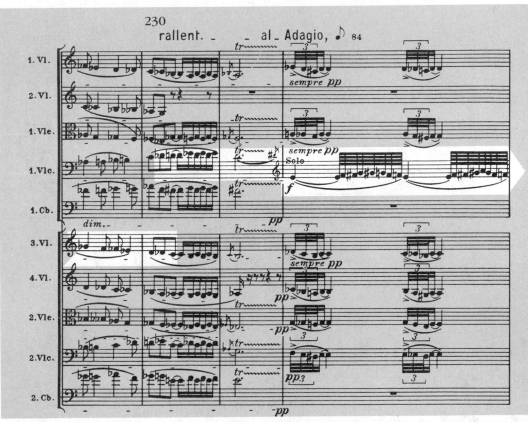

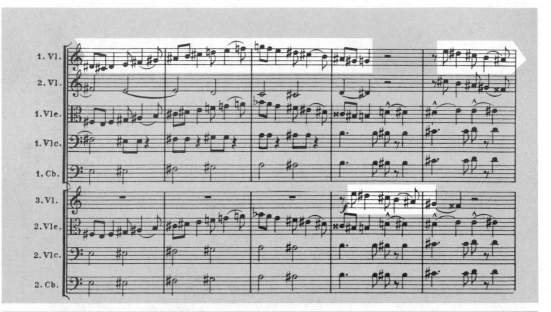

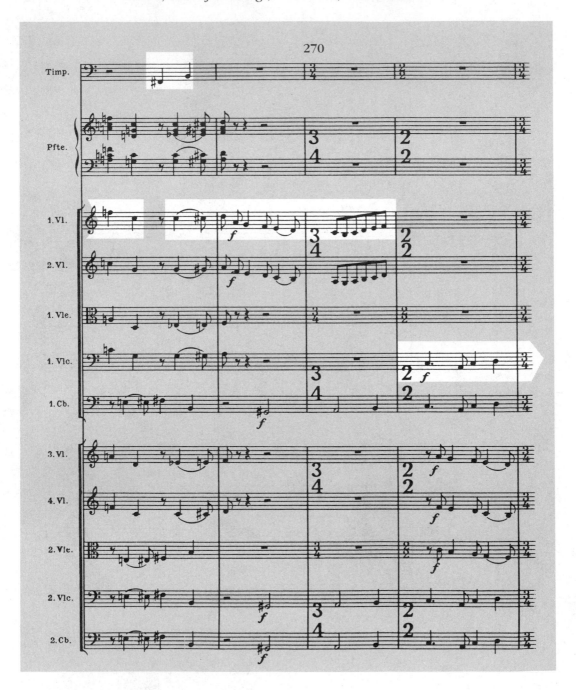

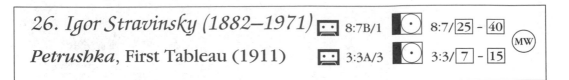

26. *Igor Stravinsky (1882–1971)*

Petrushka, First Tableau (1911)

"The Shrovetide Fair"

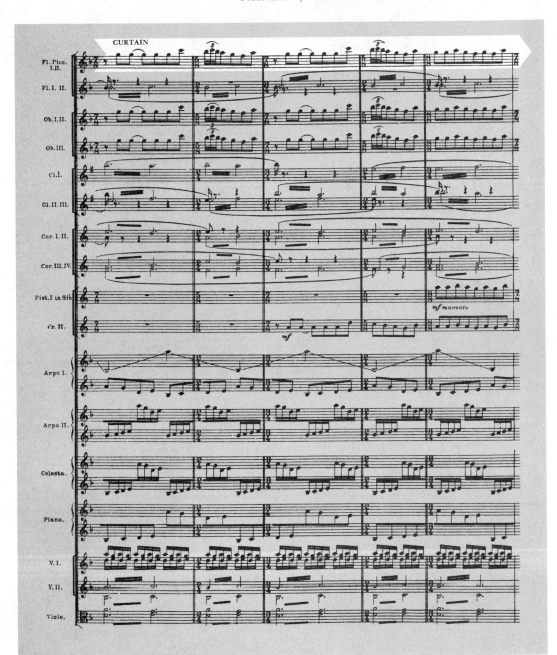

A SMALL GROUP OF TIPSY MERRYMAKERS, PRANCING, PASSES BY.

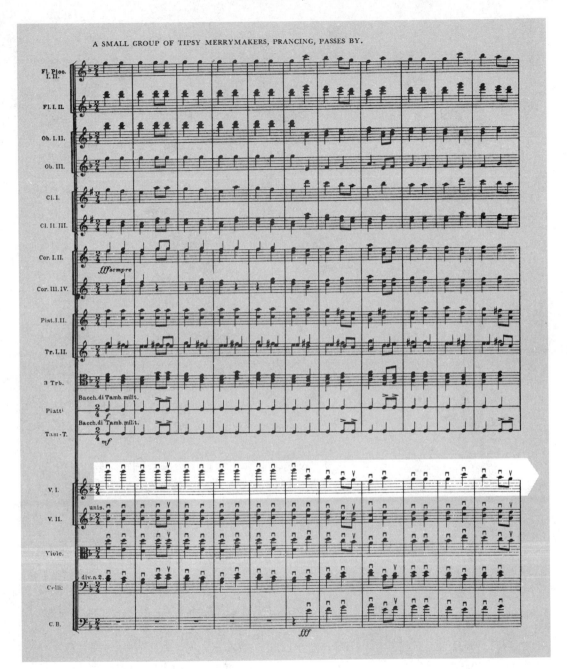

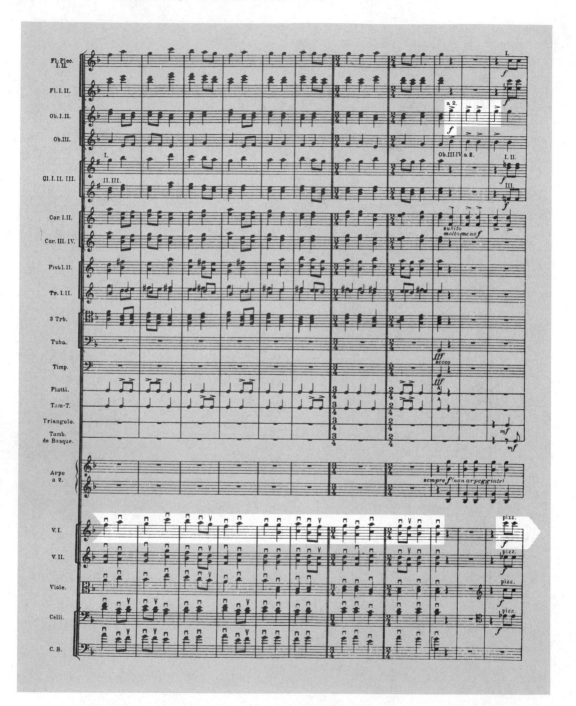

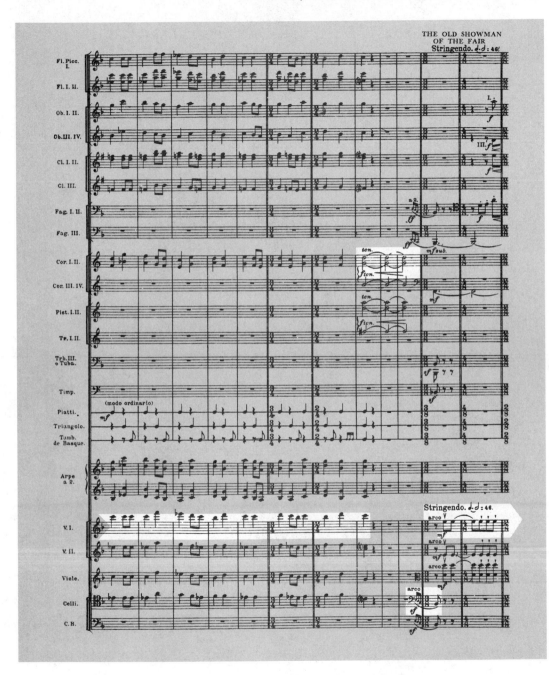

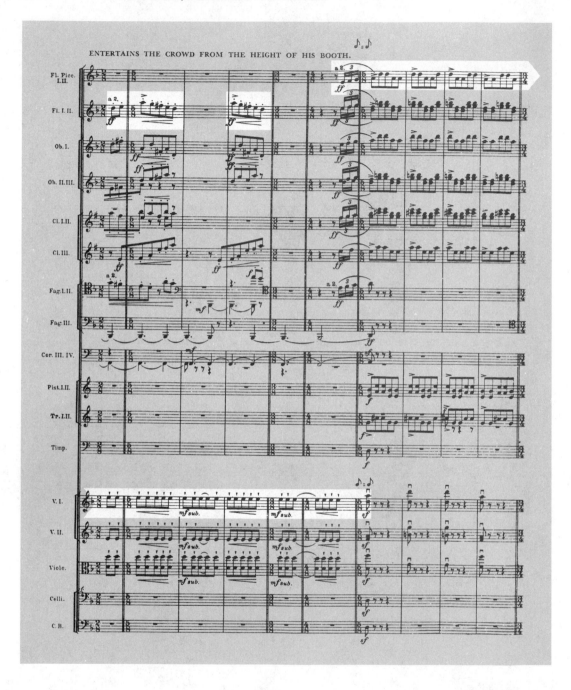

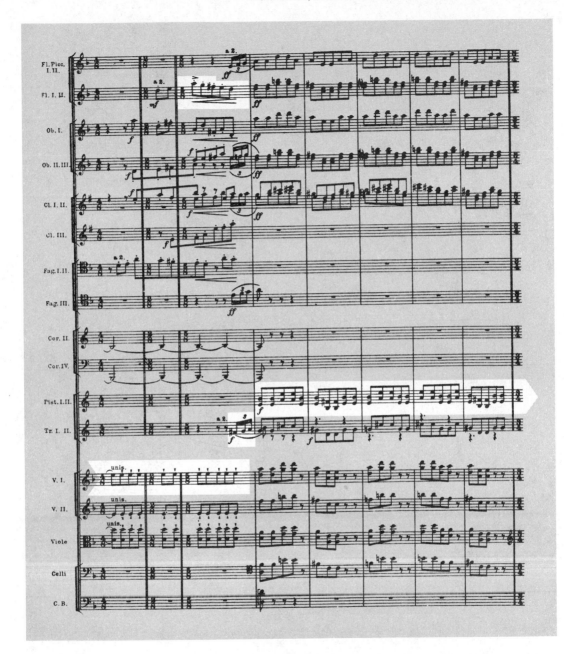

THE STREET DANCER DANCES,
BEATING TIME ON THE TRIANGLE.

*THE ORGAN-GRINDER, CONTINUING TO TURN THE CRANK WITH ONE HAND, PLAYS
THE CORNET WITH THE OTHER.

*THE ORGAN-GRINDER RESUMES PLAYING THE CORNET.

THE MUSIC BOX STOP PLAYING; THE SHOWMAN
AGAIN ATTRACTS THE ATTENTION OF THE CROWD.

THE MERRYMAKERS RETURN.

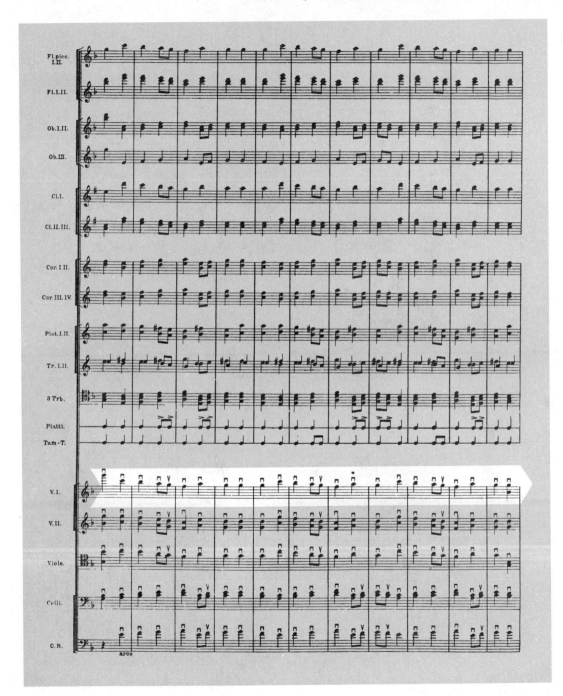

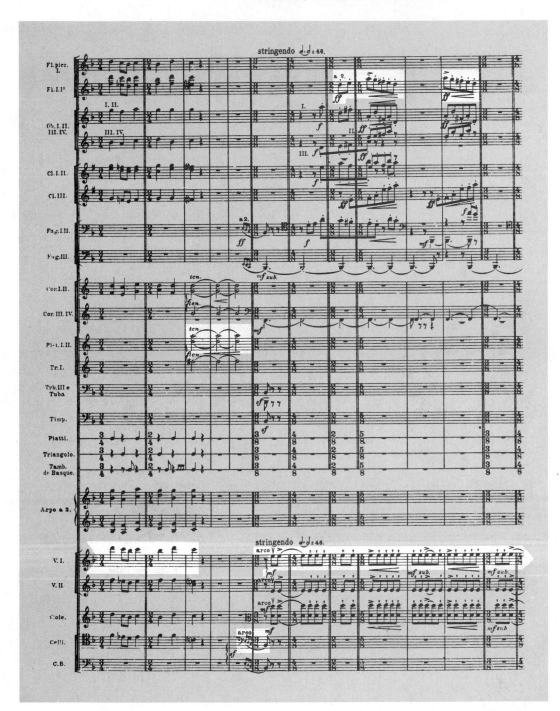

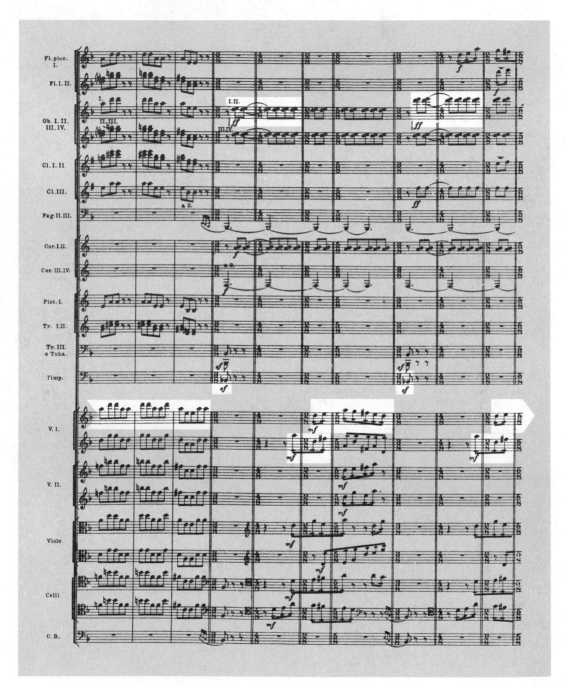

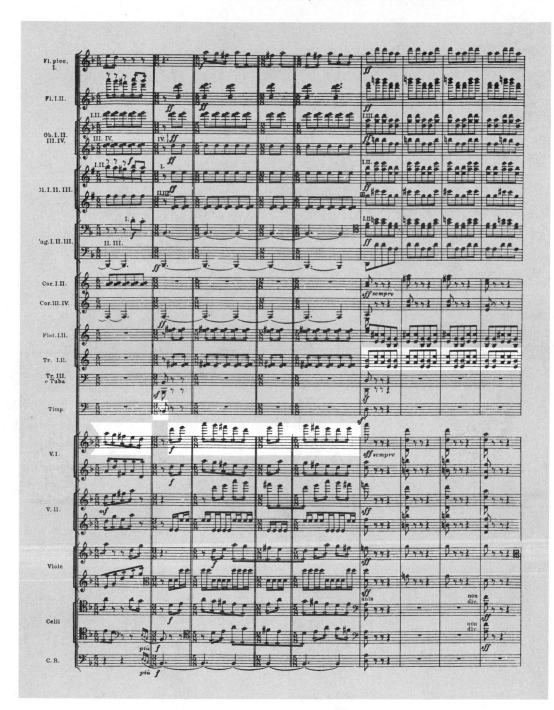

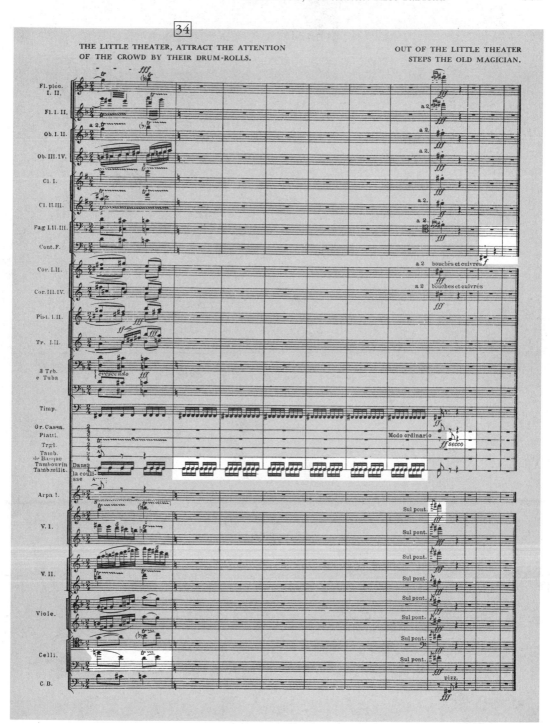

"The Magic Trick"

THE MAGICIAN PLAYS THE FLUTE.

THE CURTAIN OF THE LITTLE THEATER OPENS, AND THE CROWD SEES THREE PUPPETS:
PETRUSHKA, A MOOR, AND A BALLERINA.

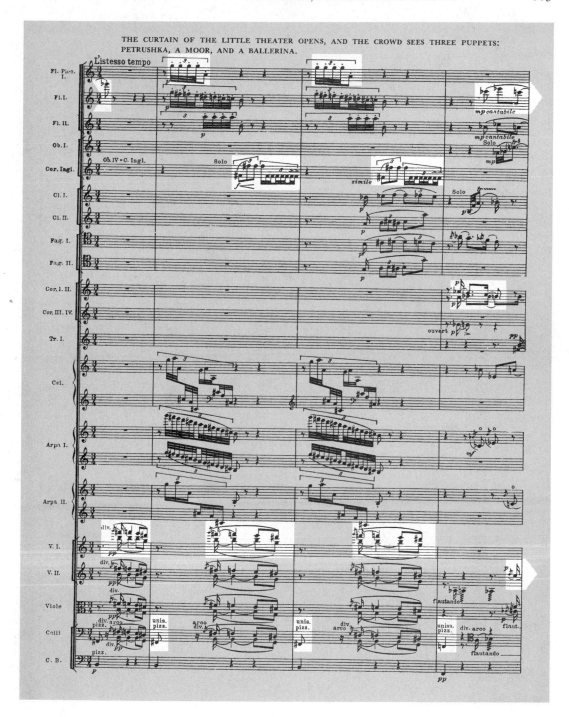

THE MAGICIAN ANIMATES THEM BY
TOUCHING THEM WITH HIS FLUTE.

"Russian Dance"

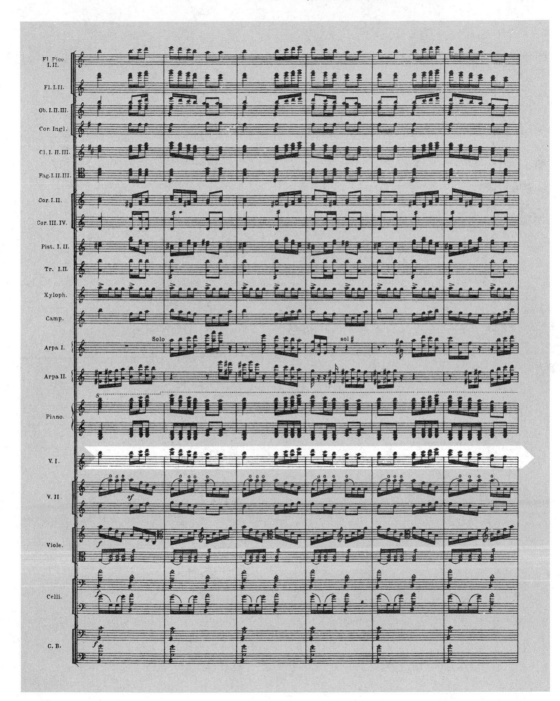

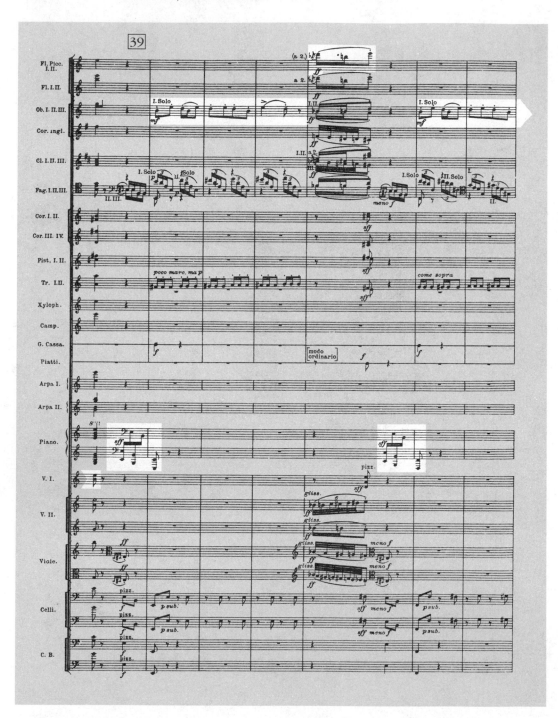

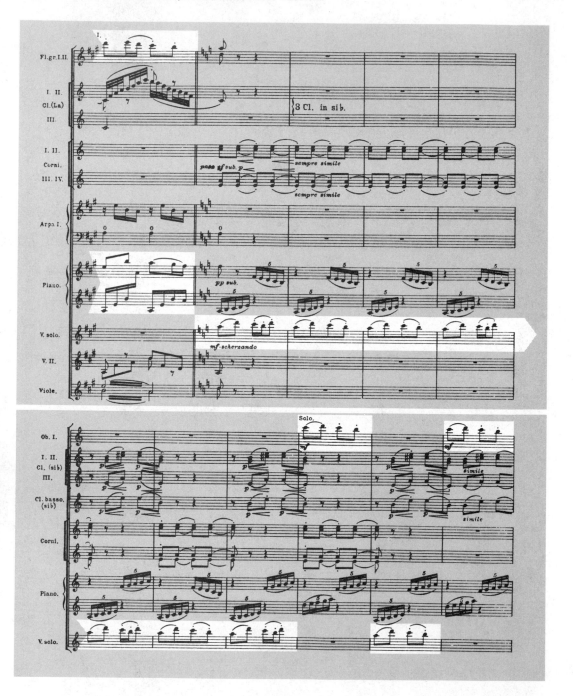

Editor's note: The last measure on this page is not played when continuing to the Second Tableau.

Editor's note: The Norton recording stops in the second measure of this page at the fermata.

27. Anton Webern (1883–1945)

 8:7A/8 8:7/ 41 - 43

Symphony, Op. 21, Second Movement (1928)

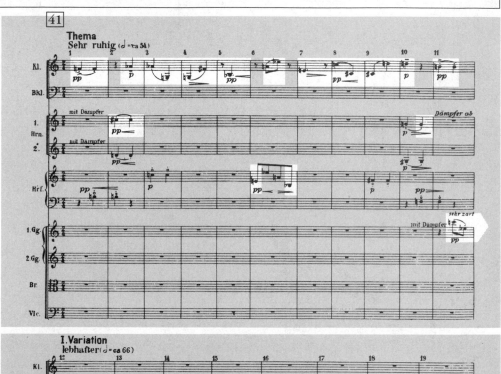

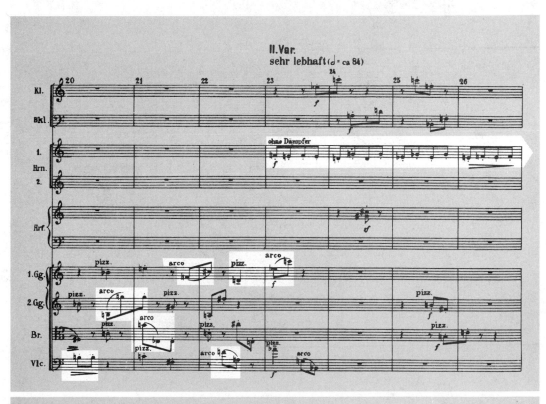

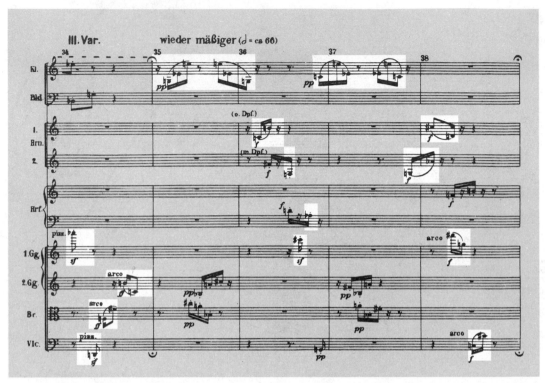

28. Alban Berg (1885–1935)

 8:7B/2 ◉ 8:7/ 44 - 47

Wozzeck, Act III, Scenes 4 and 5 (1922)

Wieder langsamer, aber nicht schleppend

255

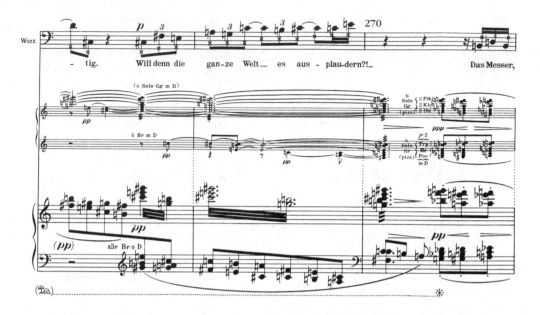

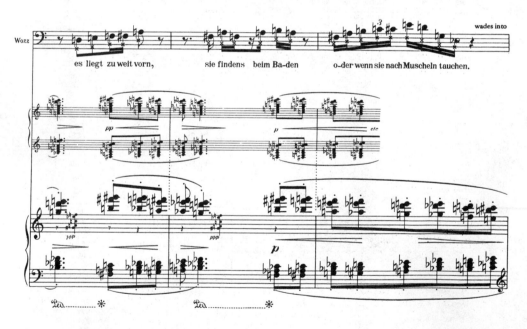

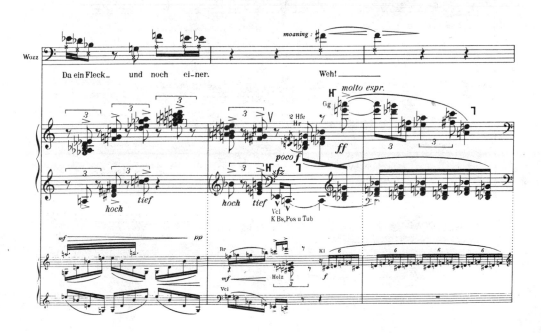

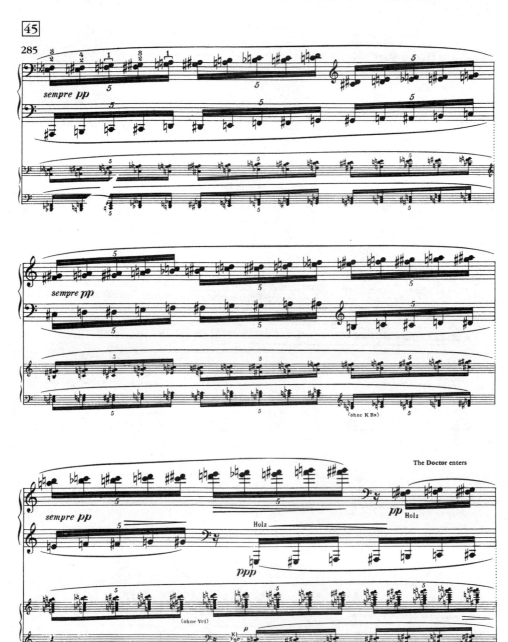

The **Captain** follows the Doctor (speaks)

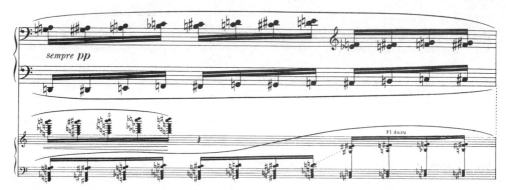

The **Doctor** (stands still): *p* Hören Sie? Dort!

Hauptmann: *p* Jesus! Das war ein Ton. (also stands still)

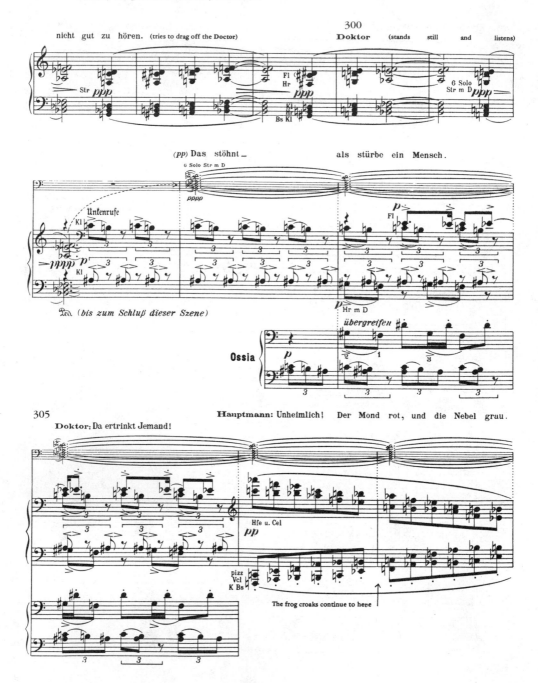

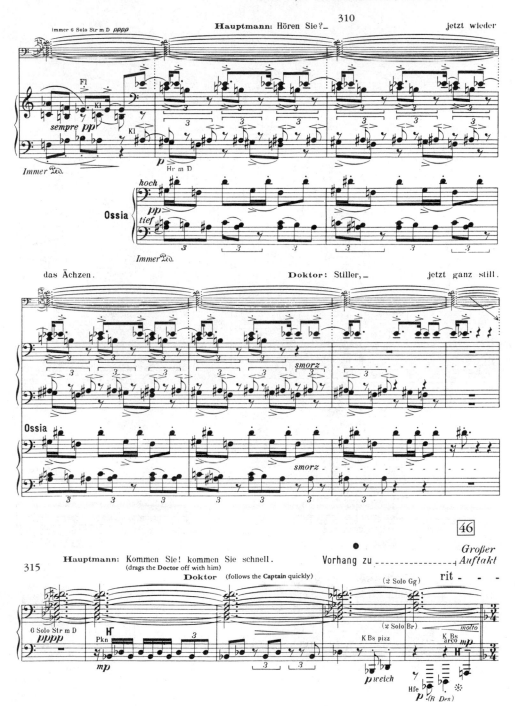

5th (last) Scene   In front of Marie's house (bright morning, sunshine)

Flowing 8ths, but with much rubato

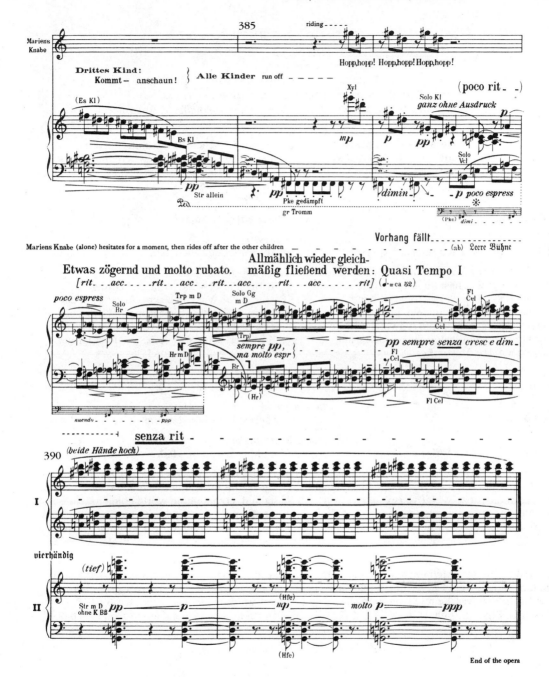

End of the opera

TEXT AND TRANSLATION

SCENE FOUR
INVENTION ON A CHORD OF SIX NOTES
PATH IN THE WOOD BY THE POND. MOONLIGHT, AS BEFORE.
(WOZZECK STUMBLES HURRIEDLY IN, THEN STOPS, LOOKING AROUND FOR SOMETHING.)

WOZZECK

Das Messer? Wo ist das Messer? Ich hab's dagelassen. Näher, noch näher. Mir graut's . . . da regt sich was. Still! Alles still und tot.	The knife? Where is the knife? I left it there. Around here somewhere. I'm terrified . . . something's moving. Silence. Everything silent and dead.

(SHOUTING)

Mörder! Mörder!	Murderer! Murderer!

(WHISPERING AGAIN)

Ha! Da ruft's. Nein, ich selbst.	Ah! Someone called. No, it was only me.

(STILL LOOKING, HE STAGGERS A FEW STEPS FURTHER AND STUMBLES AGAINST THE CORPSE)

Marie! Marie! Was hast du für eine rote Schnur um den Hals? Hast dir das rote Halsband verdient, wie die Ohrringlein, mit deiner Sünde! Was hängen dir die schwarzen Haare so wild? Mörder! Mörder! Sie werden nach mir suchen. Das Messer verrät mich!	Marie! Marie! What's that red cord around your neck? Was the red necklace payment for your sins, like the earrings? Why's your dark hair so wild about you? Murderer! Murderer! They will come and look for me. The knife will betray me!

(LOOKS FOR IT IN A FRENZY)

Da, da ist's!	Here! Here it is!

(AT THE POND)

So! Da hinunter!	There! Sink to the bottom!

(THROWS THE KNIFE INTO THE POND)

Es taucht ins dunkle Wasser wie ein Stein.	It plunges into the dark water like a stone.

(THE MOON APPEARS, BLOOD-RED, FROM BEHIND THE CLOUDS. WOZZECK LOOKS UP.)

Aber der Mond verrät mich, der Mond ist blutig. Will denn die ganze Welt es ausplaudern? Das Messer, es liegt zu weit vorn, sie finden's beim Baden oder wenn sie nach Muscheln tauchen.	But the moon will betray me: the moon is blood stained. Is the whole world going to incriminate me? The knife is too near the edge: they'll find it when they're swimming or diving for snails.

(WADES INTO THE POND)

Ich find's nicht. Aber ich muss mich waschen. Ich bin blutig. Da ein Fleck—und noch einer. Weh! Weh! Ich wasche mich mit Blut—das Wasser ist Blut . . . Blut . . .	I can't find it. But I must wash myself. There's blood on me. There's a spot here— and another. Oh, God! I am washing myself in blood—the water is blood . . . blood . . .

(DROWNS)
(THE DOCTOR APPEARS, FOLLOWED BY THE CAPTAIN.)

CAPTAIN

Halt!   Wait!

DOCTOR (STOPS)

Hören Sie? Dort!   Can you hear? There!

CAPTAIN

Jesus! Das war ein Ton!   Jesus! What a ghastly sound!

(STOPS AS WELL)

DOCTOR (POINTING TO THE POND)

Ja, dort!   Yes, there!

CAPTAIN

Es ist das Wasser im Teich. Das Wasser ruft.   It's the water in the pond. The water is calling.
Es ist schon lange Niemand ertrunken.   It's been a long time since anyone drowned.
Kommen Sie, Doktor!   Come away, Doctor.
Es ist nicht gut zu hören.   It's not good for us to be hearing it.

(TRIES TO DRAG THE DOCTOR AWAY)

DOCTOR (RESISTING, AND CONTINUING TO LISTEN)

Das stöhnt, als stürbe ein Mensch.   There's a groan, as though someone were
Da ertrinkt Jemand!   dying. Somebody's drowning!

CAPTAIN

Unheimlich! Der Mond rot, und die Nebel grau.   It's eerie! The moon is red, and the mist is grey.
Hören Sie? . . . Jetzt wieder das Ächzen.   Can you hear? . . . That moaning again.

DOCTOR

Stiller, . . . jetzt ganz still.   It's getting quieter . . . now it's stopped
                            altogether.

CAPTAIN

Kommen Sie! Kommen Sie schnell!   Come! Come quickly!

(HE RUSHES OFF, PULLING THE DOCTOR ALONG WITH HIM.)

SCENE CHANGE

INVENTION ON A KEY (D MINOR)

SCENE FIVE

INVENTION ON A QUAVER RHYTHM

IN FRONT OF MARIE'S DOOR. MORNING. BRIGHT SUNSHINE.
(CHILDREN ARE NOISILY AT PLAY. MARIE'S CHILD IS RIDING A HOBBY-HORSE.)

CHILDREN

Ringel, Ringel, Rosenkranz, Ringelreih'n,   Ring-a-ring-a-roses,
Ringel, Ringel, Rosenkranz, Ring . . .   A pocket full of . . .

(THEIR SONG AND GAME ARE INTERRUPTED BY OTHER CHILDREN BURSTING IN.)

ONE OF THE NEWCOMERS

Du, Käthe! Die Marie!   Hey, Katie! Have you heard about Marie?

SECOND CHILD

Was ist?   What's happened?

FIRST CHILD

Weisst' es nit? Sie sind schon Alle 'naus.   Don't you know? They've all gone out there.

THIRD CHILD (TO MARIE'S LITTLE BOY)

Du! Dein' Mutter ist tot!   Hey! Your mother's dead!

MARIE'S SON (STILL RIDING)

Hopp, hopp! Hopp, hopp! Hopp, hopp!   Hop, hop! Hop, hop! Hop, hop!

SECOND CHILD

Wo ist sie denn?   Where is she, then?

FIRST CHILD

Draus' liegt sie, am Weg, neben dem Teich.   She's lying out there, on the path near the
pond.

THIRD CHILD

Kommt, anschaun!   Come and have a look!

(ALL THE CHILDREN RUN OFF.)

MARIE'S SON (CONTINUING TO RIDE)

Hopp, hopp! Hopp, hopp! Hopp, hopp!   Hop, hop! Hop, hop! Hop, hop!

(HE HESITATES FOR A MOMENT AND THEN RIDES AFTER THE OTHER CHILDREN.)

END OF THE OPERA

LIBRETTO BY ALBAN BERG, AFTER GEORG BÜCHNER'S PLAY *WOYZECK* (1837)

Translated by Sarah E. Soulsby

29. *Sergei Prokofiev (1891–1953)*

▭ 8:7B/3   ◐ 8:7/48 – 49

Alexander Nevsky, Seventh Movement (1939)

30. Richard Rodgers (1902–1979)

My Funny Valentine (1937)

8:7B/4-5   8:7/50 – 53   (MW)

3:3B/2   3:3/35 – 36

50   **Original Version, from *Babes in Arms* (1937)**

Be-hold the way our fine-feath-ered friend his vir-tue doth pa-rade. Thou

know-est not, my dim-wit-ted friend, The pic-ture thou hast made. Thy

Editor's note: Shorter Norton recording and *The Norton CD-ROM Masterworks*, volume 1, include Gerry Mulligan Quartet version only.

va - cant brow and thy tous - led hair con - ceal thy good in - tent. Thou

no - ble, up - right, truth - ful, sin - cere and slight - ly dop - ey gent, you're

Refrain *(slowly, with much expression)*

My fun - ny Val - en - tine, Sweet com - ic

Val - en - tine, You make me smile with my

Gerry Mulligan Quartet Version (1953)

Transcribed by Evan Solot.

31. Louis Armstrong (c. 1898–1971) and the Savoy Ballroom Five

8:7B/6   8:7/54 – 59

West End Blues (1928), excerpt

Introduction

Chorus 1 (Solo trumpet)

Chorus 5 (Solo trumpet)

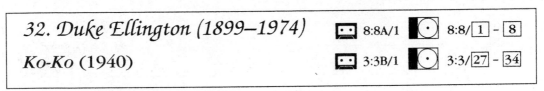

33. Aaron Copland (1900–1990)

Billy the Kid, Scene 1, *Street in a Frontier Town* (1939, orchestral suite)

8:8A/2   8:8/ 9 - 11

3:3A/7   3:3/ 24 - 26

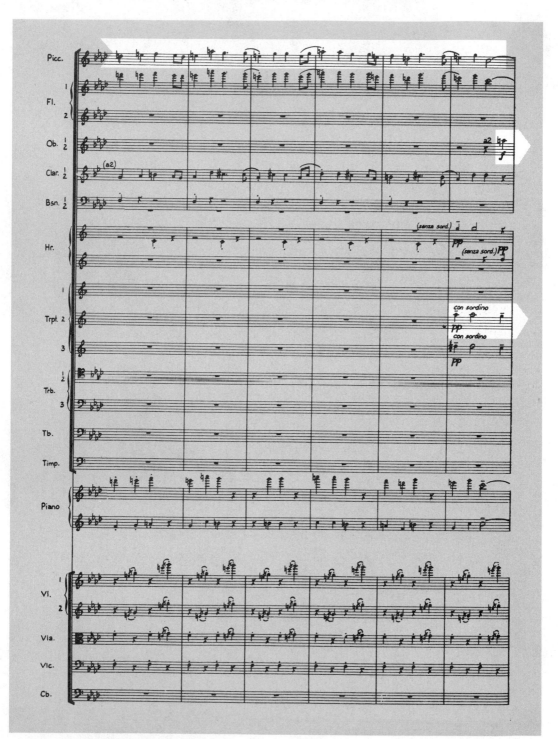

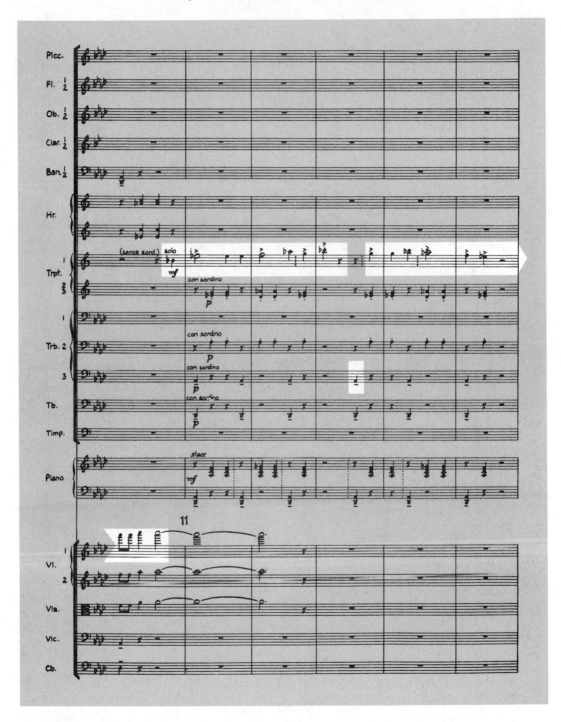

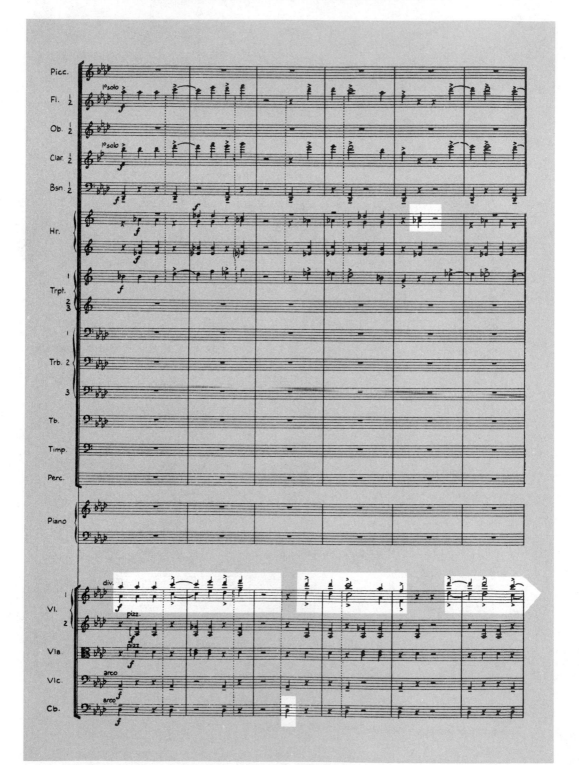

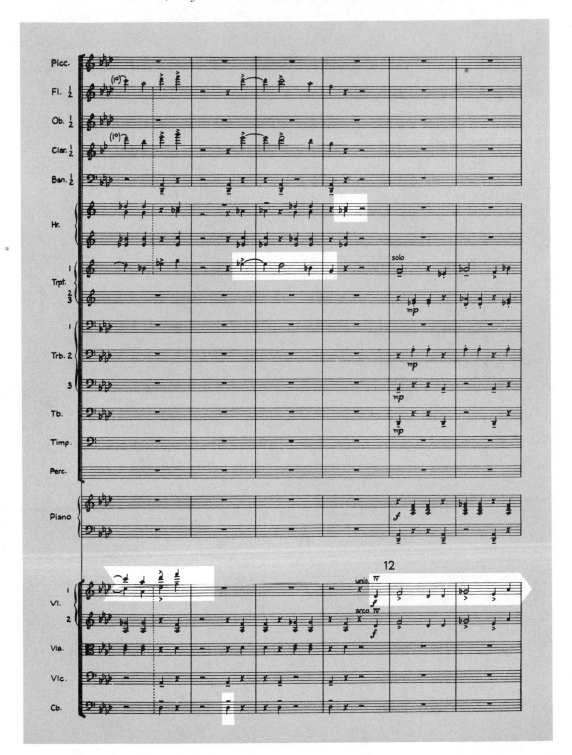

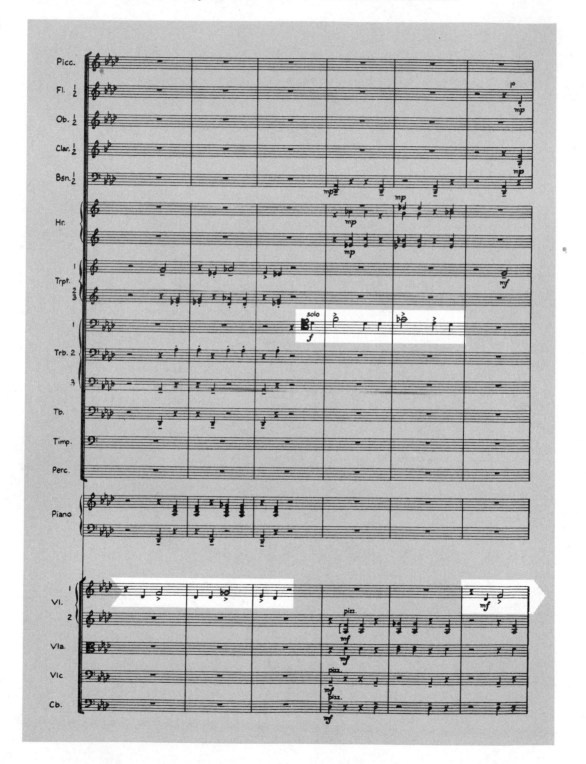

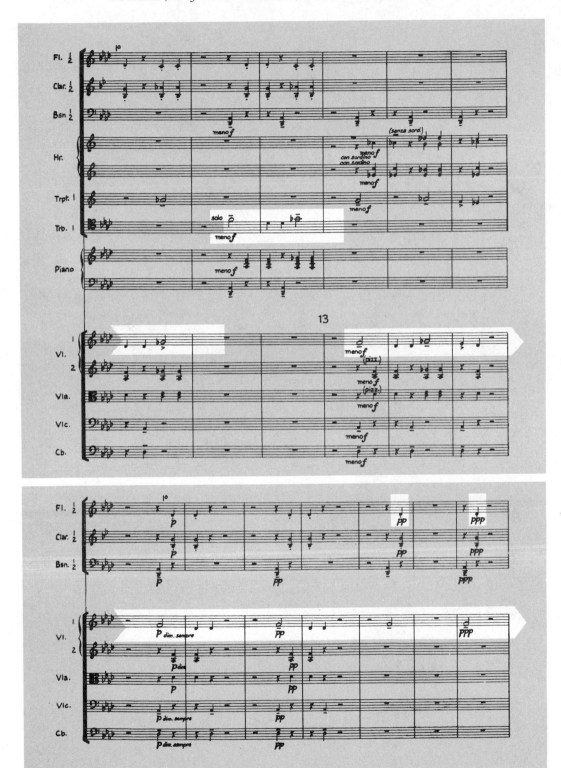

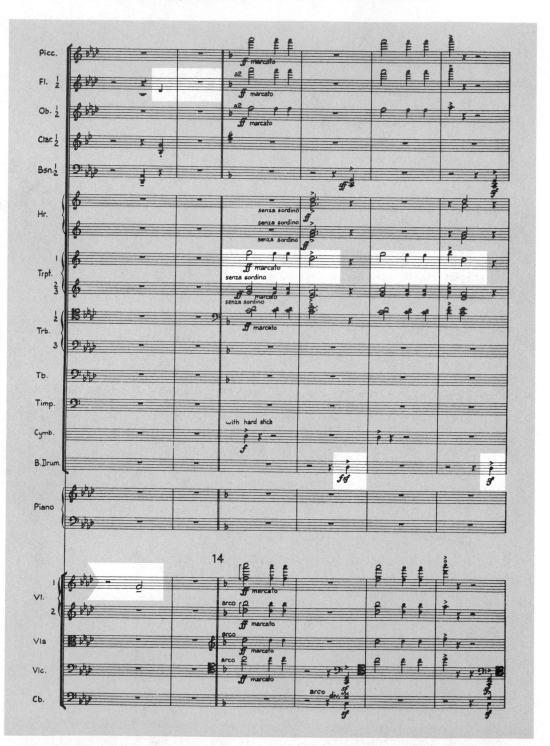

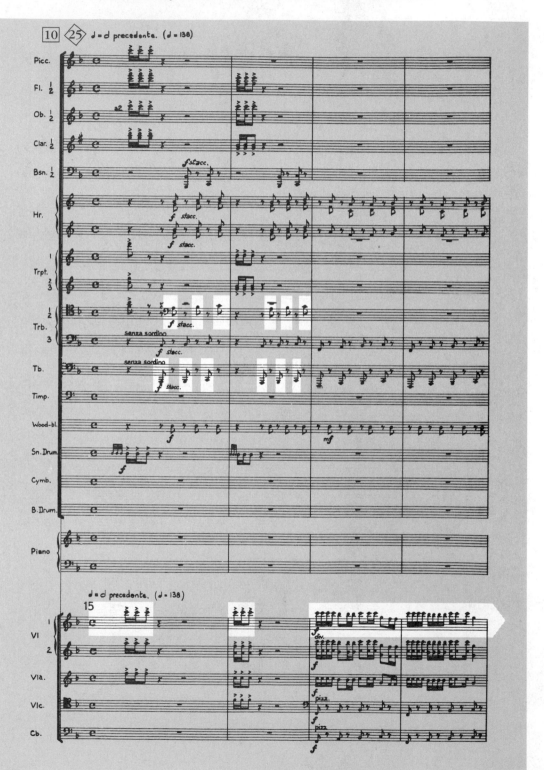

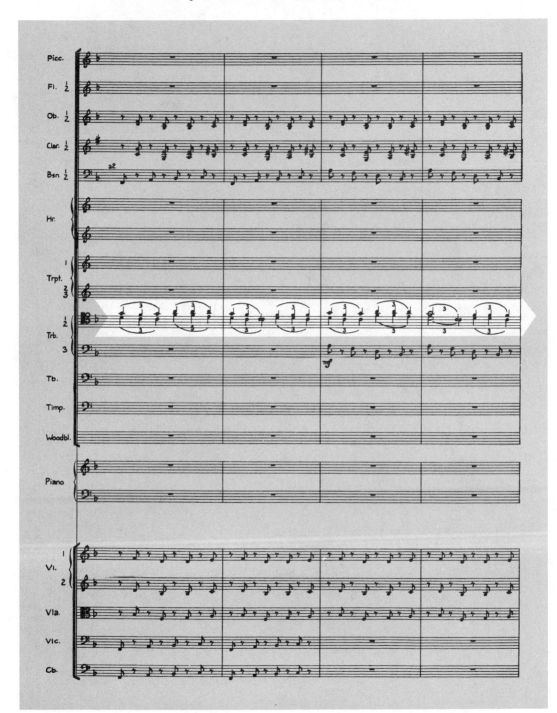

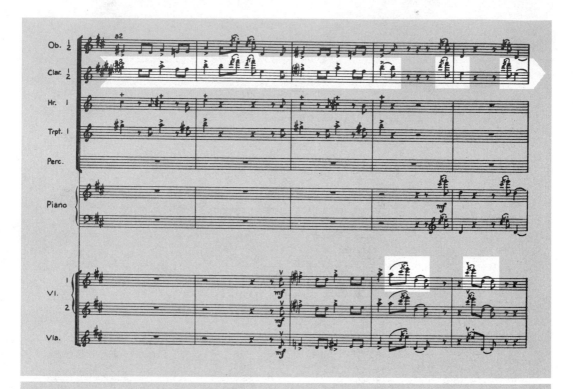

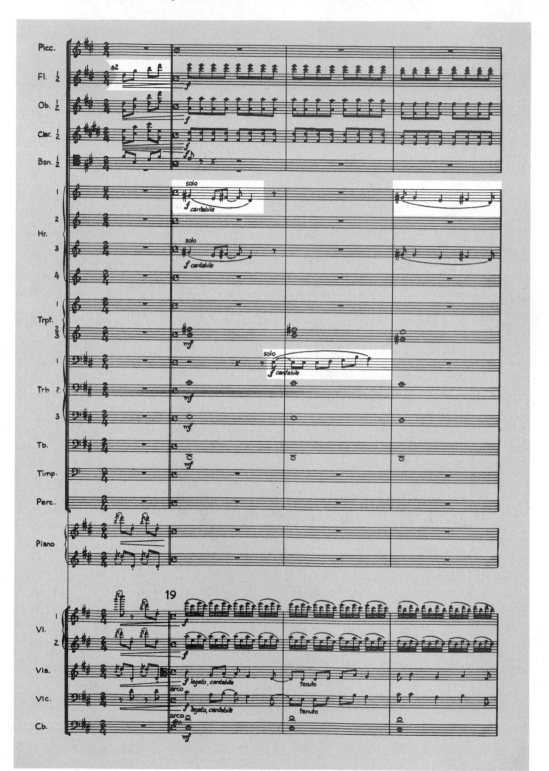

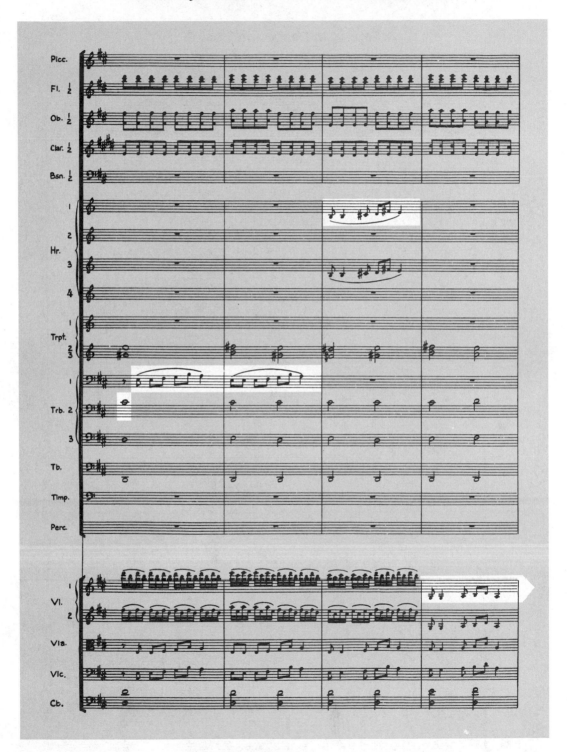

Mexican Dance and Finale

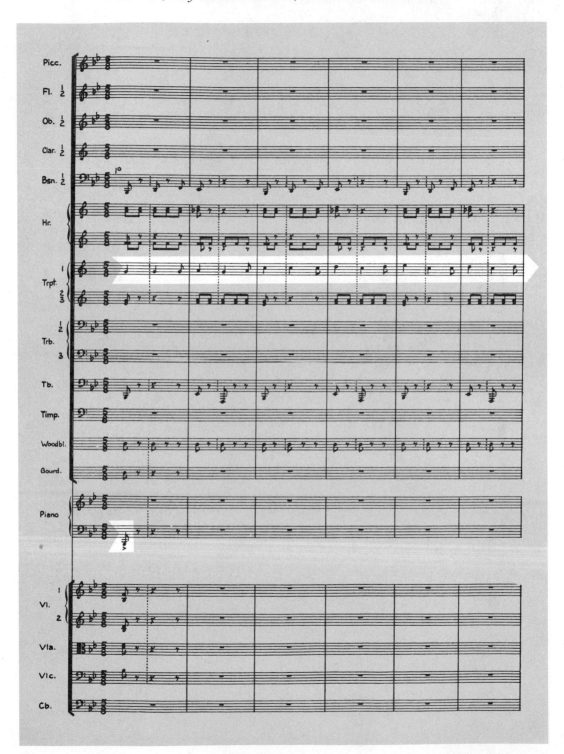

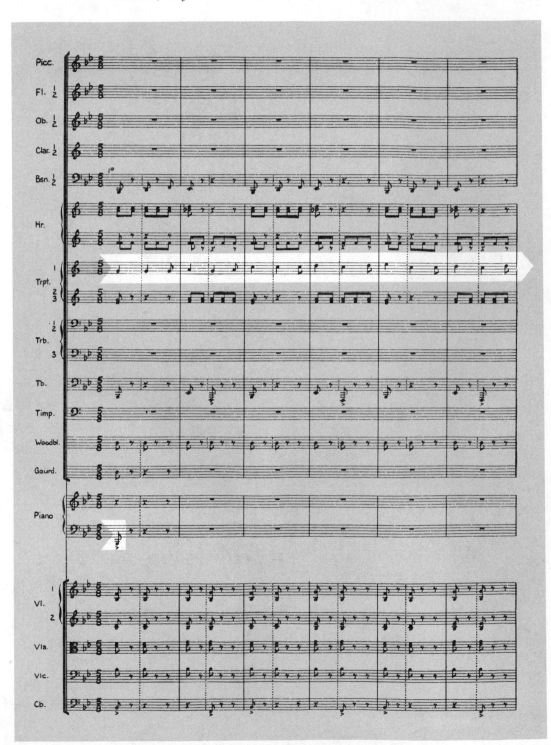

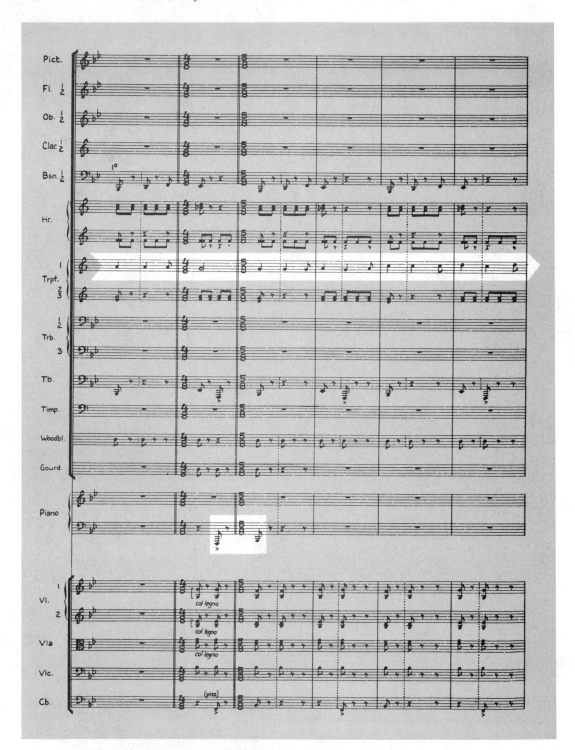

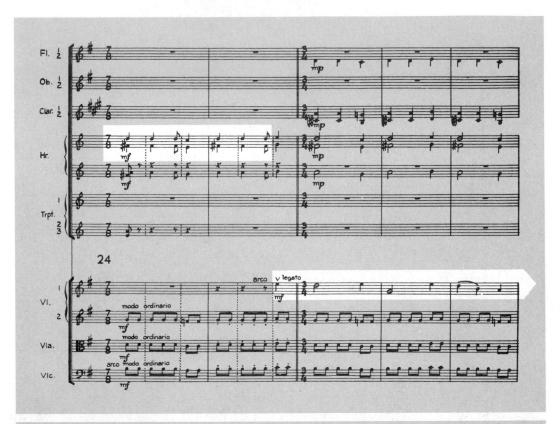

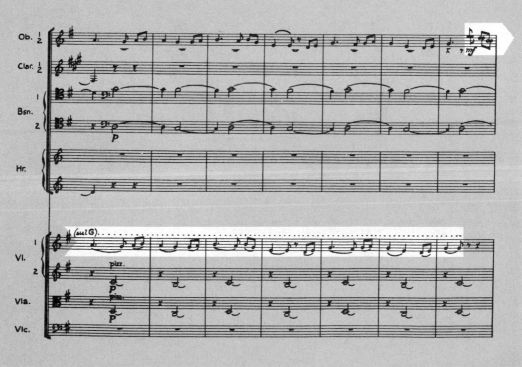

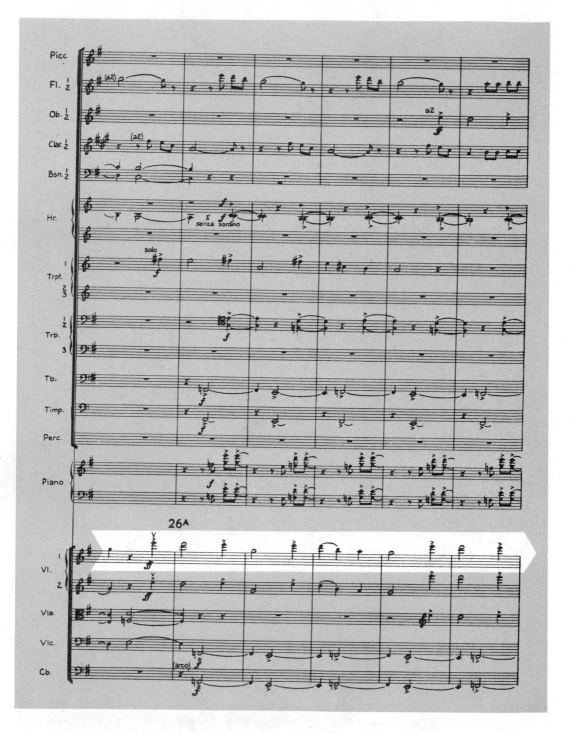

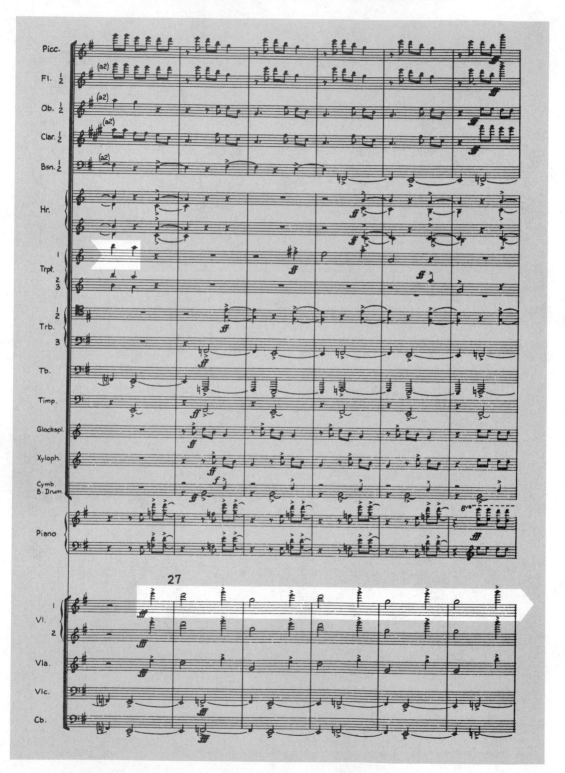

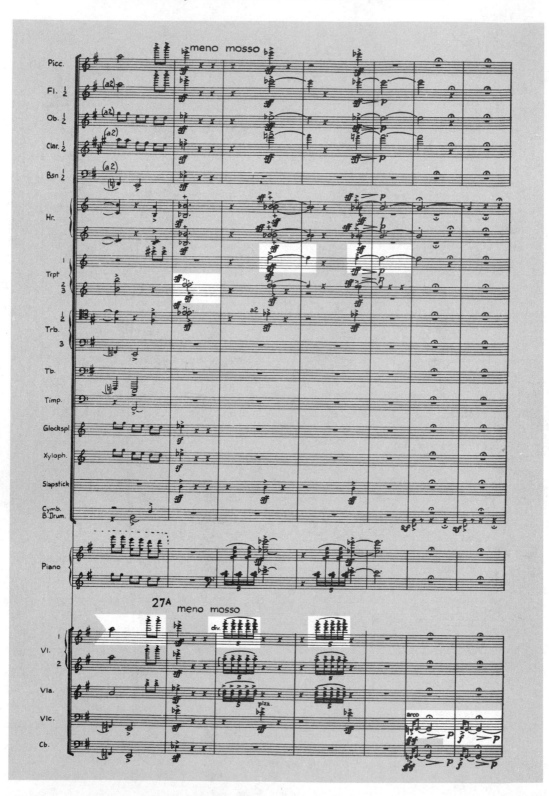

34. Ruth Crawford (1901–1953) 8:8A/3   8:8/12 – 15

Rat Riddles, from Three Songs (1933)

Accidentals affect only those individual notes before which they stand

Ruth Crawford, Rat Riddles *from* Three Songs for Voice. © *1933 New Music Edition.*
Theodore Presser Company.

Editor's note: "N.B." (*nota bene*, "note well") and "(a)!" used to mark composer's cautionary accidentals.

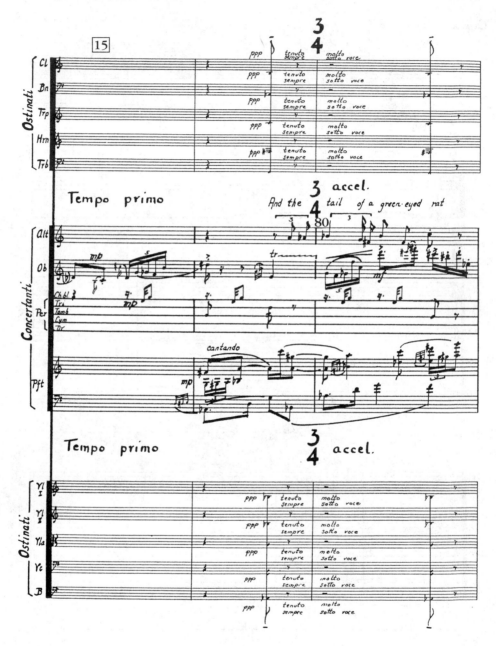

35. Witold Lutoslawski (1913–1994)

Jeux vénitiens (Venetian Games), First Movement (1961)

 8:8A/5 8:8/ 18 – 19

STRUMENTI DELL'ORCHESTRA

2 flauti (II anche flauto piccolo)
1 oboe
3 clarinetti in sib (III anche clarinetto basso in sib)
1 fagotto

1 tromba in do
1 corno in fa
1 trombone

percussione (4 esecutori)
      I 3 timpani scordati (3 dimensioni)
      II 3 tamburi (soprano, alto, tenore), tamburo rullante
      III xilofono, 3 piatti sospesi (soprano, alto, tenore), tam-tam, 5 tom-tom
      IV claves, vibrafono senza motore

arpa
pianoforte (2 esecutori; II anche celesta)

4 violini
3 viole
3 violoncelli
2 contrabbassi

DURATA ca 13'

The piccolo, xylophone, and celesta are notated an octave lower, and the double-basses an octave higher, than they sound. All the other instruments are notated at their actual pitch. In this score the signs # and b apply only to the notes they precede. Notes without accidentals should always be read as naturals.

18

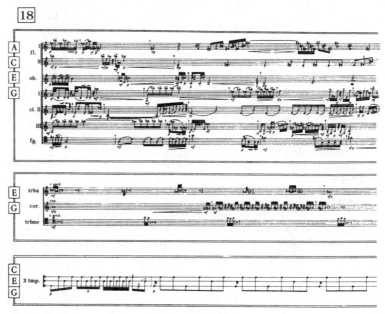

Order of performance: A B C D E F G H

Sections A C E G :

A is played by the woodwinds and percussion group; C by the woodwinds, kettledrums, and percussion; E by the woodwinds, brass, kettledrums, and percussion; G by the woodwinds, brass, kettledrums, percussion, and piano. The broken "bar lines" with a caesura above call for a caesura of optional length; on the length of the caesura will depend the density of the texture.

Duration of the particular sections: A = 12″, C = 18″, E = 6″, G = 24″. The conductor gives the sign for the beginning and end of each section (the beat showing the end of section A also indicates the beginning of section B, the beat showing the end of C, the beginning of D, etc.). When the sign for the end of each section is given, the performers must interrupt playing immediately. If by this time a player has already played his part to the end, he should repeat it

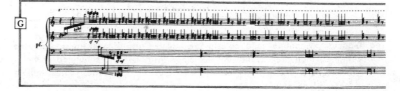

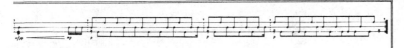

from the beginning of the section. In the following sections, which are indi-
cated by the letters in the order C, E, G, the individual parts ought not to be
played from the beginning but from any other phrase between two caesuras.
Each musician should play his part with the same freedom as if he were playing
it alone; the rhythmic values serve only as a guide, and the basic tempo is between ♪ = 140 and ♪ = 150.

Sections B D F H:

The bar lines, rhythmical values, and meter are intended merely for orientation:
the music should be played with the greatest possible freedom. The number of
notes at places like the third bar of section B in the first viola part depends on
the strength of the player's bowing (*spiccato* or preferably *ricochet*). In section
D the first violin part should be played independently of the conductor and the
rest of the ensemble.

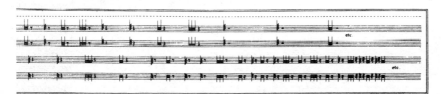

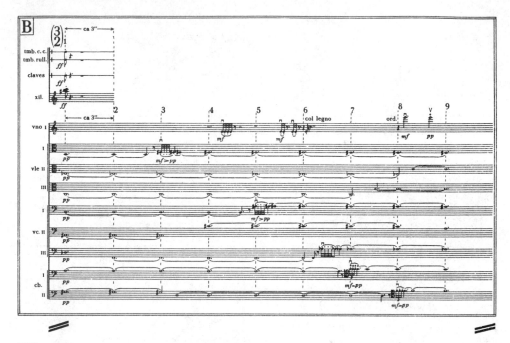

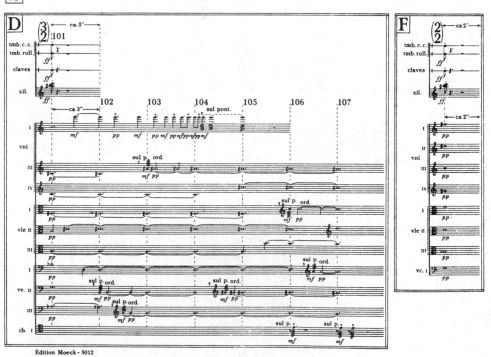

Edition Moeck - 5012

36. Elliott Carter (b. 1908)

8:8A/4   8:8/ 16 - 17

Sonata for Flute, Oboe, Cello, and Harpsichord, First Movement (1952)

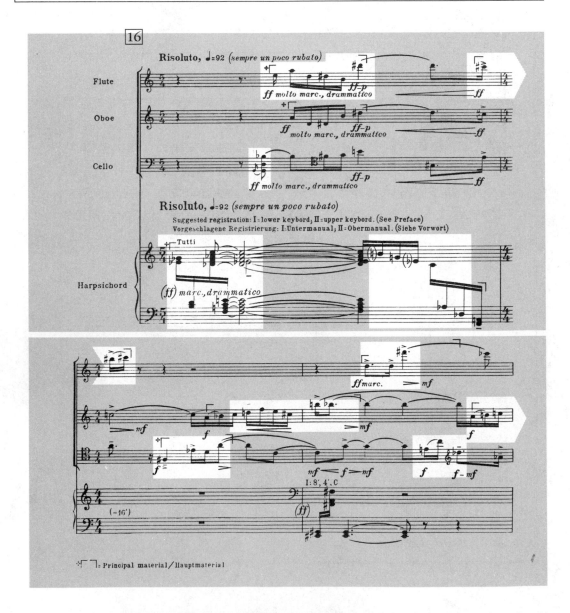

⌐┐ : Principal material/Hauptmaterial

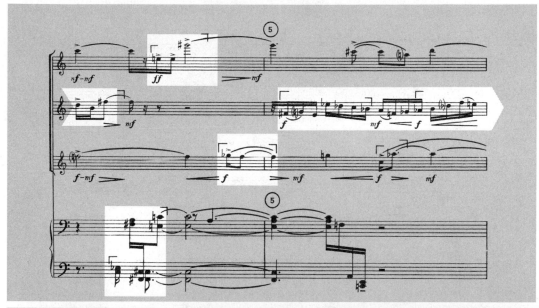

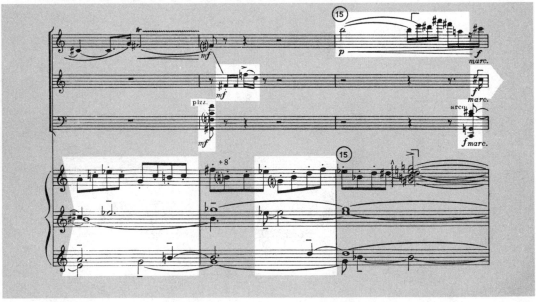

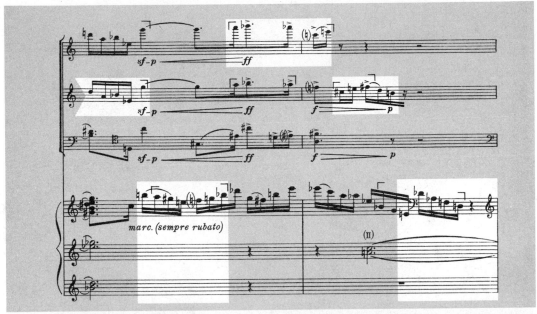

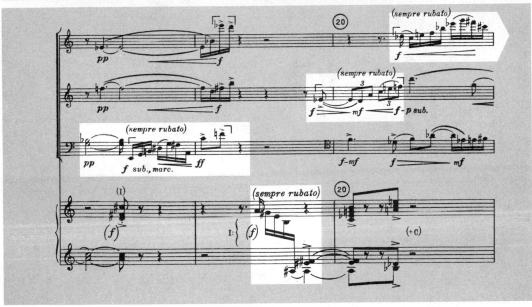

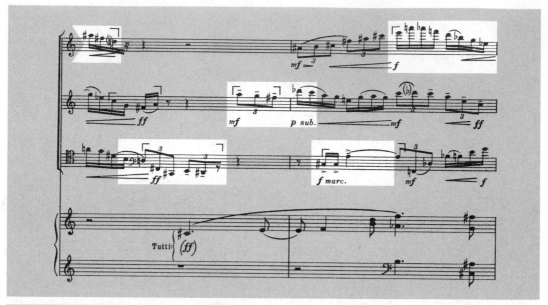

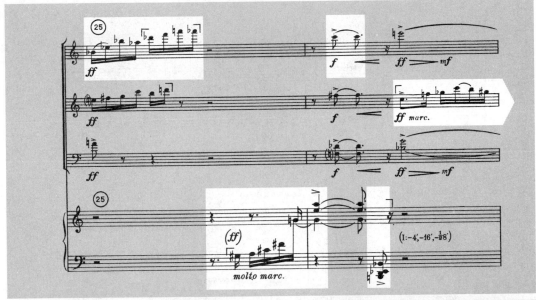

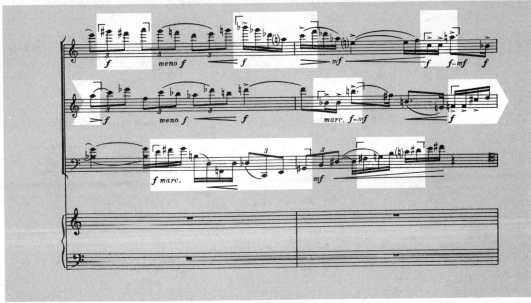

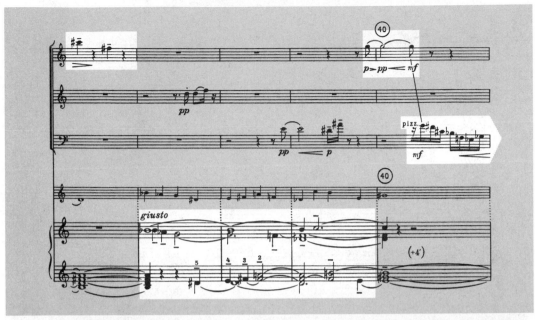

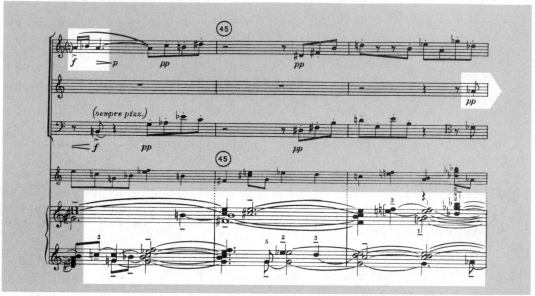

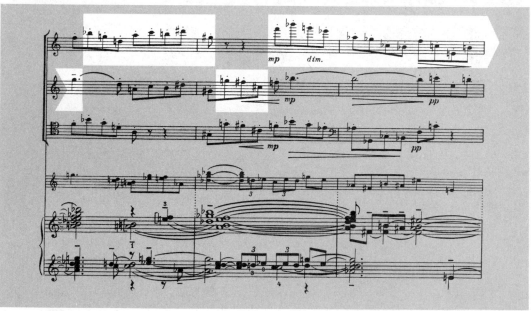

37. Milton Babbitt (b. 1916)

Phonemena, excerpt (1969-70)

Editor's note: This work was originally conceived with synthesized accompaniment. The composer prepared this piano/vocal score for study purposes.

38. Leonard Bernstein (1918–1990)

Symphonic Dances from *West Side Story* (1957/1961), excerpts

8:8A/7   8:8/ 21 – 24

3:3B/3   3:3/ 37 – 40

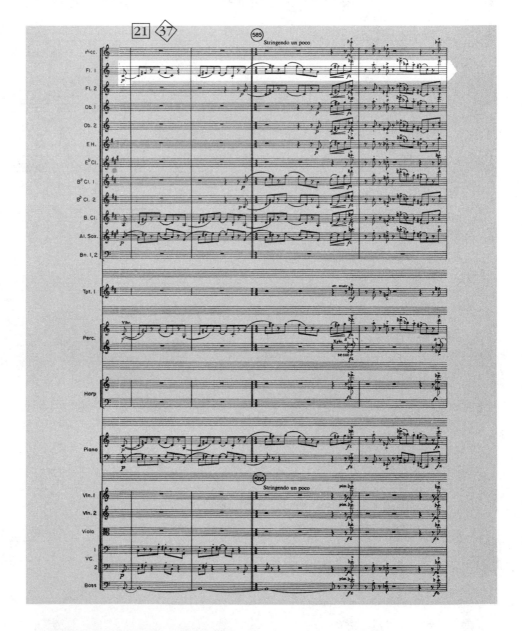

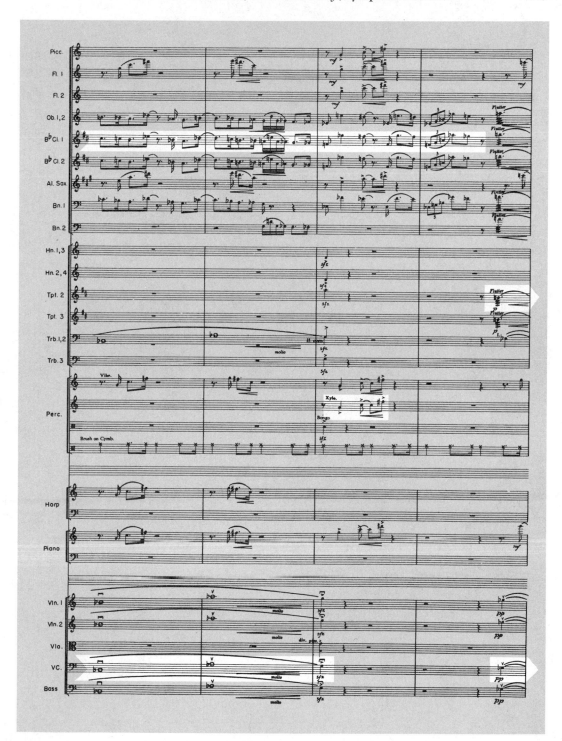

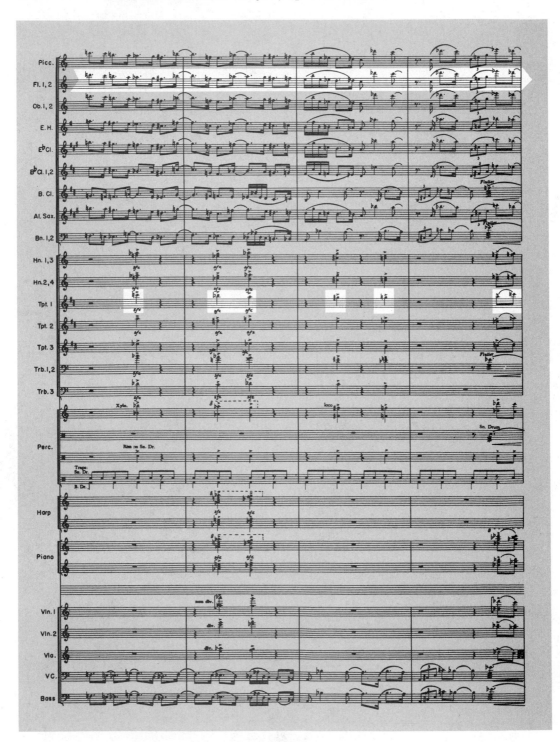

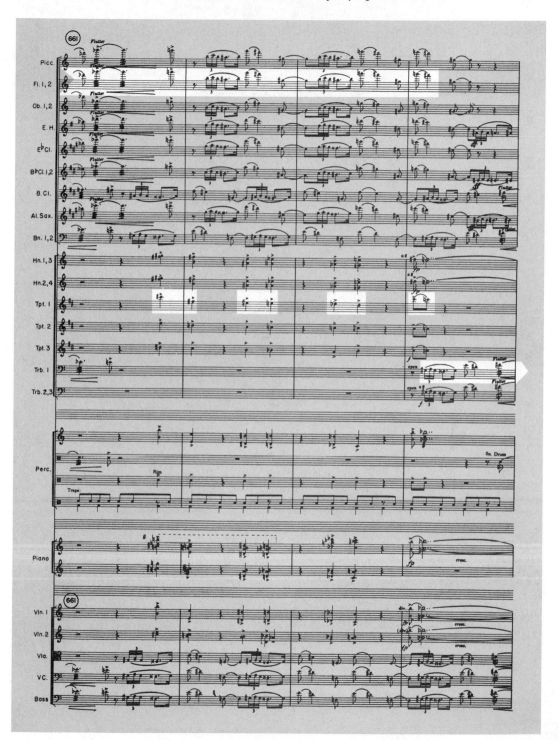

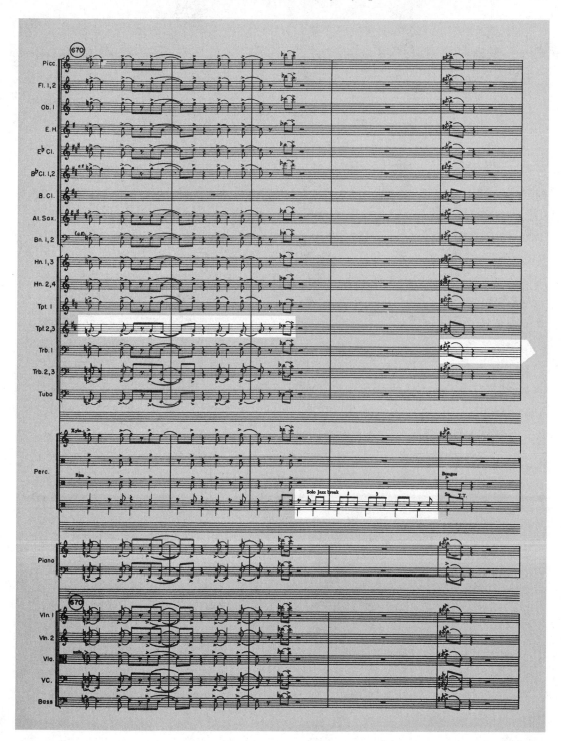

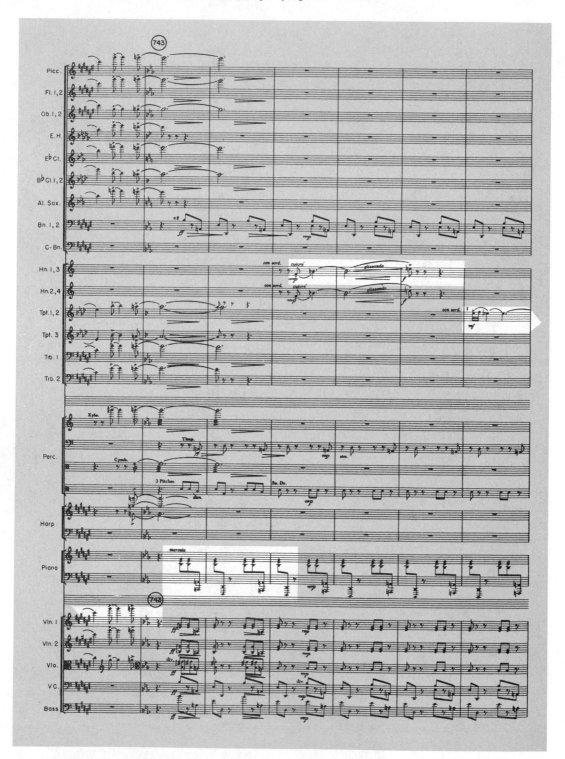

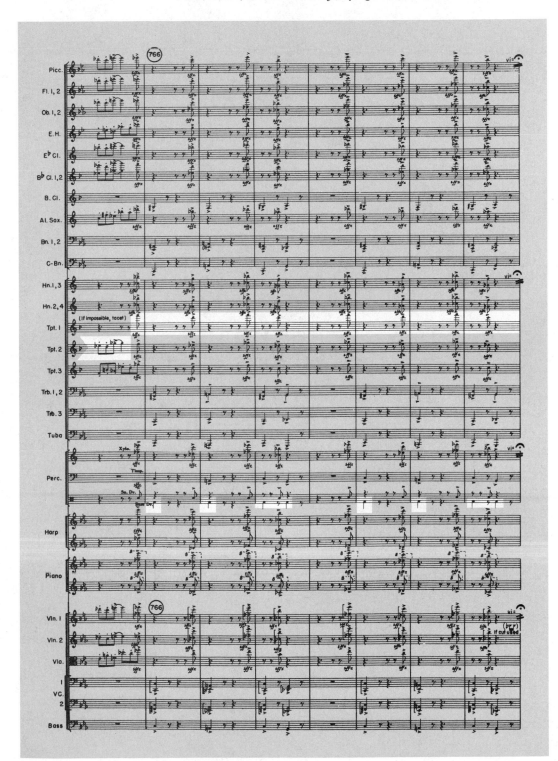

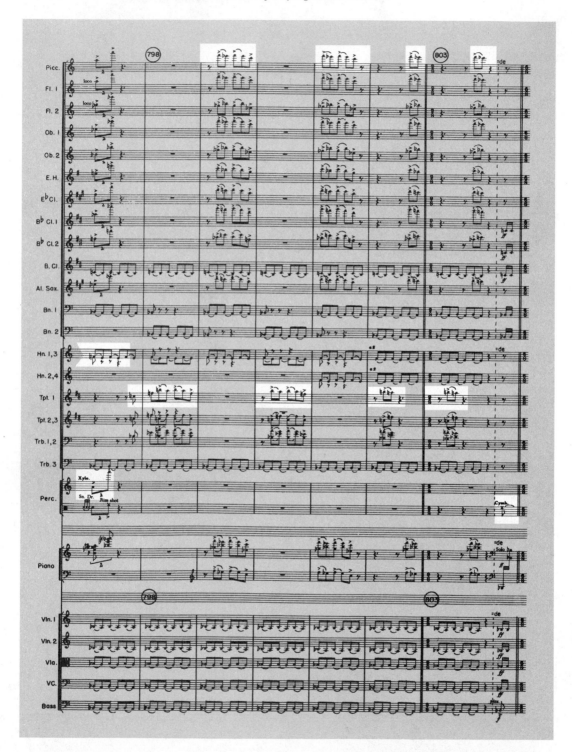

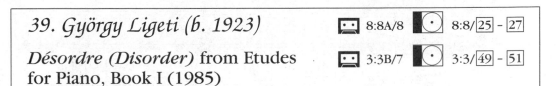

39. György Ligeti (b. 1923)

Désordre (Disorder) from Etudes for Piano, Book I (1985)

8:8A/8   8:8/ 25 - 27

3:3B/7   3:3/ 49 - 51

Composer's directions: Use the pedal very discreetly throughout the entire piece.

Composer's directions:

*Dynamic balance: the right hand should play somewhat louder than the left, so that the accented chords in both hands sound equally loud (until the end of the piece).

Gradually add more pedal (but always sparingly).

*Gradual crescendo (until the end): the accents gradually become *ff*, then *fff* (with the right hand constantly louder), the eighth notes gradually *mp*, then *mf*.

40. Pierre Boulez (b. 1925)

8:8A/9   8:8/ 28 – 30

Le marteau sans maître
(The Hammer Without a Master),
Nos. 1, 3, 7 (1953–54; revised 1957)

1. *Avant "L'artisanat furieux" (Before "Furious Artisans")*

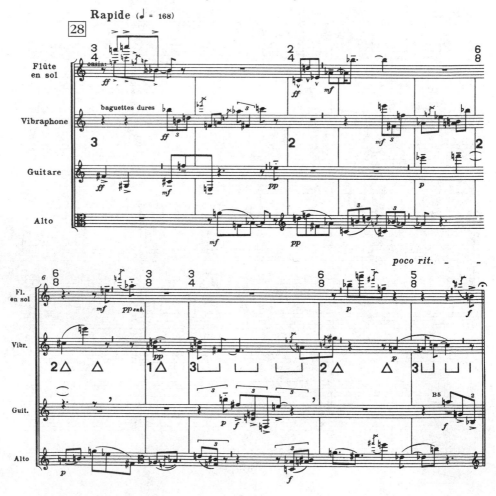

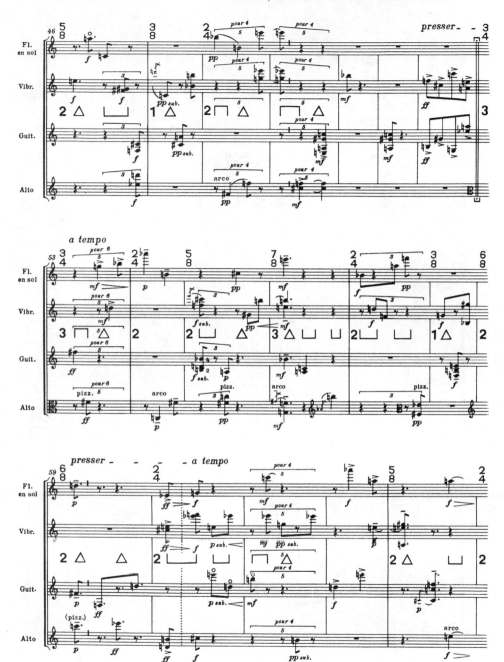

3. *L'artisanat furieux (Furious Artisans)*

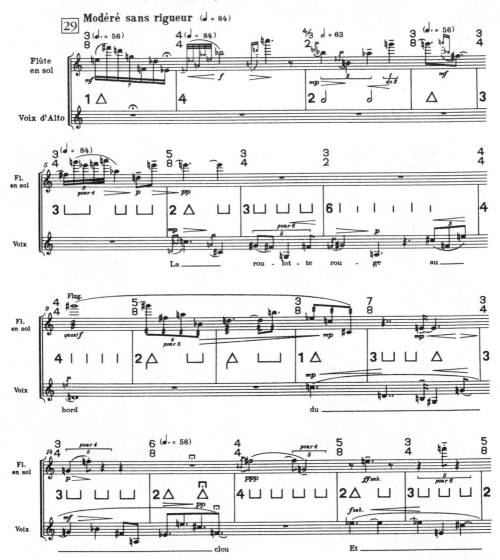

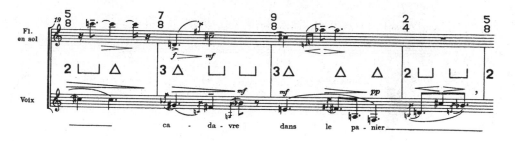

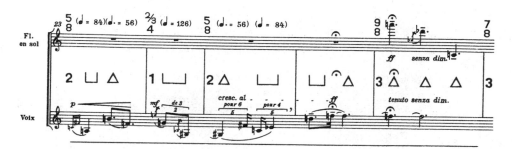

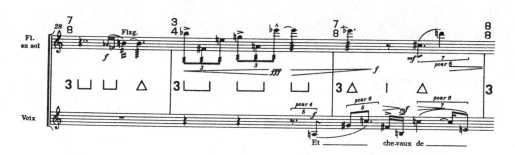

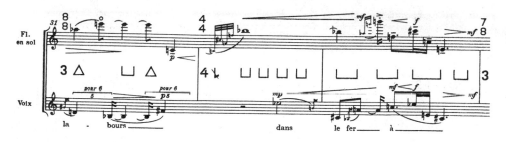

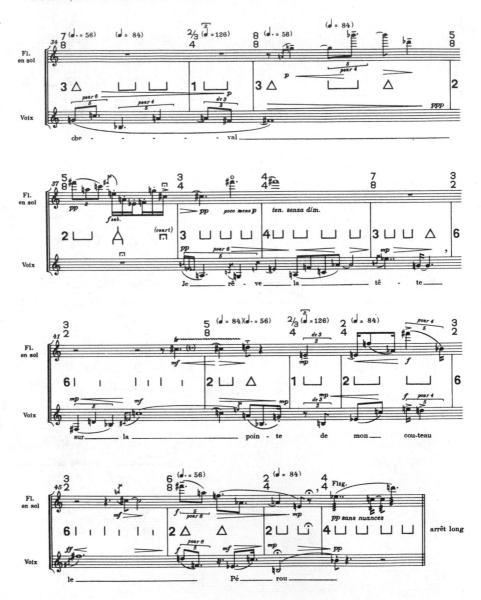

TEXT AND TRANSLATION

La roulotte rouge au bord du clou
Et cadavre dans le panier
Et chevaux de labours dans le fer à cheval
Je rêve la tête sur la pointe de mon couteau le
    Pérou

The red caravan at the prison's edge
And a corpse in the basket
And the work horses in the horseshoe
I dream of Peru with my head on the point of
    my knife

7. *Après "L'artisanat furieux" (After "Furious Artisans")*

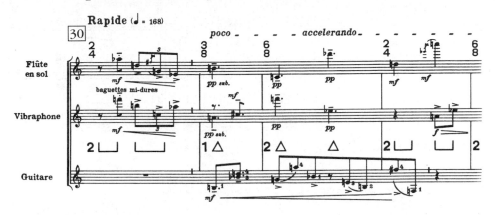

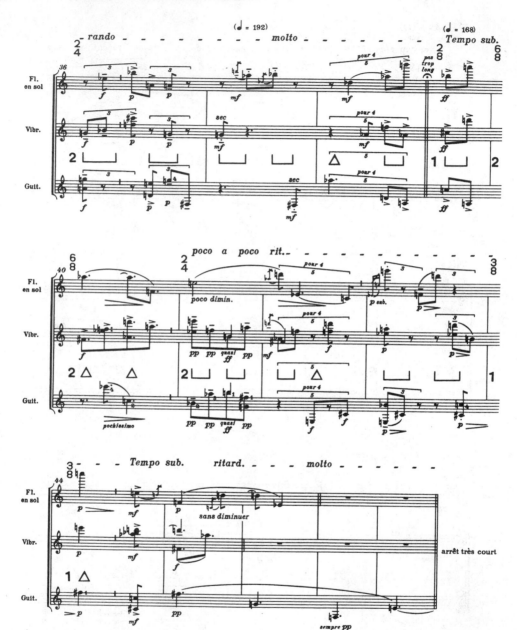

41. George Crumb (b. 1929)

Ancient Voices of Children, First Movement: *El niño busca su voz* (1970)

8:8B/1   8:8/ 31 – 33

3:3B/6   3:3/ 46 – 48

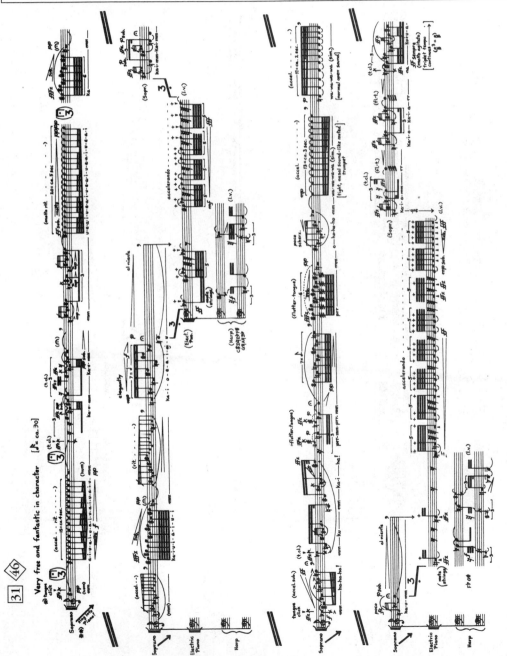

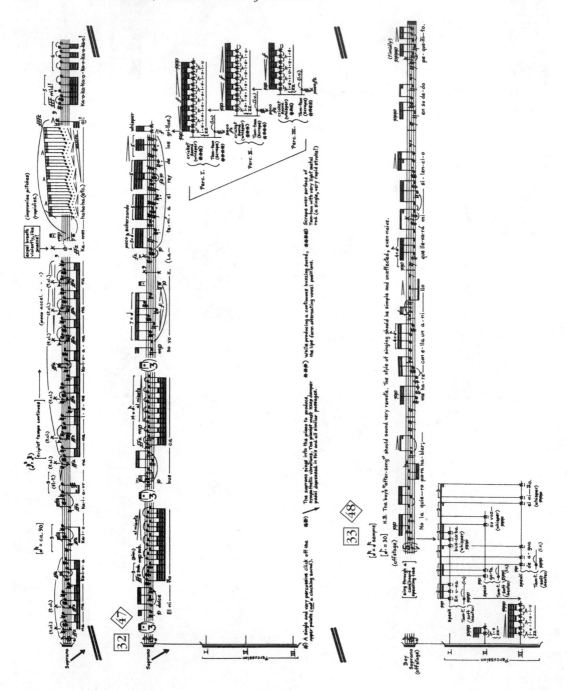

TEXT AND TRANSLATION

El niño busca su voz.
(La tenía el rey de los grillos.)
En una gota de agua
buscaba su voz el niño.

No la quiero para hablar;
me haré con ella un anillo
que llevará mi silencio
en su dedo pequeñito.

FEDERICO GARCÍA LORCA

The little boy is looking for his voice.
(The king of the crickets had it.)
In a drop of water
the little boy looked for his voice.

I don't want it to speak with;
I will make a ring of it
so that he may wear my silence
on his little finger.

Translated by W. S. Merwin

42. Joan Tower (b. 1938)

Petroushskates (1980)

8:8B/2   8:8/ 34 – 37

3:3B/9 3:3/ 55 – 58

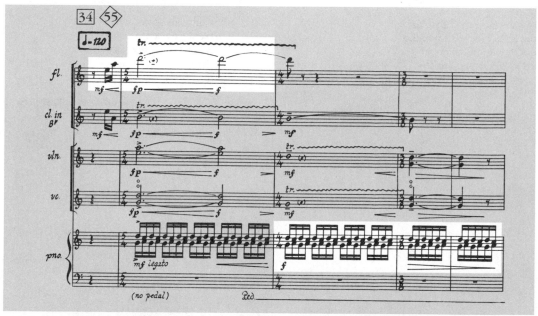

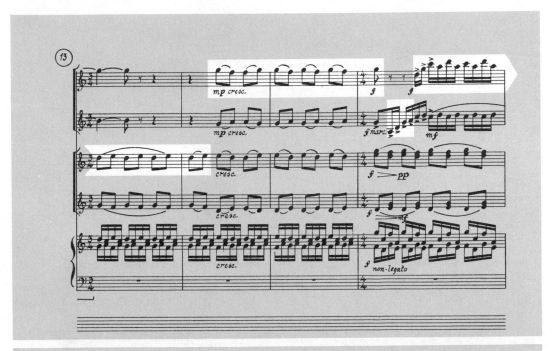

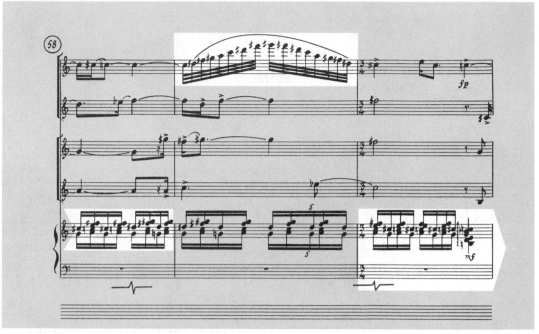

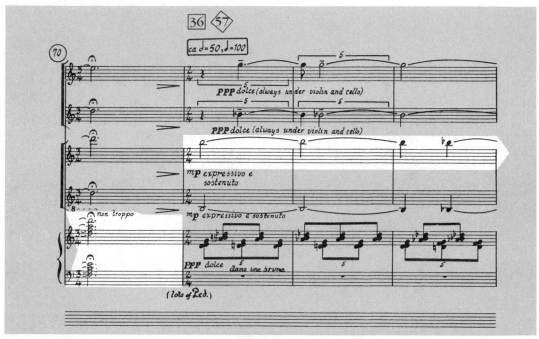

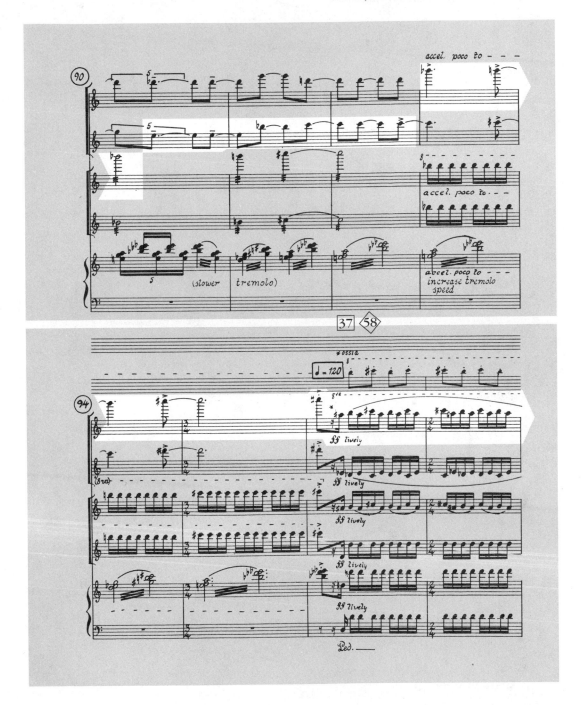

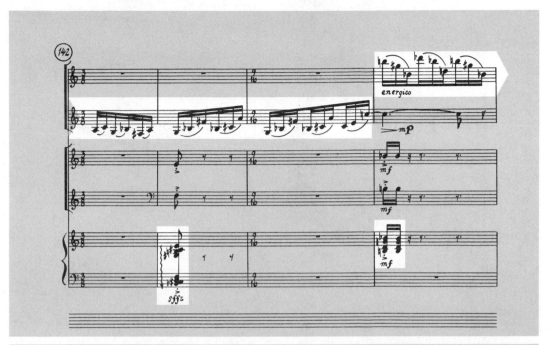

* press silently cluster of black and white notes
* keep below b♭ and catch notes with sost. pedal

sost. Ped.

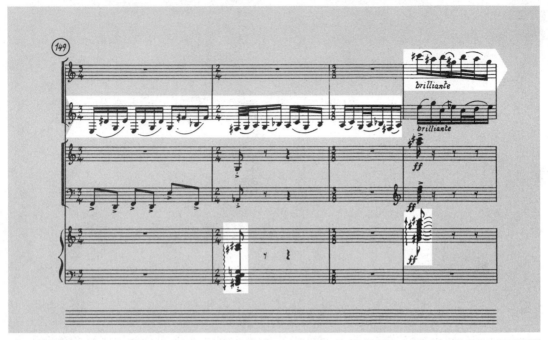

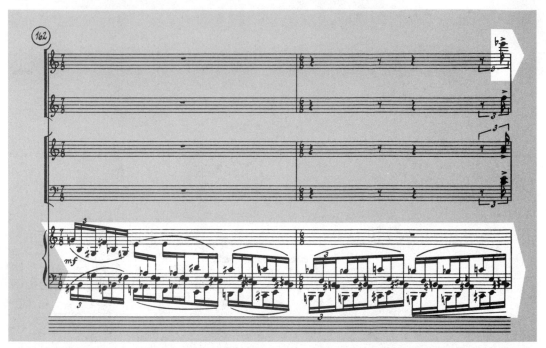

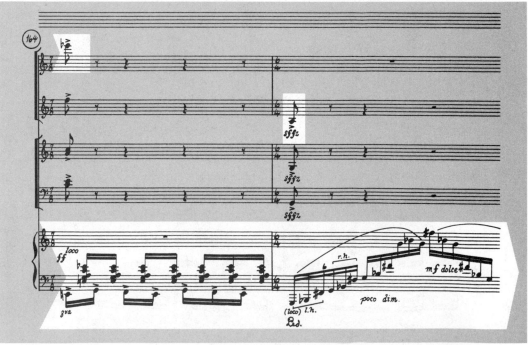

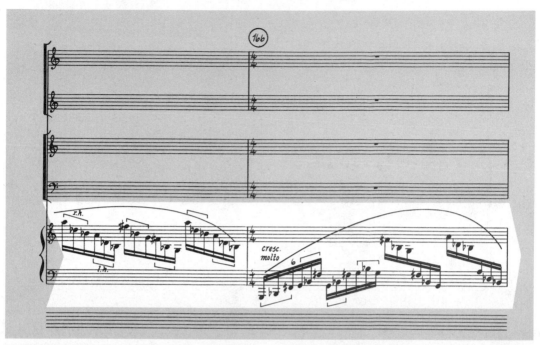

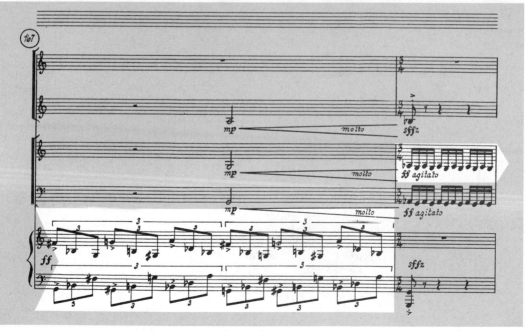

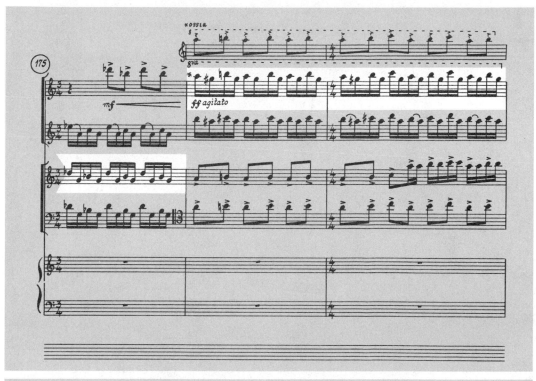

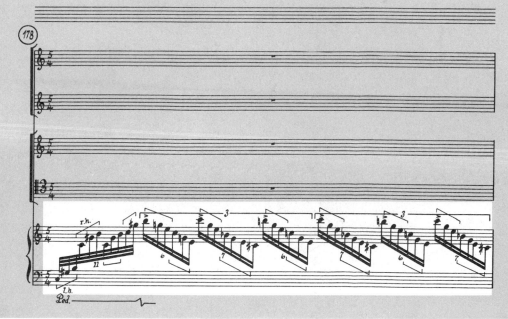

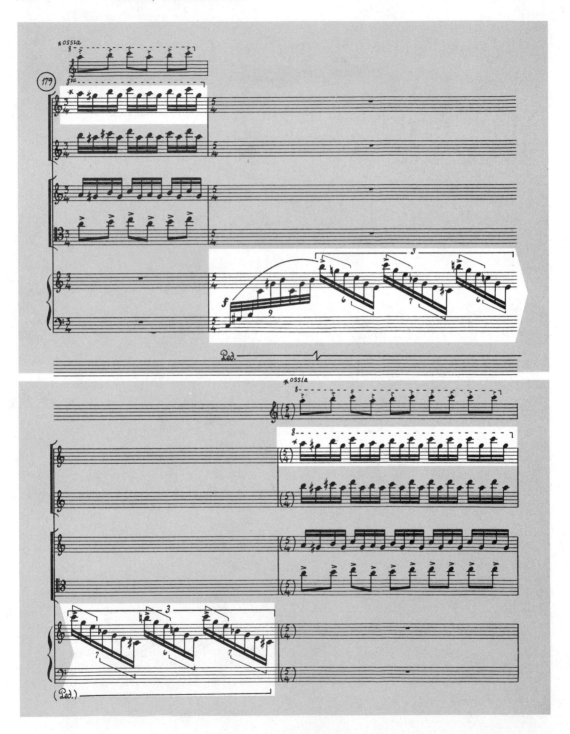

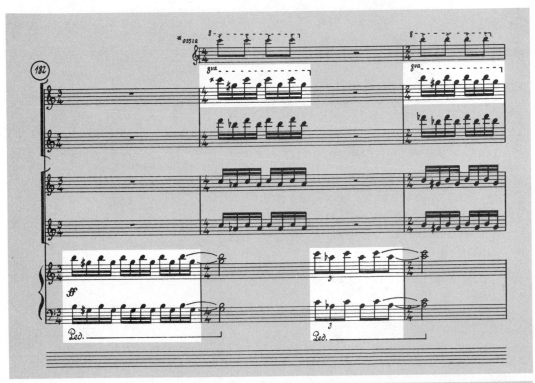

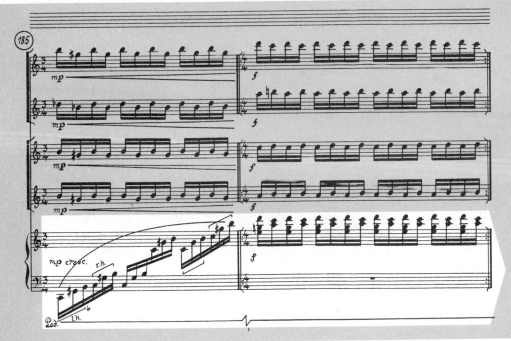

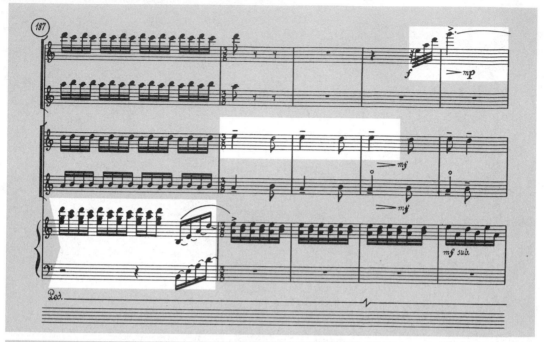

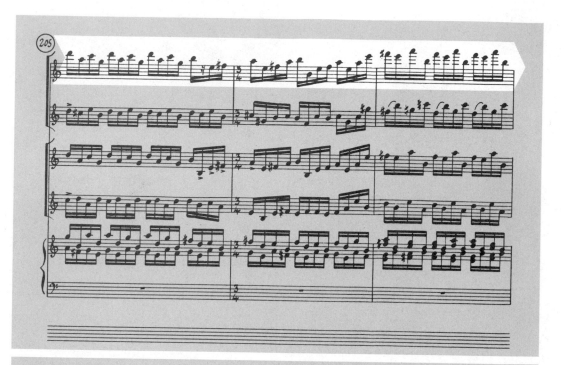

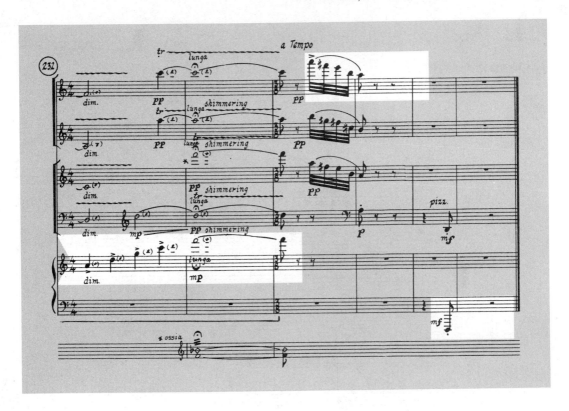

43. John Adams (b. 1947)

Nixon in China, Act I, Scene 3, Finale (1987)

928

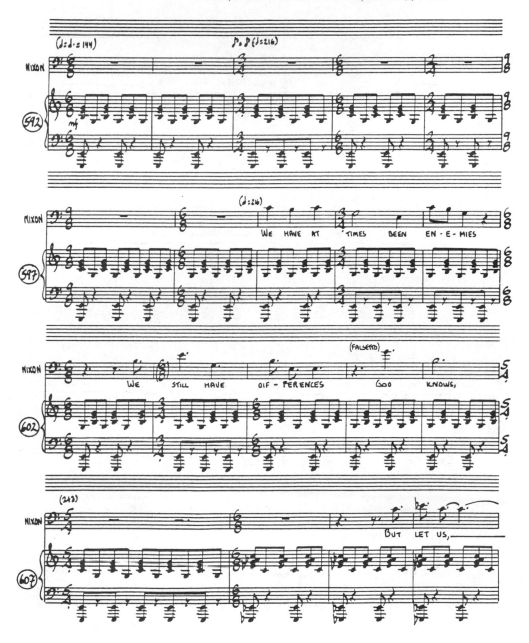

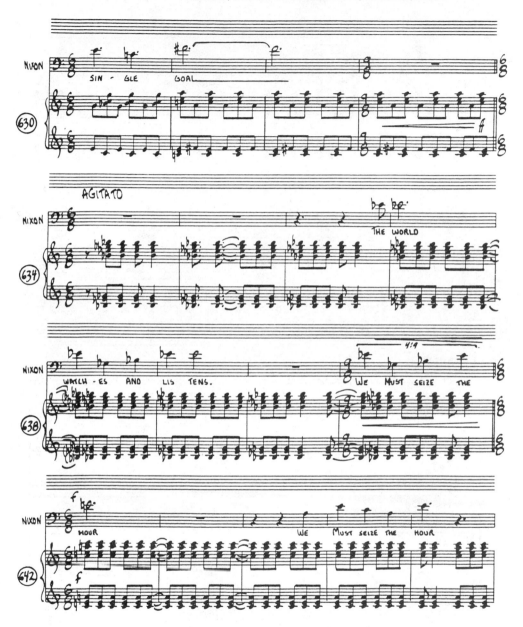

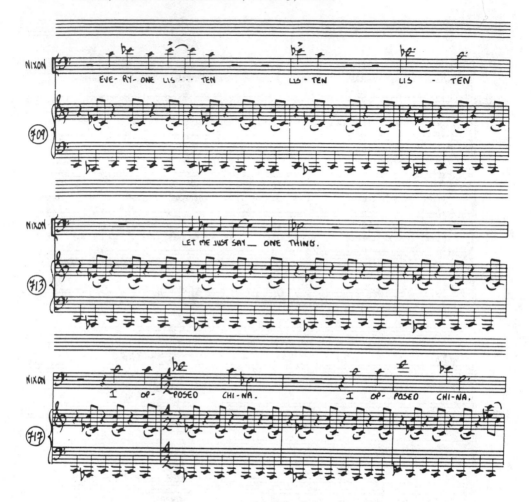

44. Tod Machover (b. 1952)

Bug-Mudra, excerpt (1989–90)

8:8B/4   8:8/⌐40⌐ – ⌐42⌐

3:3B/8   3:3/⌐52⌐ – ⌐54⌐

Composer's Note on *Bug-Mudra*

Bug-Mudra is scored for two guitarists (one electric and one acoustic) and one percussionist (who plays an electronic mallet controller and acoustic cymbals), each of whose playing is converted to MIDI data and interpreted in specially developed hyper-instrument software. (A hyper-instrument is one that is electronically enhanced based on computer monitoring of the performer's musical interpretation.) The musical result is computed according to the functions assigned to each instrument in each section and produced as sound by an array of synthesis gear. Additionally, the conductor wears a hand-and-finger-sensing device known as the Exos Dexterous Hand Master, which is used to control a second hyper-instrument system. This system interprets the hand gestures of the conductor (measuring the bend of each joint of each finger) and maps them to real-time control of a pair of automated mixers that shape the levels, panning, frequencies, etc., of the sounds from the other hyper-instruments. The major components of the entire setup are shown in the diagram on the following page.

There is also a tape part, which plays the entire length of the piece, providing time code information that controls the performance. The time base information (i.e., bars, time signatures, and tempi) is precisely maintained through the use of SMPTE time code. Thus, the hyper-instruments know exactly (within 1/100 of a second) what the current place in the performance is, as well as the beat and metric structure. This information enables the system to change behavior rapidly and in synchronization with the music. For example, in one section, the electric guitar's timbre is switched repeatedly between an electric bass sound transposed two octaves down to a synthesized guitar sound transposed two octaves up. In another case, notes are fed into the guitar synchronized with rapid notes on the tape so that the tape part sounds the correct note regardless of what the guitarist plays. Also, the fret board has been remapped so that each position produces a slightly different timbre; thus, the guitarist controls articulation, timbre, and phrase shape, while the tape controls the pitch.

The relationship between the hand gesture (controlled by the conductor wearing the Hand Master glove) and the sonic result changes in the different sections of the piece. The hand is used at times to shape complex, inharmonic spectra, the thumb is tied into the panning of one group of channels, and finger movement is mapped to levels of the different performers with an automatic smoothing function. This hyper-instrument system represents the most powerful and complex performance environment created to date.

Bug-Mudra Hyper-Instrument Performance System

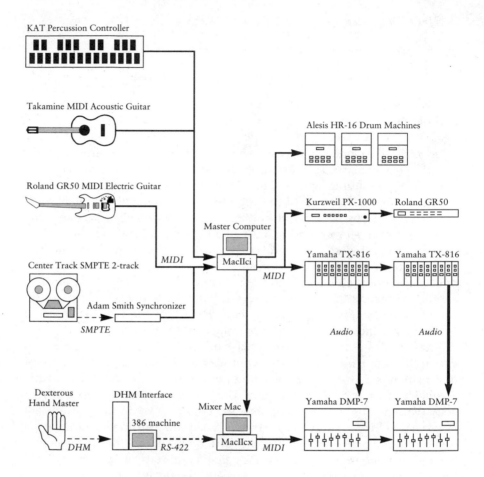

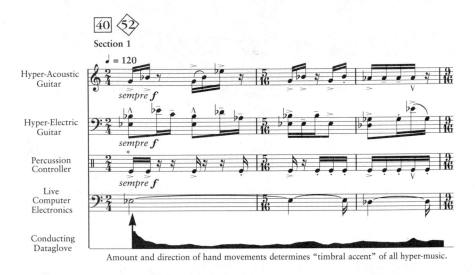

Amount and direction of hand movements determines "timbral accent" of all hyper-music.

*In non-pitched sections (no 𝄞) *any* percussion sound may be chosen and played in specified rhythm. Play on 4-octave *KAT controller* or equivalent. All these are noted on bottom line of staff. Notes above this bottom line are to be played on *acoustic cymbals*, lo-to-hi:

MACHOVER, *Bug-Mudra*: excerpt

MACHOVER, *Bug-Mudra*: excerpt

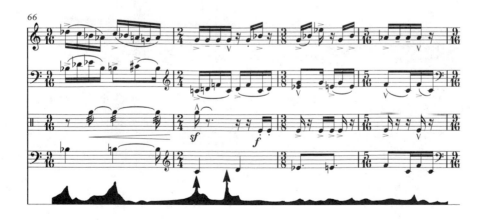

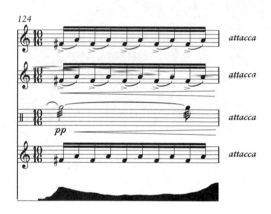

Conduct beats with dataglove (synchronizes computer part). Amount of movement (small→ large) determines degree of rhythmic quantizing (none→lots) for hyper-instruments.

*Improvise rhythm on running sixteenth notes. Constantly leave rests and pauses in texture. Place accents irregularly. Live playing will be "quantized" into exact sixteenth notes by the computer. Choose wood, claves and other dry sounds, not traditional "drum-set" material. These are generally found in octaves 2 and 3 of the KAT.

- - - (beats; movement = sync) - - -

1 E : hyper event triggered on these notes.

- - - (beats; movement = sync) - - -

- - - (beats; movement = sync) - - -

MACHOVER, *Bug-Mudra*: excerpt

- - - (beats; movement = sync) - - -

- - - (beats; movement = sync) - - -

- - - (beats; movement = sync) - - -

- - - (beats; movement = sync) - - -

984	MACHOVER, *Bug-Mudra*: excerpt

- - - (beats; movement = sync) - - -

- - - (beats; movement = sync) - - -

986

MACHOVER, *Bug-Mudra*: excerpt

--- (beats; movement = sync) ---

Hyper-electric guitar (see note below)

- - - (beats; movement = sync) - - -

Hyper-electric guitar: Until ms. 157, notes are fed automatically to 6 guitar strings. Fret = timbre. Play fast, furiously, and with great rhythmic complexity/irregularity.

Continue with beats. Arrow indicates very large downbeat; enhances accent and synchronization.

- - - (beat; arrows) - - -

994   MACHOVER, *Bug-Mudra*: excerpt

- - - (beat; arrows) - - -

Hyper-electric guitar (see note below)

**Back to improvised sixteenths (see note below)

Hyper-electric guitar: Play notes on low E string. Complex patterns transferred automatically to other strings.

**Back to improvised sixteenths, quantized by computer, again using wood sounds. Continue until measure 176.

- - - (beat; arrows) - - -

- - - (beat; arrows) - - -

--- (beat; arrows) ---

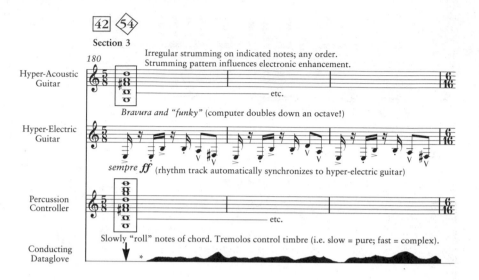

*Right-hand conducting stops. Timbre shaping of all hyper-music from dataglove. Position of hand, speed/continuity of movement, and position of fingers sculpts timbre density and determines spectral content.

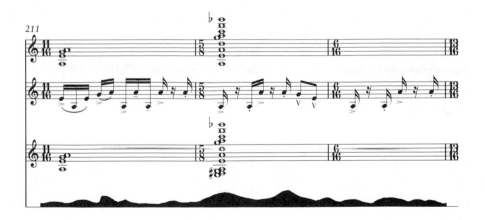

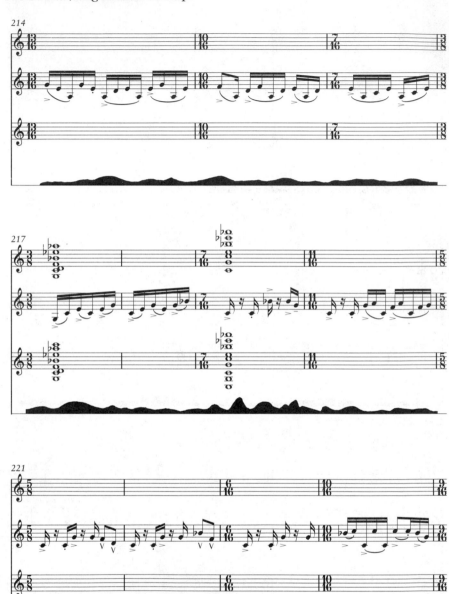

Appendix A

Reading a Musical Score

CLEFS

The music for some instruments is written in clefs other than the familiar treble and bass. In the following example, middle C is shown in the four clefs used in orchestral scores:

Treble clef   Alto clef   Tenor clef   Bass clef

The *alto clef* is primarily used in viola parts. The *tenor clef* is employed for cello, bassoon, and trombone parts when these instruments play in a high register.

TRANSPOSING INSTRUMENTS

The music for some instruments is customarily written at a pitch different from its actual sound. The following list, with examples, shows the main transposing instruments and the degree of transposition. (In some modern works—such as the Stravinsky example included in this anthology—all instruments are written at their sounding pitch.)

Instrument	Transposition	Written note	Actual sound
Piccolo Celesta	sounds an octave higher than written		
Trumpet in F	sounds a fourth higher than written		
Trumpet in E	sounds a major third higher than written		
Clarinet in E♭ Trumpet in E♭	sounds a minor third higher than written		

Instrument	Transposition	Written note	Actual sound
Trumpet in D Clarinet in D	sounds a major second higher than written		
Clarinet in B♭ Trumpet in B♭ Cornet in B♭ French horn in B♭, alto	sounds a major second lower than written		
Clarinet in A Trumpet in A Cornet in A	sounds a minor third lower than written		
French horn in G Alto flute	sounds a fourth lower than written		
English horn French horn in F	sounds a fifth lower than written		
French horn in E	sounds a minor sixth lower than written		
French horn in E♭ Alto saxophone	sounds a major sixth lower than written		
French horn in D	sounds a minor seventh lower than written		
Contrabassoon French horn in C Double bass	sounds an octave lower than written		

Bass clarinet in B♭
Tenor saxophone
  (written in treble
  clef)
	sounds a major ninth
	lower than written		

(written in bass clef)	sounds a major second lower than written		

Bass clarinet in A
  (written in treble
  clef)
	sounds a minor tenth
	lower than written		

(written in bass clef)	sounds a minor third lower than written		

Baritone saxophone
  in E♭ (written
  in treble clef)
	sounds an octave and
	a major sixth lower
	than written		

Appendix B

Instrumental Names and Abbreviations

The following tables set forth the English, Italian, German, and French names used for the various musical instruments in these scores, and their respective abbreviations (when used). Latin voice designations and a table of the foreign-language names for scale degrees and modes are also provided.

WOODWINDS

English	Italian	German	French
Piccolo (Picc.)	Flauto piccolo (Fl. Picc.)	Kleine Flöte (Kl. Fl.)	Petite flûte
Flute (Fl.)	Flauto (Fl.); Flauto grande (Fl. gr.)	Grosse Flöte (Gr. Fl.)	Flûte (Fl.)
Alto flute	Flauto contralto (fl. c-alto)	Altflöte	Flûte en sol
Oboe (Ob.)	Oboe (Ob.)	Hoboe (Hb.); Oboe (Ob.)	Hautbois (Hb.)
English horn (E. H.)	Corno inglese (C. or Cor. ingl., C.i.)	Englisches Horn (E. H.)	Cor anglais (C. A.)
E♭ clarinet	Clarinetto piccolo (clar. picc.)		
Clarinet (C., Cl., Clt., Clar.)	Clarinetto (Cl., Clar.)	Klarinette (Kl.)	Clarinette (Cl.)
Bass clarinet (B. Cl.)	Clarinetto basso (Cl. b., Cl. basso, Clar. basso)	Bass Klarinette (Bkl.)	Clarinette basse (Cl. bs.)
Bassoon (Bsn., Bssn.)	Fagotto (Fag., Fg.)	Fagott (Fag., Fg.)	Basson (Bssn.)

1013

English	Italian	German	French
Contrabassoon (C. Bsn.)	Contrafagotto (Cfg., C. Fag., Cont. F.)	Kontrafagott (Kfg.)	Contrebasson (C. bssn.)
Alto saxophone	Sassofone	Saxophon	Saxophone
Tenor saxophone			
Baritone saxophone			

BRASS

French horn (Hr., Hn.)	Corno (Cor., C.)	Horn (Hr.) [*pl.* Hörner (Hrn.)]	Cor; Cor à pistons
Trumpet (Tpt., Trpt., Trp., Tr.)	Tromba (Tr.)	Trompete (Tr., Trp.)	Trompette (Tr.)
Trumpet in D	Tromba piccola (Tr. picc.)		
Cornet	Cornetta	Kornett	Cornet à pistons (C. à p., Pist.)
Trombone (Tr., Tbe., Trb., Trm., Trbe.)	Trombone [*pl.* Tromboni (Tbni., Trni.)]	Posaune (Ps., Pos.)	Trombone (Tr.)
Bass trombone			
Tuba (Tb.)	Tuba (Tb., Tba.)	Tuba (Tb.) [*also* Basstuba (Btb.)]	Tuba (Tb.)
Ophicleide	Oficleide	Ophikleide	Ophicléide

PERCUSSION

Percussion (Perc.)	Percussione	Schlagzeug (Schlag.)	Batterie (Batt.)
Kettledrums (K. D.)	Timpani (Timp., Tp.)	Pauken (Pk.)	Timbales (Timb.)
Snare drum (S. D.)	Tamburo piccolo (Tamb. picc.)	Kleine Trommel (Kl. Tr.)	Caisse claire (C. cl.); Caisse roulante
	Tamburo militare (Tamb. milit.)		Tambour militaire (Tamb. milit.)

English	Italian	German	French
Bass drum (B. drum)	Gran cassa (Gr. Cassa, Gr. C., G. C.)	Grosse Trommel (Gr. Tr.)	Grosse caisse (Gr. c.)
Cymbals (Cym., Cymb.)	Piatti (P., Ptti., Piat.)	Becken (Beck.)	Cymbales (Cym.)
Tam-Tam (Tam.-T.)			
Tambourine (Tamb.)	Tamburino (Tamb.)	Schellentrommel; Tamburin	Tambour de Basque (T. de B., Tamb. de Basque)
Triangle (Trgl., Tri.)	Triangolo (Trgl.)	Triangel	Triangle (Triang.)
Glockenspiel (Glocken.)	Campanelli (Cmp.)	Glockenspiel	Carillon
Bells; Chimes	Campane (Cmp.)	Glocken	Cloches
Antique cymbals	Crotali; Piatti antichi	Antike Zimbeln	Crotales; Cymbales antiques
Sleigh bells	Sonagli (Son.)	Schellen	Grelots
Xylophone (Xyl.)	Xilofono	Xylophon	Xylophone
Cowbells		Herdenglocken	
Crash cymbal			Grande cymbale chinoise
Siren			Sirène
Lion's roar			Tambour à corde
Slapstick			Fouet
Wood blocks			Blocs chinois

STRINGS

English	Italian	German	French
Violin (V., Vl., Vln., Vi.)	Violino (V., Vl., Vln.)	Violine (V., Vl., Vln.); Geige (Gg.)	Violon (V., Vl., Vln.)
Viola (Va., Vl., pl. Vas.)	Viola (Va., Vla.) [pl. Viole (Vle.)]	Bratsche (Br.)	Alto (A.)
Violoncello; Cello (Vcl., Vc.)	Violoncello (Vc., Vlc., Vcllo.)	Violoncell (Vc., Vlc.)	Violoncelle (Vc.)

English	Italian	German	French
Double bass (D. Bs.)	Contrabasso (Cb., C. B.) [*pl.* Contrabassi or Bassi (C. Bassi, Bi.)]	Kontrabass (Kb.)	Contrebasse (C. B.)

OTHER INSTRUMENTS

English	Italian	German	French
Harp (Hp., Hrp.)	Arpa (A., Arp.)	Harfe (Hrf.)	Harpe (Hp.)
Piano	Pianoforte (P.-f., Pft.)	Klavier	Piano
Celesta (Cel.)			
Harpsichord	Cembalo	Cembalo	Clavecin
Harmonium (Harmon.)			
Organ (Org.)	Organo	Orgel	Orgue
Guitar		Gitarre (Git.)	
Mandoline (Mand.)			

Voice Designations

Soprano (S)
Alto (A)
Tenor (T)
Bass (B)

Singstimme	Voice
Rezitation	Voice in Sprechstimme
Chor	Chorus

Names of Scale Degrees and Modes

SCALE DEGREES

English	Italian	German	French
C	do	C	ut
C-sharp	do diesis	Cis	ut dièse
D-flat	re bemolle	Des	ré bémol
D	re	D	ré
D-sharp	re diesis	Dis	ré dièse
E-flat	mi bemolle	Es	mi bémol
E	mi	E	mi
E-sharp	mi diesis	Eis	mi dièse
F-flat	fa bemolle	Fes	fa bémol
F	fa	F	fa
F-sharp	fa diesis	Fis	fa dièse
G-flat	sol bemolle	Ges	sol bémol
G	sol	G	sol
G-sharp	sol diesis	Gis	sol dièse
A-flat	la bemolle	As	la bémol
A	la	A	la
A-sharp	la diesis	Ais	la dièse
B-flat	si bemolle	B	si bémol
B	si	H	si
B-sharp	si diesis	His	si dièse
C-flat	do bemolle	Ces	ut bémol

MODES

major	maggiore	dur	majeur
minor	minore	moll	mineur

Appendix C

Glossary of Musical Terms Used in the Scores

The following glossary is not intended to be a complete dictionary of musical terms, nor is knowledge of all these terms necessary to follow the scores in this book. However, as listeners gain experience in following scores, they will find it useful and interesting to understand the composer's directions with regard to tempo, dynamics, and methods of performance.

In most cases, compound terms have been broken down in the glossary and defined separately, as they often recur in varying combinations. A few common foreign-language particles are included in addition to the musical terms. Note that names and abbreviations for instruments and for scale degrees will be found in Appendix B.

a The phrases *a 2*, *a 3* (etc.) indicate the number of parts to be played by 2, 3 (etc.) players; when a simple number (1, 2, etc.) is placed over a part, it indicates that only the first (second, etc.) player in that group should play.

ab Off.

aber But.

accelerando (accel.) Growing faster.

accentato, accentué Accented.

accompagnando Accompanying.

accompagnemento Accompaniment.

accordato, accordez Tune the instrument as specified.

adagio Slow, leisurely.

affettuoso With emotion.

affrettare (affrett.) Hastening a little.

agitando, agitato Agitated, excited.

al fine "The end"; an indication to return to the start of a piece and to repeat it only to the point marked "fine."

alla breve Indicates two beats to a measure, at a rather quick tempo.

allargando (allarg.) Growing broader.

alle, alles All, every, each.

allegretto A moderately fast tempo (between allegro and andante).

allegrezza Gaiety.

allegro A rapid tempo (between allegretto and presto).

allein Alone, solo.

allmählich Gradually (*allmählich wieder gleich mässig fliessend werden*, gradually becoming even-flowing again).

alta, alto, altus (A.) The deeper of the two main divisions of women's (or boys') voices.

am Steg On the bridge (of a string instrument).

ancora Again.

andante A moderately slow tempo (between adagio and allegretto).

andantino A moderately slow tempo.

Anfang Beginning, initial.

anima Spirit, animation.

animando With increasing animation.

animant, animato, animé, animez Animated.

aperto Indicates open notes on the horn, open strings, and undamped piano notes.

a piacere The execution of the passage is left to the performer's discretion.

1018

appassionato Impassioned.

appena Scarcely, hardly.

apprensivo Apprehensive.

archet Bow.

archi, arco Played with the bow.

arditamente Boldly.

arpeggiando, arpeggiato (arpegg.) Played in harp style, i.e., the notes of the chord played in quick succession rather than simultaneously.

arrêt Break (as in *arrêt long*, long break).

articulato Articulated, separated.

assai Very.

assez Fairly, rather.

attacca Begin what follows without pausing.

a tempo At the original tempo.

auf dem On the (as in *auf dem G*, on the G string).

Ausdruck Expression.

ausdrucksvoll With expression.

äusserst Extreme, utmost.

avec With.

bachetta, bachetti Drumsticks (*bachetti di spugna*, sponge-headed drumsticks).

baguettes Drumsticks (*baguettes de bois*, wooden drumsticks; *baguettes d'éponge*, sponge-headed drumsticks; *baguettes dures*, hard mallets; *baguettes midures*, medium-hard mallets or drumsticks.

bass, bassi, basso, bassus (B.) The lowest male voice.

battere, battuta, battuto (batt.) To beat.

beaucoup A lot.

Becken Cymbals.

bedeutend bewegter With significantly more movement.

behaglich heiter Pleasingly serene or cheerful.

beider Hände With both hands.

ben Very.

bewegt Agitated.

bewegter More agitated.

bisbigliando, bispiglando (bis.) Whispering.

bis zum Schluss dieser Szene To the end of this scene.

blasen Blow.

Blech Brass instruments.

bogen (bog.) Played with the bow.

bois Woodwind.

bouché Muted.

breit Broadly.

breiter More broadly.

brilliante Brilliant.

brio Spirit, vivacity.

burden Refrain.

cadenza (cad., cadenz.) An extended passage for solo instrument in free, improvisatory style.

calando (cal.) Diminishing in volume and speed.

calma, calmo Calm, calmly.

cantabile (cant.) In a singing style.

cantando In a singing manner.

canto Voice (as in *col canto*, a direction for the accompaniment to follow the solo part in tempo and expression).

cantus An older designation for the highest part in a vocal work.

capriccio Capriciously, whimsically.

cedendo Yielding.

cédez Slow down.

changez Change (usually an instruction to retune a string or an instrument).

chiuso See *gestopft*.

chromatisch Chromatic.

circa (ca.) About, approximately.

coda The last part of a piece.

col, colla, colle, coll' With the.

colore Colored.

come prima, come sopra As at first, as previously.

commodo Comfortable, easy.

con With.

corda String; for example, *seconda (2a) corda* is the second string (the A string on the violin).

corto Short, brief.

court Short.

crescendo (cres.) An increase in volume.

cuivré Played with a harsh, blaring tone.

da capo (D.C.) Repeat from the beginning.

dal segno (D.S.) Repeat from the sign.

Dämpfer (dpf.) Mutes.

dazu In addition to that, for that purpose.

de, des, die Of, from.

début Beginning.

deciso Determined, resolute.

declamando In a declamatory style.

decrescendo (decresc., decr.) A decreasing of volume.

dehors Outside.

delicato Delicate, delicately.

dem To the.

détaché With a broad, vigorous bow stroke, each note bowed singly.

deutlich Distinctly.

d'exécution Performance.

diminuendo, diminuer (dim., dimin.) A decreasing of volume.

distinto Distinct, clear.

divisés, divisi (div.) Divided; indicates that the instrumental group should be divided into two parts to play the passage in question.

dolce Sweetly and softly.

dolcemente Sweetly.

dolcissimo (dolciss.) Very sweetly.

dolore, doloroso With sorrow.

Doppelgriff Double stop.

doux Sweetly.

drammatico Dramatic.

drängend Pressing on.

dreifach Triple.

dreitaktig Three beats to a measure.

dur Major, as in *G dur* (G major).

durée Duration.

e, et And.

eilen To hurry.

ein One, a.

elegante Elegant, graceful.

Empfindung Feeling.

energico Energetically.

espansione Expansion, broadening.

espressione With expression.

espressivo (espr., espress.) Expressively.

etwas Somewhat, rather.

expressif Expressively.

facile Simple.

falsetto Male voice singing above normal range, with light sound.

feroce Fierce, ferocious.

fin, fine End, close.

Flatterzunge (Flzg.), flutter-tongue A special tonguing technique for wind instruments, producing a rapid, trill-like sound.

flebile Feeble, plaintive, mournful.

fliessend Flowing.

forte (f) Loud.

fortepiano (fp) Loud, then soft immediately.

fortissimo (ff) Very loud (*fff* indicates a still louder dynamic).

forza Force.

forzando (fz) Forcing, strongly accented.

forzandissimo (ffz) Very strongly accented.

fou Frantic.

frappez To strike.

frei Freely.

freihäng., freihängendes Hanging freely. An indication to the percussionist to let the cymbals vibrate freely.

frisch Fresh, lively.

fuoco Fire.

furioso Furiously.

furore Fury, rage.

ganz Entirely, altogether.

Ganzton Whole tone.

gedämpft (ged.) Muted.

geheimnisvoll Mysteriously.

geschlagen Pulsating.

gestopft (gest.) Stopping the notes of a horn; that is, the hand is placed in the bell of the horn to produce a muffled sound. Also *chiuso*.

geteilt (get.) Divided; indicates that the instrumental group should be divided into two parts to play the passage in question.

getragen Sustained.

gewöhnlich As usual.

giocoso Humorous.

giusto Moderately.

glissando (gliss.) Rapid scales produced by running the fingers over all the strings.

gradamente Gradually.

grande Large, great.

grandezza Grandeur.

grandioso Grandiose.

grave Slow, solemn; deep, low.

grazioso Gracefully.

Griffbrett Fingerboard.

grosser Auftakt Big upbeat.

gut Good, well.

Hälfte Half.

Hauptzeitmass Original tempo.

hauteur réelle In the octave notated, designation for transposing French horns.

hervortreten Prominent.

hoch High, nobly.

Holz Woodwinds.

Holzschlägel Wooden drumstick.

im gleichen Rhythmus In the same rhythm.

immer Always.

in Oktaven In octaves.

insensibilmente Slightly, imperceptibly.

intensa Intensely.

istesso tempo Duration of beat remains unaltered despite meter change.

jeu Playful.

jusqu'à Until.

kadenzieren To cadence.

klagend Lamenting.

kleine Little.

klingen To sound.

komisch bedeutsam Very humorously.

kurz Short.

langsam Slow.

langsamer Slower.

languendo, langueur Languor.

l'archet See *archet*.

largamente Broadly.

larghetto Slightly faster than largo.

largo A very slow tempo.

lasci, lassen To abandon.

lebhaft Lively.

lebhafter Livelier.

legatissimo A more forceful indication of *legato*.

legato Performed without any perceptible interruption between notes.

légèrement, leggieramente Lightly.

leggierissimo Very light.

leggiero (legg.) Light and graceful.

legno The wood of the bow (*col legno gestrich*, played with the wood).

lent Slow.

lentamente Slowly.

lento A slow tempo (between andante and largo).

l.h. Abbreviation for "left hand."

liricamente Lyrically.

loco Indicates a return to the written pitch, following a passage played an octave higher or lower than written.

Luftpause Pause for breath.

lunga Long, sustained.

lusingando Caressing.

ma, mais But.

maestoso Majestic.

marcatissimo (marcatiss.) With very marked emphasis.

marcato (marc.) Marked, with emphasis.

marcia March.

marschmässig, nicht eilen Moderate-paced march, not rushed.

marziale Military, martial, march-like.

mässig Moderately.

mässiger More moderately.

melodia Melody.

même Same.

meno Less.

mezzo forte (mf) Moderately loud.

mezzo piano (mp) Moderately soft.

mindestens At least.

misterioso Mysterious.

misura Measured.

mit With.

moderatissimo A more forceful indication of *moderato*.

moderato, modéré At a moderate tempo.

moins Less.

molto Very, much.

mordenti Biting, pungent.

morendo Dying away.

mormorato Murmured.

mosso Rapid.

moto Motion.

mouvement (mouv., mouvt.) Tempo.

muta, mutano Change the tuning of the instrument as specified.

nach After.

naturalezza A natural, unaffected manner.

nel modo russico In the Russian style.

neuen New.

nicht Not.

niente Nothing.

nimmt To take; to seize.

noch Still.

non Not.

nuovo New.

obere, oberer (ob.) Upper, leading.

oder langsamer Or slower.

offen Open.

ohne   Without.

ondeggiante   Undulating movement of the bow, which produces a tremolo effect.

ordinario (ord., ordin.)   In the usual way (generally canceling an instruction to play using some special technique).

ossia   An alternative (usually easier) version of a passage.

ôtez vite les sourdines   Remove the mutes quickly.

ottava   Octave (as in *8va*, octave higher than written; *8 basso, 8 bassa,* octave lower than written; *16 va,* two octaves higher than written).

ottoni   Brass.

ouvert   Open.

parte   Part (*colla parte, colle parti,* the accompaniment is to follow the soloist[s] in tempo).

passionato   Passionately.

passione   Passion, emotion.

Paukenschlägel   Timpani stick.

pavillons en l'air   An indication to the player of a wind instrument to raise the bell of the instrument upward.

pedal, pedale (ped., P.)   (1) In piano music, indicates that the damper pedal should be depressed; an asterisk indicates the point of release (brackets below the music are also used to indicate pedaling); (2) on an organ, the pedals are a keyboard played with the feet.

per   During.

perdendosi   Gradually dying away.

pesante   Heavily.

peu   Little, a little.

piacevole   Agreeable, pleasant.

pianissimo (pp)   Very soft (*ppp* indicates a still softer dynamic).

piano (p)   Soft.

piena   Full.

più   More.

pizzicato (pizz.)   The string plucked with the finger.

plötzlich   Suddenly, immediately.

plus   More.

pochissimo (pochiss.)   Very little, a very little.

poco   Little, a little.

poco a poco   Little by little.

ponticello (pont.)   The bridge (of a string instrument).

portamento   Continuous smooth and rapid sliding between two pitches.

portando   Carrying.

position naturel (pos. nat.)   In the normal position (usually canceling an instruction to play using some special technique).

possibile   Possible.

precedente   Previous, preceding.

precipitato   Rushed, hurried.

premier mouvement (1er mouvt.)   At the original tempo.

prenez   Take up.

préparez   Prepare.

presque   Almost, nearly.

presser   To speed up.

prestissimo   A more forceful indication of *presto.*

presto   A very quick tempo (faster than allegro).

prima, primo   First, principal.

punto   Point.

quarta   Fourth.

quasi   Almost, as if.

quinto   Fifth.

rallentando (rall., rallent.)   Growing slower.

rapidamente   Quickly.

rapide   Rapid, fast.

rapidissimo (rapidiss.)   Very quickly.

rasch   Quickly.

rascher   More quickly.

rauschend   Rustling, roaring.

recitative, recitativo (recit.)   A vocal style designed to imitate and emphasize the natural inflections of speech.

rein   Perfect interval.

resonante   Resonating.

respiro   Pause for breath.

retenu   Held back.

revenir au tempo   Return to the original tempo.

r.h.   Abbreviation for "right hand."

rianimando   Reanimating.

richtig   Correct (*richtige Lage,* correct pitch).

rien   Nothing.

rigore di tempo   Strictness of tempo.

rigueur   Rigor, strictness.

rinforzando (rf, rfz, rinf.)   A sudden accent on a single note or chord.

risoluto   In a resolute or determined manner.

ritardando (rit., ritard.) Gradually slackening in speed.

ritenuto (riten.) Immediate reduction of speed.

ritmato, ritmico Rhythmic.

ritornando, ritornello (ritor.) Refrain.

rubato A certain elasticity and flexibility of tempo, consisting of slight accelerandos and ritardandos according to the requirements of the musical expression.

ruhig Quietly.

saltando Leaping.

sans Without.

Schalltrichter Horn.

scherzando (scherz.) Playful.

schlagen To strike in a usual manner.

Schlagwerk Striking mechanism.

schleppen, schleppend Dragging.

Schluss Cadence, conclusion.

schnell Fast.

schneller Faster.

schon Already.

Schwammschägeln Sponge-headed drumstick.

scorrevole Flowing, gliding.

sec, secco Dry, simple.

secunda Second.

sehr Very.

semplice Simple.

semplicità Simplicity.

sempre Always, continually.

senza Without.

sforzando (sf., sfz.) With sudden emphasis.

sforzandissimo (sff, sffz) With very loud, sudden attack.

simile (sim.) In a similar manner.

sin Without.

Singstimme Singing voice.

sino al Up to the . . . (usually followed by a new tempo marking, or by a dotted line indicating a terminal point).

si piace Especially pleasing.

smorzando (smorz.) Dying away.

sofort Immediately.

soli, solo (s.) Executed by one performer.

sonoro Sonorous, resonant.

sopra Above; in piano music, used to indicate that one hand must pass above the other.

soprano (S.) The voice classification with the highest range.

sordini, sordino (sord.) Mute.

sostenendo, sostenuto (sost.) Sustained.

sotto voce In an undertone, subdued, under the breath.

sourdine (sourd.) Mute.

soutenu Sustained.

spiel, spielen Play (an instrument).

Spieler Player, performer.

spirito Spirit, soul.

spiritoso In a spirited manner.

spugna Sponge.

staccato (stacc.) Detached, separated, abruptly, disconnected.

stentando, stentare, stentato (stent.) Delaying, retarding.

stesso The same.

Stimme Voice.

stimmen To tune.

strascinare To drag.

straziante Agonizing, heart-rending.

Streichinstrumente (Streichinstr.) Bowed string instruments.

strepitoso Noisy, loud.

stretto In a non-fugal composition, indicates a concluding section at an increased speed.

stringendo (string.) Quickening.

subito (sub.) Suddenly, immediately.

sul On the (as in *sul G*, on the G string).

superius In older music, the uppermost part.

sur On.

tacet The instrument or vocal part so marked is silent.

tasto Fingerboard (as in *sul tasto*, bow over the fingerboard).

tasto solo In a continuo part, this indicates that only the string instrument plays; the chord-playing instrument is silent.

tempo primo (tempo I) At the original tempo.

teneramente, tenero Tenderly, gently.

tenor, tenore (T.) The highest male voice.

tenuto (ten., tenu.) Held, sustained.

tertia Third.

tief Deep, low.

timbre Tone color.

touche Key; note.

toujours Always, continually.

tranquillo   Quietly, calmly.

tre corde (t.c.)   Release the soft (or *una corda*) pedal of the piano.

tremolo (trem.)   On string instruments, a quick reiteration of the same tone, produced by a rapid up-and-down movement of the bow; also a rapid alternation between two different notes.

très   Very.

trill (tr.)   The rapid alternation of a given note with the diatonic second above it. In a drum part, it indicates rapid alternating strokes with two drumsticks.

tromba   Trumpet (as in *quasi tromba*, trumpet-like).

Trommschlag (Tromm.)   Drumbeat.

troppo   Too much.

tutta la forza   Very emphatically.

tutti   Literally, "all"; usually means all the instruments in a given category as distinct from a solo part.

übergreifen   To overlap.

übertonend   Drowning out.

umstimmen   To change the tuning.

un   One, a.

una corda (u.c.)   With the "soft" pedal of the piano depressed.

und   And.

unison (unis.)   The same notes or melody played by several instruments at the same pitch. Often used to emphasize that a phrase is not to be divided among several players.

unmerklich   Imperceptible.

velocissimo   Very swiftly.

verklingen lassen   To let die away.

vibrare   To sound.

vibrato (vibr.)   To fluctuate the pitch on a single note.

vierfach   Quadruple.

vierhändig   Four-hand piano music.

vif   Lively.

vigoroso   Vigorous, strong.

violento   Violent.

viva, vivente, vivo   Lively.

vivace   Quick, lively.

vivacissimo   A more forceful indication of *vivace*.

voce   Voice (as in *colla voce*, a direction for the accompaniment to follow the solo part in tempo and expression).

volles Orch.   Entire orchestra.

vorbereiten   Prepare, get ready.

Vorhang auf   Curtain up.

Vorhang zu   Curtain down.

vorher   Beforehand, previously.

voriges   Preceding.

Waltzertempo   In the tempo of a waltz.

weg   Away, beyond.

weich   Mellow, smooth, soft.

wie aus der Fern   As if from afar.

wieder   Again.

wie zu Anfang dieser Szene   As at the beginning of this scene.

zart   Tenderly, delicately.

Zeit   Time; duration.

zögernd   Slower.

zu   The phrases *zu 2, zu 3* (etc.) indicate the number of parts to be played by 2, 3 (etc.) players.

zum   In addition.

zurückhaltend   Slackening in speed.

zurücktreten   To withdraw.

zweihändig   With two hands.

Appendix D

Concordance Table for Recordings and The Enjoyment of Music *Listening Guides*

The following table provides cross-references to the Listening Guides (LG) in the various versions of *The Enjoyment of Music*, seventh edition, by Joseph Machlis and Kristine Forney (New York: W.W. Norton, 1995). The following abbreviations are used throughout: C for the Chronological version; S for the Standard version, and Sh for the Shorter version. The table also summarizes the location of each work and its individual movements within the various recordings sets (see "Note on Recordings," p. xiv). Because of copyright restrictions, several contemporary works included on the recordings and in the Listening Guides do not appear in *The Norton Scores*.

| Listening Guides | | | | Norton Scores | 8-CD | 8-Cas | 3-CD | 3-Cas |
C	Sh	S	Composer, Title	Page	Set	Set	Set	Set
36	—	29	MENDELSSOHN, *A Midsummer Night's Dream*, Overture	62	5/13	5A/3	—	—
37	20	2	SCHUBERT, *Erlkönig (Erlking)*,*	1	5/1	5A/1	2/20	2A/4
38	—	3	BRAHMS, *Vergebliches Ständchen (Futile Serenade)*	247	5/47	5B/4	—	—
39	21	4	CHOPIN, Polonaise in A-flat major, Op. 53*	117	5/24	5A/5	2/27	2A/5
40	—	5	CHOPIN, Prelude in E minor, Op. 28, No. 4	116	5/22	5A/4	—	—
41	—	6	LISZT, *Wilde Jagd (Wild Hunt)*, Transcendental Etude No. 8	168	5/35	5A/6	—	—
42	22	7	C. SCHUMANN, Scherzo in D minor, Op. 10	226	6/6	6A/2	2/31	2B/1

*Included in *The Norton CD-ROM Masterworks*, Volume I.

Listening Guides			Composer, Title	Norton Scores Page	8-CD Set	8-Cas Set	3-CD Set	3-Cas Set
C	Sh	S						
43	23	8	BERLIOZ, *Symphonie fantastique*, Fifth Movement	8	5/8	5A/2	2/37	2B/2
44	24	9	MUSORGSKY, *Pictures at an Exhibition*					
			Promenade	317	6/23	6B/1	—	—
			The Hut on Fowl's Legs	322	6/24	6B/2	—	—
			The Great Gate of Kiev	352	6/27	6B/2	2/42	2B/3
45	—	10	BRAHMS, Symphony No. 4, Fourth Movement	252	6/12	6A/3	—	—
46	—	11	DVOŘÁK, Symphony No. 9 in E minor, *From the New World*, Second Movement	424	6/43	6B/6	—	—
47	—	12	R. SCHUMANN, Piano Concerto in A minor, First Movement	127	5/28	5B/1	—	—
48	25	13	BRAHMS, *A German Requiem*, Fourth Movement	236	5/42	5B/3	2/49	2B/4
49	26	14	VERDI, *La traviata*					
			Act II, Finale (complete)	189	6/1	6A/1	—	—
			Act II, Finale (second part only)	200	—	—	3/1	3A/1
50	27	15	WAGNER, *Die Walküre*					
			Act III, "Farewell" and "Magic fire" music	179	5/38	5B/2	—	—
			Act III, "Magic fire" music (only)	183	—	—	2/54	2B/5
51	—	16	BIZET, *Carmen*, Act I (excerpt)	283	6/15	6A/4	—	—
52	28	17	LEONCAVALLO, *Pagliacci*, Act I, Canio's Aria*	442	6/46	6B/7	2/56	2B/6
53	—	18	TCHAIKOVSKY, *The Nutcracker*					
			March	377	6/34	6B/3	—	—
			Dance of the Sugar Plum Fairy	401	6/37	6B/4	—	—
			Trepak	410	6/40	6B/5	—	—
54	—	54	MAHLER, *Das Lied von der Erde (The Song of the Earth)*, Third Movement	447	6/48	6B/8	—	—
55	—	55	STRAUSS, *Der Rosenkavalier (The Cavalier of the Rose)*, Act III, Trio	489	7/5	7A/2	—	—
56	29	56	DEBUSSY, *Prélude à "L'après-midi d'un faune" (Prelude to "The Afternoon of a Faun")*	458	7/1	7A/1	3/3	3A/2

*Included in *The Norton CD ROM Masterworks*, Volume I.

Listening Guides				Norton Scores	8-CD	8-Cas	3-CD	3-Cas
C	Sh	S	Composer, Title	Page	Set	Set	Set	Set
57	—	57	RAVEL, *Chansons madécasses (Songs of Madagascar)*, Second Movement	570	7/19	7A/6	—	—
58	30	58	STRAVINSKY, *Petrushka*					
			First Tableau (complete)	628	7/25	7B/1	—	—
			First Tableau (first part only)*	628	—	—	3/7	3A/3
59	31	59	SCHOENBERG, *Pierrot lunaire*					
			No. 18, "Der Mondfleck"*	499	7/7	7A/3	3/16	3A/4
			No. 21, "O alter Duft aus Märchenzeit"	505	7/9	7A/4	3/18	3A/5
60	—	60	BERG, *Wozzeck*, Act III, Scenes 4 and 5	692	7/44	7B/2	—	—
61	—	61	WEBERN, Symphony, Op. 21, Second Movement	684	7/41	7A/8	—	—
62	—	62	PROKOFIEV, *Alexander Nevsky*, Seventh Movement	717	7/48	7B/3	—	—
63	32	63	BARTÓK, *Music for Strings, Percussion, and Celesta*, Fourth Movement	578	7/21	7A/7	3/20	3A/6
64	—	64	IVES, *The Fourth of July*, from *A Symphony: New England Holidays*	509	7/11	7A/5	—	—
65	—	65	CRAWFORD, *Rat Riddles*, from Three Songs (1933)	799	8/12	8A/3	—	—
66	33	66	COPLAND, *Billy the Kid*, Scene 1, *Street in a Frontier Town*	758	8/9	8A/2	3/24	3A/7
67	—	67	LOUIS ARMSTRONG AND THE SAVOY BALLROOM FIVE, *West End Blues*	737	7/54	7B/6	—	—
68	34	68	ELLINGTON, *Ko-Ko*	739	8/1	8A/1	3/27	3B/1
69	35	69	RODGERS, *My Funny Valentine*					
			Original Version	730	7/50	7B/4	—	—
			Gerry Mulligan Quartet Version*	734	7/52	7B/5	3/35	3B/2
70	36	70	BERNSTEIN, Symphonic Dances from *West Side Story*, excerpts: *Cool* (Fugue) & "Rumble"	840	8/21	8A/7	3/37	3B/3
71	—	71	DYLAN, *Mister Tambourine Man* by the Byrds	—	8/43	8B/5	—	—
72	37	72	*Black Magic Woman/Gypsy Queen* by Santana	—	8/44	8B/6	3/41	3B/4
73	38	73	*That's Why I Choose You* by Ladysmith Black Mambazo	—	8/46	8B/7	3/43	3B/5

*Included in *The Norton CD-ROM Masterworks*, Volume I.

C	Listening Guides Sh	S	Composer, Title	Norton Scores Page	8-CD Set	8-Cas Set	3-CD Set	3-Cas Set
74	—	74	CARTER, Sonata for Flute, Oboe, Cello, and Harpsichord, First Movement	822	8/16	8A/4	—	—
75	—	75	BOULEZ, *Le marteau sans maître (The Hammer Without a Master)*					
			No. 1	880	8/28	8A/9	—	—
			No. 3	886	8/29	8A/10	—	—
			No. 7	889	8/30	8A/11	—	—
76	—	76	LUTOSŁAWSKI, *Jeux vénitiens (Venetian Games)*, First Movement	817	8/18	8A/5	—	—
77	39	77	CRUMB, *Ancient Voices of Children*, First Movement	893	8/31	8B/1	3/46	3B/6
78	40	78	LIGETI, *Désordre (Disorder)*, from Etudes for Piano, Book I	875	8/25	8A/8	3/49	3B/7
79	—	79	BABBITT, *Phonemena* (excerpt)	833	8/20	8A/6	—	—
80	41	80	MACHOVER, *Bug-Mudra* (excerpt)	961	8/40	8B/4	3/52	3B/8
81	42	81	TOWER, *Petroushskates*	896	8/34	8B/2	3/55	3B/9
82	—	82	ADAMS, *Nixon in China*, Act I, Scene 3, Finale	928	8/38	8B/3	—	—

Index of Forms and Genres